King Cnut and the
Viking Conquest
of England

King Cnut and the Viking Conquest of England

W. B. BARTLETT

AMBERLEY

This edition published 2018

Amberley Publishing
The Hill, Stroud
Gloucestershire, GL5 4EP

www.amberley-books.com

British Library Cataloguing in Publication Data.
A catalogue record for this book is available from the British Library.

ISBN 978 1 4456 8289 1 (paperback)
ISBN 978 1 4456 4592 6 (ebook)

Map design by Thomas Bohm, User design.
Typesetting and Origination by Amberley Publishing.
Printed in the UK.

Contents

	Maps and Genealogical Tables	6
	Introduction	11
	Prelude: A Viking Saga	13
1	England: The Long Road to Conquest (991–1002)	39
2	Sweyn Forkbeard: From Raider to King (1002–1014)	73
3	Cnut of Denmark: The Prince without a Land (1014–1015)	108
4	Ironsides: Battle to the Death (1015–1016)	129
5	King of England: Victory and Kingship (1016–1018)	161
6	King of Denmark: The Years of Consolidation (1018–1027)	189
7	Emperor of the North: The Years of Greatness (1027–1034)	222
8	Cnut the Great: A Life Assessed (1035)	258
	Bibliography	284
	Notes	287
	Acknowledgements	299
	Index	301
	About the Author	316

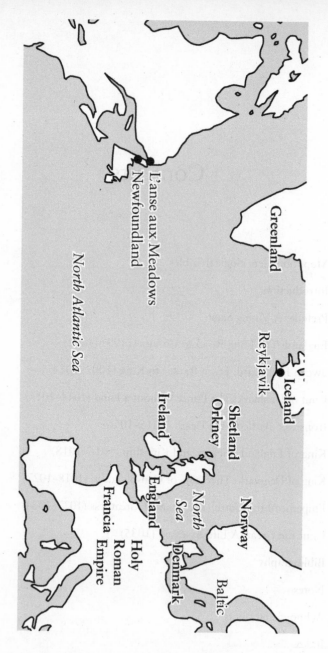

The North Atlantic in the Viking Age. (*Author collection / Amberley Archive*)

Scandinavia in the Viking Age. (*Author collection / Amberley Archive*)

The British Isles in the Viking Age. (*Author collection / Amberley Archive*)

Gorm the Old
(before 900–c. 958,
King of Denmark c. 936–c. 958

Harald Bluetooth
(c. 935–985/6, King of Denmark
c. 958–985/986

Sweyn Forkbeard
(c. 960–1014, King of Denmark 985–1014

Harald II (King of Denmark 1014–18)	Cnut (995?–1035, King of England 1016–1035 of Denmark 1018–1035)	=	Ælfgifu [1] of Northampton	=	[2] Emma of Normandy (c. 985–1052)	Estrith

Sweyn
(c. 1019–1074,
King of
Denmark
(1047–1074)

	Sweyn Cnutsson	Harold Harefoot (1016–1040, King of England 1035–1040)		Harthacnut (c. 1018–1042, King of England 1040–42)	Gundhild

Genealogy of Cnut. (*Author collection / Amberley Archive*)

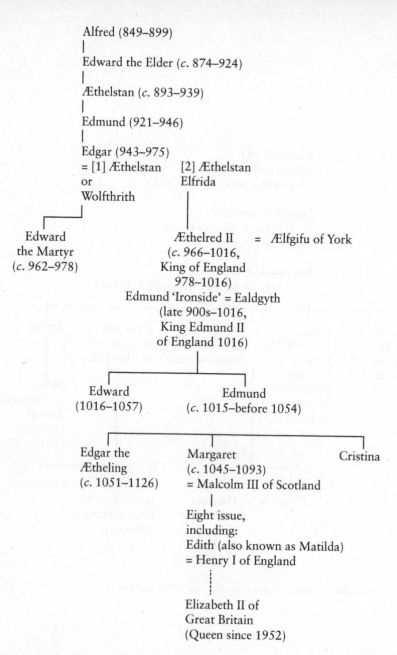

Alfred (849–899)
|
Edward the Elder (c. 874–924)
|
Æthelstan (c. 893–939)
|
Edmund (921–946)
|
Edgar (943–975)
= [1] Æthelstan   [2] Æthelstan
or   Elfrida
Wolfthrith

Edward   Æthelred II   = Ælfgifu of York
the Martyr   (c. 966–1016,
(c. 962–978)   King of England
                       978–1016)
            Edmund 'Ironside' = Ealdgyth
            (late 900s–1016,
            King Edmund II
            of England 1016)

Edward   Edmund
(1016–1057)   (c. 1015–before 1054)

Edgar the   Margaret   Cristina
Ætheling   (c. 1045–1093)
(c. 1051–1126)   = Malcolm III of Scotland

                       Eight issue,
                       including:
                       Edith (also known as Matilda)
                       = Henry I of England

                       Elizabeth II of
                       Great Britain
                       (Queen since 1952)

Genealogy of Edmund Ironside. (*Author collection / Amberley Archive*)

Introduction

Since the Vikings seized the attention of historians and archaeologists in the Victorian era, fascination with them has never left us. Succeeding generations re-craft views of them to meet the needs of the time. Often there is a sinister undertone to all this: Hitler was quick to seize on the Viking motifs made popular in Germany in a different context by men like Richard Wagner. Most recently, show business has focused on the exploits of the semi-mythical Viking war-chief Ragnar Lodbrok ('Hairy Breeches') to make the story fresh for the latest generation, whilst Bernard Cornwell's historical novels on Uhtred of Bebbanburgh have struck a chord with readers young and old.

If the story of the Vikings still strikes a chord with us, and grabs the attention of film-makers and literary craftsmen alike, a book that seeks to understand the most successful 'real-life' Scandinavian king of the entire Viking epoch would seem long overdue. Cnut is widely referred to as 'The Great' in Denmark though the moniker is reserved pretty much exclusively for King Alfred in Britain. Here, Cnut is best remembered for a possibly apocryphal story about his vain attempts to turn back the sea, which is unfortunate given the great sweep of his reign, which had a huge impact on Britain and Scandinavia and in a different way on wider European affairs too.

Some of this is probably due to the fact that Cnut is Danish rather than English. It is understandable perhaps that a non-English king should not automatically be granted the high status that the acts of his reign might otherwise demand in England. There is a sense of damaged national pride in this; no one likes celebrating the prowess of someone who has bested them. But go to Scandinavia and the situation is different. The greatness of Cnut and his family is celebrated with much less embarrassment there.

If Cnut is little remembered in England, the events that led to his triumph 1,000 years ago are equally lacking in prominence in the collective English memory. I was recently reading a book on the Roman invasion of Britain. Written by a respected historian, it included a statement that there have only ever been two successful invasions of England: Roman and Norman. If a historian can overlook Cnut's conquest of 1016, then little wonder that it has escaped the consciousness of the general public.

These two thoughts are behind the writing of this book: the need to raise the profile of an unfairly overlooked king of England (and Denmark) and a timely reminder of a forgotten conquest as its millennium is at hand. Both elements provide fascinating storylines and what follows is an attempt to recreate them and give them their proper place in history. It is a fascinating tale and one that is long overdue a retelling.

A Viking Saga

It was, according to the *Anglo-Saxon Chronicles*, sometime in the reign of King Beorhtric of Wessex, who ruled from 786 to 802,[1] that Beaduheard, his reeve in Dorsetshire, received news that three ships had landed 'in the island which is called Portland'.[2] These vessels carried parties of strangers, men of a type who had not been seen in the country before. No one knew why they had landed and Beaduheard's job was to bring them in for questioning to determine their motives.

We do not know very much about Beaduheard but perhaps we can be allowed some speculation. The Wessex in which he lived was a Christian realm but pagan antecedents in the region were not very far in the past. The great epic *Beowulf* had been written down probably not long before in Northumbria or Mercia but was almost certainly drawn from a much older oral tradition. As he made the short journey to the coast, perhaps after enjoying a last drink in the mead-hall before he left, words from that epic may have resonated with Beaduheard. In *Beowulf* these words were uttered by a sentry when seeing men in a strange craft for the first time: 'Strangers, you have steered this steep craft through the sea-ways, sought our coast. I see you are warriors; you wear that dress now. I must ask who you are.'[3]

A conscientious official who was determined to see that the strangers got up to no mischief, Beaduheard had ridden to the coast in order to compel the unannounced visitors to come with him to the king's town of Dorchester just a few miles off to explain themselves. Possibly the request, though justified in terms of honouring the king or ensuring that law and order was kept, was made in a haughty manner. Or maybe the men on the receiving end of the summons were just no respecter of any kind of authority. In any event the dutiful reeve's blood was soon staining the sands red, the first known English victim of a Viking raid.

This was an act of piracy, no doubt disconcerting but not necessarily of particular note in what were very bloody times indeed. This was an era when warfare within a fragmented England was still a regular feature. It was in all probability a chance encounter, a case of the king's reeve being in the wrong place at the wrong time. No doubt the event registered on the consciousness of the people of England but it was probably seen as an unwelcome act of violence that was essentially a one-off.

But the incident paled into insignificance against what happened just a few years later in 793, a year when 'there were immense flashes of lightning and fiery dragons were seen flying in the air', portents of something terrible.[4] Aidan's monastery of Lindisfarne, where the holiest of English saints, Cuthbert, was buried, was on a tidal island off the coast of Northumbria and was one of the most sacred places in Europe, let alone England. In this year, this holy of holies fell prey to Viking raiders, its monks drowned in the sea or forced naked out of the abbey, its treasures looted, its fabric left in flames.

The smoke that billowed up into the sky over the burning abbey took on the appearance of a funeral pyre. The shockwaves from Lindisfarne's fall reverberated across the Continent. In Paris, the prominent English scholar and ecclesiastic Alcuin of York lamented that 'never before has such terror appeared in Britain. Behold the church of St Cuthbert, splattered with the blood of God's priests, robbed of its ornaments.'

What made this so awful was that this was no chance encounter. This was a plum prize waiting to be picked and the raiders must have known exactly where they were headed when they set out to raid it. This act was cold, calculating and deliberate. Further terrible raids followed in the succeeding years and decades, increasing in intensity until the purpose of the assaults seemed to change. From being hit-and-run incursions that maybe shook the very foundations of the kingdoms of England to the core from time to time but then dissipated, in succeeding decades a greater threat emerged. The raiders, primarily from Denmark or Norway (though there were probably what we would now call Swedes too), came in greater numbers and they started to stay for longer. It was not too long before they began to take up residence. This was no longer about raiding, it was about conquest.

The Vikings, or the Northmen (the *vikingar* in Old Norse), were not just raiders. They were also undoubtedly intrepid adventurers and magnificent opportunists. Their impact was felt as far east as the Russian steppes and as far west as Iceland, Greenland and (briefly) Newfoundland. Even the great city of Constantinople felt their presence; Viking graffiti from the ninth century can still be seen scratched into the hallowed stonework of the church/mosque of Hagia Sofia; for lovers of trivia, the name of the undisciplined visitor was Halfdan.

What to call these raiders is something of a problem. They were not often described as 'Vikings' at the time, either by themselves or by those that they came into contact with. The very derivation of the word is a subject for debate. Some say it is linked to the Viken, a district in southern Norway that was most definitely connected to a number of what we would call Vikings. The Old Norse *vik* means 'bay', a geographical feature certainly linked to their raiding and seafaring activities, so that is another possible source. In the same language *vikingr* means an individual who is away from home whilst to go viking refers to being in a group of such people.

In Anglo-Saxon a *wicing* referred to any individual of piratical tendencies, and that might include those we know as Vikings. Interestingly, though, the term is used only five times in the *Anglo-Saxon Chronicle* and each time it appears to be in a relation to a raiding party rather than a full-blown army.[5] None of these terms was very regularly applied in most of the chronicles of the time though. Latin texts talk about 'Northmen', 'Danes', 'pirates' and 'pagans', Old English to 'Danes', 'Northmen' and 'heathens'. In Welsh and Old Irish they are 'foreigners', divided into white and black groups, perhaps based on which part of Scandinavia they came from. But it was as Vikings that they would become known in more recent times and so they will often be called in the saga that follows.[6]

The Scandinavian interlopers left a permanent mark on England. A number of everyday words still in use in English today have their origins in the Far North: anger, fellow, husband, sister, egg, root, skill, skin, sky, wing, thrive, ill and die for example. Place names too betray a similar origin; those ending in –by, such as Derby, Grimsby and Whitby, all have Scandinavian antecedents (by-law, still in common English usage, means the law of the village) as do those ending in –thorp.[7] Viking ancestry is in the DNA of Britain (for they had a huge impact in Scotland and Ireland as well as England), both metaphorically and literally. There is even a debt to the Vikings for half the days of the week which were named after their gods: Tuesday (Tyr), Wednesday (Odin), Thursday (Thor) and Friday (Freyja).

Mention of the 'Danes', as Viking raiders of England are often called, can be misleading. Just as England as we now call it was still in the process of formation at the time, so too was Scandinavia. The term 'Scandinavia' itself is subject to some ambiguity, though hereafter it broadly means what we now call Norway, Sweden and Denmark. By the opening years of the eleventh century Denmark was still a relatively new united polity, just a few generations old as a centralised territory that we might loosely call a state.

Norway was actually slightly older, founded by King Harald Fairhair in the late ninth century. Central Sweden meanwhile possessed the oldest Scandinavian monarchy of all.[8] Around this time, Scandinavian kings started to emerge. There was already a strong and independent-minded group of jarls (earls) in place below these men and it is highly likely that many of them were not happy with this development. Indeed, it is not impossible that it breathed life into renewed Viking raiding activities as those threatened by the rise of kingly power sought opportunities to flex their muscles elsewhere.

Oftentimes the ruler of Denmark would also be overlord of parts of what are now Norway and Sweden too, especially the south-western district of Scania – locally Skåne – in modern Sweden, separated from modern Denmark only by the narrow Øresund Strait; this district did not become part of modern Sweden until formally ceded by Denmark in the Treaty of Roskilde of 1658. However, this was typically an uncertain state of affairs that did not last for long without being challenged. Great war-chiefs, the jarls or earls as we might call them, still wielded considerable power in the countries of the North and their loyalty to a central power and a king was far from consistent or secure, as the story that follows will demonstrate very well. In fact, uncertain loyalties were very much a feature in both Scandinavia and England at the time.

There is no doubt that the Vikings were a group of people with many facets. Some historians bemoan the fact that the chroniclers of the time see Viking activities in a rather one-dimensional way; one who wrote in the second half of the twentieth century observed that the chroniclers in their approach adopted an 'emphasis on the destructive effects of the [Viking] movement in western Europe, and [they] neglect its contributions on the countries affected, [and as a result] these chroniclers produced for the contemporary world and posterity alike a picture at once incomplete, lurid and distorted'.[9]

Whilst it is true to say that the chroniclers do indeed not focus on the wider picture, and the Vikings were certainly accomplished traders as well as raiders, these criticisms are perhaps relatively easy to make from the safe distance of a thousand years in time. Yet it is also true that the *Anglo-Saxon Chronicles*, our prime source for the history of England at the time, were, by definition, written primarily with an English/Anglo-Saxon audience in mind (and then were written down some decades after the period to which they relate).

To those who were likely to be interested in such matters back then, it was what the Vikings did in England that was of primary interest. And in this respect it is perhaps very understandable that entries in the *Anglo-Saxon Chronicles* focus on the acts of devastation that the raiders were responsible for during the first decades of the eleventh century in particular. There seem to be plenty of them to refer to. It was difficult for chroniclers who were invariably monks to get too excited about the positive cultural contributions of the Vikings when they had done so much damage to the Church and the countries which they raided.

And anyway, supporting evidence for the ferocity of Viking attacks, and the damage that they did, can be found in the much more prosaic form of charters. The following preamble to one, written in 1005 – long before the Viking invasions that shattered the already fragile peace of the kingdom of King Æthelred had reached their terrifying peak – is so informative that it is worth quoting at length:

> I, Æthelred, in the company of the priests of God and our counsellors, contemplating with the pacific gaze of a religious mind, and with good will the anger of God raging with ever increasing savagery against us, have decreed that he should be appeased with the unremitting performance of good works and that there should be no desisting from his praises. And since in our days we suffer the fires of war and the plundering of our riches, and from the cruel depredations of barbarian enemies engaged in ravaging our country and from the manifold sufferings inflicted on us by pagan races threatening us with extermination we perceive that we live in perilous times ... it greatly behoves us ... to give the utmost care and attention to the profit of our souls.[10]

'The anger of God', 'increasing savagery against us', 'the fires of war', 'the plundering of our riches', 'the cruel depredations of barbarian enemies', 'ravaging our country', 'manifold sufferings', 'pagan races threatening us with extermination', 'perilous times' .... These words and phrases are salutary antidotes to the arguments of safely distant modern historians who postulate that the impact of the Vikings raids has been much overplayed.

What exactly motivated the Vikings to first launch their horrifying raids towards the end of the eighth century is a matter of debate. Land hunger has been suggested as one motive as an expanding population outgrew the limited farmable land in Scandinavia but historians are not always convinced by this argument. The heroic-epic culture of the Vikings was another, more probable factor; their history is sometimes, in its written form, indecipherable from myth. As one poem put it,

Cattle die, kinsmen die,
Finally dies one-self;
But never shall perish the fame of him
Who has won a good renown.[11]

In truth it was probably a combination of a number of motivations that drove the Vikings to undertake their overseas adventures; one historian listed fame, profit, change, adventure, land, women, danger, destruction, service, comradeship, command and irresponsibility as amongst the possible factors that drove Viking opportunism and expansionism.[12]

Another very basic reason for their raiding also presents itself: they were able to. Their swift, shallow-draft ships could land on the smallest of beaches, disgorge the crew of raiders on an unsuspecting monastery or village, help themselves to what they wanted, and then disappear again before cumbersome defence plans could be activated. Their ships were nimble and flexible, everything that their foes were not: to stand on the decks of even a modern reconstruction of such a vessel is to feel at once both its beauty and its terrifying efficiency. It is almost a cliché that it was their ships that gave the Vikings such power, but being a cliché does not make it untrue. They took full advantage of the superiority that their maritime skills gave them. When they saw great wealth allied to divided government, as they did in Francia after the reign of Charlemagne in the ninth century or in England at the beginning of the eleventh century, they were like sharks scenting blood.

There was no standing army to resist these raids in England and any defence or counter-attack was normally the responsibility of the levy (or militia) of each county, men who were on the spot; such bands of part-time warriors were called a *fyrd* by the English. Such stopgap measures were usually all that could be done in a practical sense; logistically it would be impossible to get a national army together to fight a raiding party that would not helpfully stand still and wait for retribution until the central government (such as it was) was ready to respond. Therefore, generally speaking local forces had to do what they could to protect their own kith and kin.

There was no doubting the ferocity of their attacks for those in their path. The Vikings at this stage were still pagan and there was little room for Christian niceties (dubious then anyway, even in the Christian world); the violence of their assaults could not be doubted. As one lurid example, Norse saga writers speak of a horrific practice called the 'blood eagle'. This was a ceremony in which an unfortunate captive would have his abdomen cut open, his ribs separated from his spine and his lungs pulled out and spread across his back, making him look like an eagle (or so it was said). Not every historian accepts that such brutal butchery actually happened, an early reminder of the difficulty of separating fact from fiction when we consider the history of the Vikings; but the story quickly caught on.

The early Viking raids on England hit home hard. Their chances of success were heightened by the fact that Britain as a whole was fragmented as the ninth century began. Separate kingdoms existed in England; and Wales, Scotland and Ireland were independent of the Anglo-Saxons and equally divided internally too. This allowed the Vikings to cherry-pick targets, suggesting a good knowledge of the regions that they were raiding. It was notable how difficult it was – relatively speaking – for the Vikings to be successful when their foe was united as happened in England under Alfred the Great or in early eleventh-century Ireland when the great king Brian Boru came to the fore.

The thunderbolt impact of the Viking raid on Lindisfarne in 793 was followed by more lightning strikes soon after: on the great monastery at Jarrow in Northumbria, once the home of the Venerable Bede, the founder of English history; on that at Iona, off the west coast of Scotland and sacred to the memory of the blessed Columba; on Lambey near Dublin; and in Wales. All parts of Britain seemed to be in danger. Progressively the intensity of the raids increased, as did the length of time that the raiders stayed in the lands that they attacked, and the ability of the English and their neighbours to resist weakened. To some it must have seemed as if Armageddon was at hand or, to use instead its Viking equivalent, Ragnarok, 'an age of lust, of axe and sword, and of crashing shields, of wind and wolf ere the world crumbles'.[13]

Over time the danger increased still further as large chunks of English territory fell under the sway of the Vikings, increasingly invaders and settlers rather than raiders, lured by the prospect of fertile land that was not well-defended. By 878, so bad had things become that it seemed that the last vestiges of Saxon resistance were about to be extinguished forever across all of England. By this time Alfred, King of the West Saxons, was hidden away in the marshes of the Isle of Athelney in Somerset. Here he was virtually alone, completely abandoned and apparently with no hope of fighting back, marooned in the midst of a sea of hopelessness. But then, in an incredible about-turn, he managed to gather an army and win a great victory over the Danes. He forced them to convert to Christianity and expelled them from Wessex. It was a remarkable reversal of fortunes but it also set a very difficult precedent for later English kings to try and emulate. He would be a very hard act to follow.

This was not the end of the Viking invasions, though, and not even the beginning of the end. Alfred's successes merely brought stability to some specific parts of England. The Danes established their own permanent settlements in the Midlands and the east of England in a region eventually called the Danelaw. Here they retained the use of their own Danish customary law until the reign of King Henry II in the twelfth century. This included the use of a jury system, which appeared in the Danelaw before it was adopted in Anglo-Saxon England.

At the time England was therefore effectively divided. However, in the years that followed ever more ambitious military expeditions were launched from the Anglo-Saxon lands of Wessex and western Mercia in an attempt to unify England. By 927 Æthelstan, perhaps one of England's greatest rulers, had managed to subsume within his realm all English territory including Northumbria in the far north of the country. As a result he became perhaps the first ruler to be able to justifiably claim the title of 'King of England'.[14] This even impressed the Norwegian king Harald Fairhair, who sent an embassy to the English king that brought with them the gift of a Viking ship.

In this process, something unexpected happened. The Danes of the Danelaw came to accept a strong English king and work with him; for his part the monarch seems to have accepted the need to work cooperatively with the subjects of Scandinavian ancestry that he had taken over. Viking raids further north continued but they typically came from raiders of Norwegian origin, especially those who had settled in Ireland. From time to time, other enemies of the English would ally with the Irish-based Vikings, such as when in 937 an epic battle at Brunanburh saw an alliance of Irish Vikings, Scottish troops and men of the Strathclyde Welsh (from the south-west of Scotland) decimated by an English army.

The newly unified English kingdom seemed to go from strength to strength, though unification was as yet not secure enough to be considered permanent. In 973, King Edgar was crowned at Bath, an imperial city to perhaps serve as a suitable backdrop for a man with imperial pretensions. This was not a coronation to mark the start of his reign but rather one to mark its peak. This not only marked Edgar down formally as King of England; soon after at Chester he took the homage of other rulers such as the kings of Strathclyde and of the Scots who collectively rowed him along the River Dee whilst he took the helm, a powerful symbolic moment. Now a king of all of Anglo-Saxon England was also spreading his claims to suzerainty further north beyond the dilapidated boundary marker of Hadrian's Wall.

What characterised this period in English history was not just the enormous successes of Edgar but also the lack of Viking raids during it. This was in marked contrast to periods both before and after his time as king. There were several reasons for this. First of all, England was a much tougher nut to crack than she had been and therefore easier targets would be more welcome to the Vikings, who were significantly driven by opportunism. It should be noted though that even in his time there were some Viking adventurers in England, such as the splendidly named Thorgils Skarthi – Thorgils of the Harelip – who established himself at Scarborough; or Kormak Fleinn, 'The Arrow', who acted similarly at Flamborough Head.

Secondly, there was trouble closer at home to distract the raiders with warfare inside Scandinavia and pressure on the borders of Denmark from Germany. This perhaps kept men in Scandinavia who might otherwise have been active overseas. But the absence of concerted external pressure on England was so marked that Edgar would become known as 'the Peaceable'. No wonder that later generations would regard this as a Golden Age.

England could now be regarded to some extent as a unified entity though still very young as one. The ruling house was still of the Wessex royal bloodline. At a time when ancestry was all, princes of the royal blood traced their descent back to Cerdic, cited by the *Anglo-Saxon Chronicles* as the first King of Wessex in around 519. Cerdic himself supposedly traced his ancestry back to Woden/Odin (though intriguingly his name is Celtic); he also claimed descent from Adam of Garden of Eden fame, which shows as well as anything just how mixed up Christianity and paganism were at the time. Both elements of the bloodline were in their own way important. Although there had been a number of changes of direction where the line of succession would veer slightly off course (for example, on occasion the late king's brother would succeed him rather than his son), the dynastic connection continued down over the centuries remarkably intact.

Despite Edgar's successes, England was still a long way from being a united country. Soon after the historic meeting at Chester, a new law code was issued by Edgar to strengthen the fledgling nation. One particular clause stated that 'this measure is to be common to all the nation, whether Englishmen, Danes or Britons, in every province of my dominions'.[15] There were, then, formally three different races present in those dominions and the idea of one truly coherent entity called 'England', let alone 'Britain', was still really a long way off.

These were volatile times. Even the greatest dynasties in Europe during this period could be subject to rapid and unexpected decline; the mighty Carolingian empire of Charlemagne did not take long to start to unravel after his death in 814. A strong man held a kingdom together; there were not yet strong constitutional institutions in place to guarantee continuity and stability if such a man died although in contrast, administrative structures in England in particular were well developed. Constitutional crises on the death of a king were frequent and one such was about to occur.

Edgar died in 975 at Winchester, a premature demise which no doubt shocked the country as he was only in his early thirties. His reign had already been very successful and there had been the promise of much more to come. But this was a symptom of a curse that seemed to hang over the Anglo-Saxon kings, many of whom during this period did not enjoy good health and died before their time. Edgar left behind him several sons. The oldest, Edward, was regarded by some as being illegitimate but there were others born from his union with his second wife Ælfryth (better known now perhaps by her Norman name of Elfrida). It seems likely that Elfrida wanted power for her son but the presence of another older half-brother barred the way and the crown passed to Edward instead of her surviving son, Æthelred. But the disappointed half-brother was only to be temporarily deprived of his prize. Young Æthelred's story had only just begun; and what a tale of woe, treachery and disappointment it would be.

Even during Edgar's life, there were very clear signs that the children from this second 'marriage' with Elfrida took precedence over those of the first. The exact position of Edward's mother, Edgar's earlier wife, is a subject of debate; she may well have been considered a concubine, a not uncommon state of affairs for the period. This meant that her legal rights were limited and that a later legitimate 'wife' took precedence, as did her offspring. The evidence for this suggestion concerning the doubtful status of Edward's mother is striking because it comes not from the pens of chroniclers, men who were very susceptible to bias and often more story-tellers than historians, but from dry, dusty documentary evidence from other sources much less likely to be fanciful.

So for example, in 966 Edgar and his council had met at Winchester to celebrate the re-foundation of the New Minster there. A charter was issued to confirm the Minster's rights and privileges. What was significant to our story is not what it actually said but rather who witnessed this document. Top of the list of course was King Edgar. His formidable Archbishop of Canterbury, Dunstan, came next. It was the third name though that was in some ways of most interest. It was Edmund Ætheling (the word for a prince of the royal blood or, literally 'throneworthy'), child of Edgar and Elfrida, described pointedly as 'the legitimate son of the aforementioned king' and still a babe in arms.

Edward, the elder brother, came next, described as 'begotten by the same king'. No mention of legitimacy here, a significant contrast. The fact that he came next in line after his younger brother was no mere accident; it was a very deliberate hierarchical process that was taking place here.[16] During Edgar's reign these were clear signs of the way that the king was thinking and that his children from Elfrida took precedence over those from his previous relationship. But now the king was dead and the world of Elfrida and her son Æthelred (the above-mentioned Edmund Ætheling had subsequently died in infancy) was turned on its head.

The Norman Conquest of England in 1066 was a relatively quick process. Not so the eventual conquest of England by Cnut fifty years earlier. It was a final victory that was the culmination of decades of raiding that had progressively ratcheted up the pressure, moving the objective of the Vikings from opportunistic pillaging to outright subjugation.

Back then England was a very different country to the one we would recognise from more recent times. Only recently had the different Anglo-Saxon and Danish territories in the kingdom been united under the English crown when the 'Danelaw' in the East Midlands was brought under the control of the English Crown. And it is very debatable that the concept of 'nationhood' as we would recognise it actually existed in England in a form that we would be familiar with.

For centuries Angles, Saxons and Jutes (who eventually faded into obscurity) had progressively carved out territories in England and would recognise a cultural affinity with each other but this was vastly different than thinking they were one nation. What gelled the young England together was the strength of its leader and he was of course a mortal. Without a strong hand at the tiller, an Alfred, an Æthelstan, an Edgar for example, the newly created bonds that loosely tied England together could quickly snap as if they were made of the flimsiest string. So on the death of a king, even a strong one, the fabric of the fledgling nation could quickly start to unravel.

Such was the case in 975. Edgar's demise in that year exposed serious weaknesses in the English monarchy and from then on for over 100 years each death of a king led to a succession dispute; the idea of a strong and united England proved to be little more than a mirage. The principle of strictly hereditary succession was not yet firmly established – King Alfred had succeeded his elder brother as king even though the latter had four infant sons. This situation turned out to be England's Achilles Heel. At a time when the king was the ultimate decision-maker in the country and wielded significant power, this was little short of a catastrophe as the death of a ruling monarch more often than not led to fierce infighting.

There were frequently very evident inter-regional tensions too. Wessex and Mercia did not always see eye-to-eye as they jostled for position as the supreme power in England. On the other hand, western Mercia was firmly in the Anglo-Saxon camp whilst eastern Mercia was largely made up of the Danelaw. Northumbria stood to a considerable extent aloof and distant with a significant degree of independent-minded thinking in evidence. There were divisions within her borders too, with the southern part – Deira – effectively dominated by those of Scandinavian origin and the northern element, Bernicia, associated with the Angles who had been there for some centuries. In other words, England was something of a patchwork quilt.

Northumbria was remote from the rest of England and often hard to get to due to poor roads, especially in bad weather which was not uncommon. It was always wise to expect trouble in the region too; William of Malmesbury noted centuries later that kings of England would not travel there without a retinue that was much larger than normal. Such journeys were anyway infrequent. In the north-west, Cumbria was not even a part of England at all and formed part of the British kingdom of Strathclyde at this time.

So England was as yet far from fully unified and rules of succession were very imprecise. As if to make the point, Edward's accession in 975 was not unopposed but it was nevertheless he who finally became king after a certain amount of jostling for position. It was a resolution of sorts but it would not last. Three years later, Edward was dead, 'martyred' in the words of the *Anglo-Saxon Chronicles*.[17] And perhaps this is the point at which the long journey to the Danish conquest of England began.

Edward was very young when he became king, probably about thirteen years of age; his half-brother Æthelred was perhaps only seven, which made him an unlikely candidate. However, at that time twelve was widely considered to be the age of maturity; a law of Æthelstan decreed that anyone over that age could be executed for theft.[18] This would give Edward some reason to hope for support over the claims of his younger brother.

Despite this, Edward's claim to be king was not uncontested. The status of his mother continued to be questioned, and there were at the time of his accession some elements in England who wanted his half-brother to succeed instead of him. Foremost amongst these, it was suggested, was his stepmother Elfrida, a not at all unreasonable assumption not only for maternal reasons but also because she would have effective control over her son during his minority.[19] One thing that Elfrida most certainly did not lack was ambition.

For three years after Edward's accession England limped on with barely concealed undercurrents of resentment evident from those who still wanted Æthelred to be king, not because of his personal qualities but for what they themselves would gain from a regime change. An unconvincing spirit of compromise led to a brooding, dark atmosphere in England. Tension was in the air and it was about to be unleashed with fierce and fatal force. One March day in 978 a violent explosion occurred, a vile act that was to shake the country like an earthquake and leave its foundations shaking for decades until they finally collapsed. The writer of the Peterborough version of the *Anglo-Saxon Chronicles* wrote in horror of the death of Edward:[20]

> No worse deed for the English race was done than this was, since they first sought out the land of Britain. Men murdered him, but God exalted him. In life he was an earthly king; after death he is now a heavenly saint. His earthly relatives would not avenge him, but his Heavenly father has much avenged him.[21]

How much of this is true depends on how reliable the *Anglo-Saxon Chronicles* are as a source. The oldest surviving versions of the *Anglo-Saxon Chronicles* are frustratingly short of detail. They were described by a historian of the early twentieth century as being 'meagre and disappointing' for periods of Cnut's reign.[22] It is worth pointing out that the reference to Chronicles in the plural is not a misprint; the versions are in places completely different and therefore to refer to a Chronicle in the singular, as is the norm, can be very misleading indeed. There are significant differences in the various versions but nevertheless this very rare survival of historical records written in the vernacular is a national treasure to be proud of.

They are not the only writings providing evidence of the events of the time. But in this case further details of the death of Edward come only from accounts written a century or two later and must therefore be treated with a due degree of caution. The *Anglo-Saxon Chronicles* give a rare more or less contemporary insight into these troubled times. But these later histories have added many dashes of colour, though whether the picture has been distorted as a result is a moot point. Certainly the most 'popular' versions have his stepmother at the heart of the events that led to Edward's 'martyrdom'.

A composite presentation of some of these later accounts has Edward out hunting for game in the forests of the Isle of Purbeck in Dorset. His day's hunting completed (it was 18 March 978), he returned to the royal lodge at Corfe, supposedly on the hill where the great ruined castle of more recent medieval vintage now stands. He was tired after the day's hunt but his companions were still out enjoying the chase and he was alone. His stepmother Elfrida came out to greet him and offered him a goblet of wine. Even as he was drinking it, one of her attendants crept up behind him and stabbed him in the back. The chronicler Henry of Huntingdon even has Elfrida sticking the knife in him herself whilst he was downing a drink that she had offered him.[23]

Edward was not killed outright and he put spurs to his horse. But the wound was mortal. As his panic-stricken steed took flight, weakened through loss of blood, the dying king fell. As he did so, his foot caught in his stirrup. He was dragged along the track, through the woods, his lifeblood oozing out of him and leaving a tell-tale trail of red streaks behind him on the ground. The horse at last stopped, the king's battered body still hanging out of the stirrup.

Then, as so often in the stories of the time, the miraculous took over. The murdered king's body was buried hastily in marshy ground but a vision came to a blind woman who lived nearby. During the night her sight was miraculously restored and she was led to the slain king's body. The news broke that Edward had been murdered. Due to this and other miracles, the king came to be regarded as a saint.

According to William of Malmesbury, those who visited his grave received evidence of divine approbation for the dead king.

The lame walked, the dumb regained their speech, the sick were restored to health. It was said that a spring appeared from the ground near his grave and that invalids who bathed in it were miraculously cured of their afflictions. Buried soon after, allegedly in the house of a peasant rather than on sacred ground (the Church of St Edward in Corfe Castle now supposedly marks the spot of this humble dwelling), his remains were then reinterred in Wareham. Later they were translated to the far more significant site of the nunnery at Shaftesbury.[24]

A great procession accompanied the body from Wareham to Shaftesbury; in the bad winter weather current at the time the journey seems to have taken at least a week (leaving Wareham on 13 February 979, the cortege did not arrive until the 20th even though it was only a journey of about thirty miles).[25] By his death, the young, untried and untested king was transformed into a saintly hero. On the other hand, by his murder the supporters of the new king, Æthelred, were from the start up against it, a situation reinforced by the shabby and unholy way that Edward's body had been treated.

This is so far a straightforward 'black-and-white' analysis of events that makes a saint of the slain king, a demon of his stepmother and a usurper of his half-brother. As is usually the case in history, there are suggestions that the 'real' story is rather different or at least more complex. Writing a life of St Oswald just a few decades after Edward's murder, the monk Byrhtferth lamented the 'shipwreck' that had overtaken England after the death of the great Edgar, castigating the supposedly saintly Edward for his violent tempers in which, allegedly, he mercilessly beat his servants.[26]

The murder of her stepson in close proximity to herself was of course potentially embarrassing to Elfrida. Eventually, she sent her close ally ealdorman Ælfhere of Mercia[27] to escort his body from Wareham to the more significant location of Shaftesbury. Although some early accounts suggest that the slaughtered king's body had been burned, now the ealdorman had Edward's body disinterred and it was found to be miraculously intact.

For the alleged murderess, this was far from a happy time. Her horse refused to carry her when she tried to approach the tomb of her stepson, stopping dead in its tracks and frozen to the spot despite the urgency of Elfrida's attempts to move it. The queen, a beautiful woman it was said, took to penitence in her attempts to atone for her crimes. In later years she dressed in hair-cloth, slept at night on the ground without a pillow and generally mortified her flesh in any way she could as a mark of her remorse. But any repentance – if such it genuinely was – did little good, and as a result 'the country for a long time after groaned under the yoke of barbarian servitude'.[28] In other words, England was punished by the Almighty for her sins. And the Vikings would be God's avengers.

So – if we believe William of Malmesbury – it was the wicked stepmother, that eternal archetype, who called down the wrath of the Vikings. It was unlikely to have been any such thing of course, even if all these accusations were true (and certainly not all modern historians are convinced that they are). Such claims and equal and opposite counter-claims were a standard motif for medieval chroniclers. This perception of divine judgement and punishment would very much shape the views of contemporary writers; even Alcuin wondered whether Lindisfarne had been sacked in retribution for the sins of local people. Such men sought around for adequate explanations for any disasters that shook the country from time to time, whether natural or man-made. They were much less interested in writing up a factual account of what had actually happened than in searching for answers in the sins of men and the avenging acts of the Almighty directed at them.

That said, there appear to be several incontrovertible facts that can be agreed upon from this unsavoury sequence of events. First of all, the main beneficiaries of the killing of Edward were Æthelred and his ambitious stepmother, who would play a key part in the rule of the country whilst he was still a minor. This gave both a strong motive, though Æthelred's youth argues against him playing any significant active part in the plot.

Secondly, the killers – who in such a public act must have been known to many and especially to the queen if the events took place on her doorstep – were never brought to justice, hence the allusion in the *Anglo-Saxon Chronicles* to the non-punishment of Edward's murderers. This again does not present Elfrida in an especially positive light as she was the power behind the throne during the new king's formative years.

In fact, the murder of Edward put the young Æthelred in a much-compromised position right from the outset. Such an act of regicide and fratricide meant that he ruled with blood on his hands. This outrage demanded a response; the killers must be brought to justice. But no such justice was ever meted out. If Elfrida was indeed responsible for the assassination, it is not hard to see why this was the case.

In the absence of any attempt to right the wrong, it was almost inevitable in the context of the times that Edward would increasingly be seen as an innocent and even saintly youth, his deficiencies ignored and ironed out, his virtues magnified to a ridiculous extent. The road to martyrdom and even sainthood was already being travelled rapidly by the shade of the murdered Edward. His shadow would loom over Æthelred for the rest of his reign, a giant and omnipresent spectre to haunt him for the remainder of his days.

With Edward out of the way, young Æthelred was duly installed as king in Kingston-upon-Thames on the fourteenth day after Easter in 979. The gap of over a year from Edward's murder suggests that the beneficiaries of the crime were keen to avoid taking too quick an advantage of the situation in case it gave the 'wrong' impression, though delayed coronations were not unheard of in Anglo-Saxon times. Any suggestion of hesitation hints at ongoing opposition to Æthelred's accession even in the absence of a viable male candidate as an alternative.[29] Best remembered by his later nickname 'Æthelred the Unready', he was formally declared King Æthelred II, Æthelred I being an elder brother and predecessor of Alfred the Great in the ninth century.

Kingston-on-Thames may seem an unlikely place for a coronation now, but it had in fact been the site of several such ceremonies during the tenth century, including that of the great Æthelstan. It was to the west of London on the river from which it took its name, and its regal title hinted at its royal associations. Most importantly it stood on the borders of Wessex and Mercia and was therefore the ideal symbolic spot to celebrate a kingship that in theory united the two powerhouses of Anglo-Saxon England as one.

Despite the alleged treachery which had led to the removal of the late king, there was said to be 'great rejoicing' in the land at Æthelred's accession.[30] But all was not well, for in the words of the Winchester version of the *Anglo-Saxon Chronicles*, 'that same year a bloody cloud was seen, many times in the likeness of fire; and it appeared most of all at midnight; and it was formed thus of various beams; then when it became day it glided away'.[31] A blood-red cloud was indeed a suitable portent for the long but troubled reign that lay ahead.

Other stories of Æthelred's coronation suggest that from the start this was considered to be an ill-starred reign. Archbishop (later Saint) Dunstan was the foremost churchman of his day and one of the most striking characters of the late Saxon period. A man who allegedly physically battled with and got the better of devils disguised in the form of beautiful women was unlikely to be phased by the prospect of crowning a boy-king usurper.

During the coronation ceremony it was said that Dunstan, after placing the crown on Æthelred's head, was moved to prophesy, saying that because he had gained the crown by murdering his brother, 'the sword shall not depart from your house, but shall rage against you all the days of your life, cutting off your seed, until your kingdom becomes the kingdom of an alien, whose customs and tongue the nation which you rule knows not. And your sin, and the sin of your mother, and the sin of the men who were parties to her wickedness, shall be expiated only by long continued punishment.'[32] Written long after the events that they describe, these words probably owe much to hindsight.

Nevertheless, it was an interesting prophecy. In the end, Æthelred's reign, certainly in its later years, would be marked by persistent fighting, infighting and bloodshed. The line of his people would indeed almost die out, as his son Edmund would be amongst the last of the male line and on his death England would fall into the hands of an alien conqueror. The Anglo-Saxon dynasty would be overturned not by one but by two foreign peoples, with strange customs and tongues – first Danes, then Normans. These years were vital in shaping the events that forged modern England.

Having thundered his predictions at the presumably terrified king and his horrified mother at the coronation, Dunstan's career was over. Rather than accept all the dire prognostications he made as being completely reliable, we might do better to bear in mind that Dunstan was no natural friend of Æthelred as they were later opposed on a number of issues concerning the Church. But Dunstan now retired from public life and on his death became one of the most revered saints of the English people until a later archbishop called Thomas à Becket would take his place in their affections.

It did not take long for something more substantial than a blood-red cloud to materialise when an old threat, not much seen in the glorious later years of Edgar's reign, returned. In the year 980 Southampton was ravaged by a Viking 'ship-army', as was Thanet and, later in the same year, Chester. In 981, Padstow and other parts of Cornwall and Devon were the target. In the years that followed other parts of England are mentioned as being under attack: Portland in Dorset, Watchet in Somerset for example. Raids were frequent and widespread. The timing is unlikely to have been fortuitous and is best explained by assuming that the raiders sensed renewed weaknesses in England that they were confident of exploiting.

Yet some context is also important here. The fact that the places which were raided were individually listed in the *Anglo-Saxon Chronicles* suggests that these were as yet unusual events and were not that widespread. Further, their location, far from London, made it difficult for any national response, and although Æthelred's popularity would clearly not benefit from the raids, the prime responsibility for fighting off the attackers was a local one. These events were irritating and at a local level undoubtedly terrifying. But they were as yet far from being apocalyptic on a national scale.

These were generally unhappy times for many people in the country. For there was not just a Viking threat to worry about: a 'great pestilence' killing off large numbers of cattle appeared in 986. If God were indeed taking revenge for the murder of the martyr King Edward he was doing so ruthlessly. But it was in 991 that matters really began to go badly wrong. In that year Olaf Tryggvason, later King of Norway, led ninety-three ships to Folkestone, from there to Sandwich and then onwards across Kent. Making his way north of the Thames, he was soon after faced by an English army led by a local ealdorman, a high-ranking royal official by the name of Byrhtnoth, at Maldon in East Anglia.

It was on 10 or 11 August that the two armies met (there are slightly conflicting accounts as to the exact date). As a result of that battle we have one of the earliest classics in English literature. It is a 325-line fragment of a poem that has not survived complete into modern times; but what remains is a glorious extract which allows us to peer directly into the soul of the Anglo-Saxon world. Maldon is on the River Blackwater in Essex and Byrhtnoth was one of a particular breed of English leaders who wished to meet fire with fire. Here he faced a Viking raiding party with his men, an event that was subsequently immortalised in verse.

The poem is more a work of literature than of history and this means that it should not necessarily be taken as a literal rendition of the battle any more than, say, an Arthurian epic should be thought of as an accurate outline of a later medieval war. It is an epic, part of the great saga tradition that the Vikings knew so well but of which the Anglo-Saxon world also supplies a superb example in the form of *Beowulf*. But on the other hand the remaining fragment gives a convincing glimpse into the world of the Anglo-Saxons at war.

The poem has ealdorman Byrhtnoth – described by another source as a tall, grey-haired man, which would be consistent with a warrior of around sixty years of age – marshalling his troops by the river, arranging their shield-wall, the *scildburh*, behind which they would face the enemy, a traditional Anglo-Saxon battle tactic. As he and his retainers stood ready for the attack, a messenger came out from the 'sea-thieves' to demand money, in return for which the Norse host would go away: 'no need to slaughter each other if you be generous to us'.

There is at least a hint of reality here, for as we shall see the standard Viking tactic for a time afterwards (as it had indeed been in the past) was for these raiding parties to seek money; they were more than happy to be bought off rather than fight but if no money was forthcoming then fight they would, with vigour. But Byrhtnoth would have none of this defeatist talk and responded in heroic fashion: 'his shield raised aloft, brandishing a slender ash-wood spear, speaking words wrathful and resolute did he give his answer' (long ash-wood spears seem to have held some special significance and may have been associated with leaders). Defiantly he spoke: 'Tell your people this spiteful message, that here stands undaunted an Earl with his band of men who will defend our homeland, Æthelred's country, the lord of my people and land.'

The tide kept the enemies apart for a while, but when it started to draw back the English were in a strong position, keeping guard over a narrow causeway which the Viking force had to cross if they wished to proceed. An emissary of the Vikings now asked the English to let them cross so that there might be a fair fight, a suggestion that Byrhtnoth acceded to. It was a proud and defiant gesture, daring the enemy to come over and fight; although if Byrhtnoth actually acted this way, he appears to have been a rather rash battle leader.[33]

With their way now clear, the 'wolves of slaughter' made their way across. Within a short time, 'murderously sharpened spears flew. Bows were busily at work, shields received spears. Fierce was that onslaught.' Great men fell; Wulfmaer, kinsman of Byrhtnoth, was cruelly hewn down, but the English resolutely fought on, even though their leader was wounded by a spear thrust.

However, Byrhtnoth's reprieve was only temporary and another spear soon struck home. He slumped to the ground, dying, and several of his loyal retinue fell with him. But then, a surprise. Rather than fight to the death in a glorious losing cause, a few of the Anglo-Saxon force broke and ran. Some of them are named, Godwin and Godwig amongst them. But others ran to the aid of their dying lord and gave their lives up. One of them, Leofsonu, swore, 'I will not flee a foot's space, as my desire is to advance further, avenge in battle-strife my lord and friend.'

The fighting was fierce and intense and many men fell on both sides. But the battle was clearly going against the English. It was then that an old retainer, Byrhtwold, spoke up. Brandishing his spear, he spoke the following immortal words: 'Our hearts must grow resolute, our courage more valiant, our spirits must be greater, though our strength grows less.'[34]

It was a battle cry to the English that echoes down the centuries, an evocation of that bulldog spirit for which later generations of Byrhtwold's countrymen would be famous, an early-day appeal to the 'Dunkirk spirit'. So saying, he charged into the eye of the storm, selling his life dearly in an effort to avenge his slain lord or die in the attempt. It was a typically 'English' gesture one might think: a glorious defiant act in the face of certain defeat and death. Yet it also shows that not all of the Anglo-Saxon people had yet lost the will to fight: as one writer remarked, 'What could be more welcome in Æthelred's reign, with its treachery and intrigues, than for Englishmen to be reminded of the ancient values of the Germanic warrior: loyalty, courage and generosity?'[35]

The death of Byrhtnoth was a great symbolic blow. As an ealdorman of some thirty-five years' standing, he was a well-known and respected figure in the country who as a supporter of the Benedictine reform movement in England had been a generous benefactor of the abbey at Ely (where indeed he was laid to rest). He had been an associate of the great so-called Æthelstan Half-king, an East Anglian noble who was perhaps the greatest non-regal secular figure of tenth-century Anglo-Saxon England, as his name suggests. It would not have helped that his body was mutilated after death: when the monks of Ely recovered it, they found that his head had been hacked off and kept by the Vikings as a gruesome trophy of war.[36] The shockwaves which followed the defeat and the loss of such men would have shaken Æthelred's court alarmingly, however much gloss a great work of literature might try to put on it by stressing its heroic aspects.

And so the Battle of Maldon was lost, along with many another battle during these tumultuous years. As the English found their strength sapping away as if a debilitating and terminal illness was eating at the fabric of the country, so did the Viking host grow ever stronger. As they scented weakness in their prey, they moved in for the kill.

There is some circumstantial evidence that the defeat at Maldon marked a sea-change in England. For in 993, just two years later, there were two major policy changes on the part of Æthelred. Firstly, his mother Elfrida, a powerful personality from what we can gauge, who had effectively been in exile from the court for nine years after her dominated son attempted to break out from her shadow, reappeared at his side. Secondly, the king had been a strong defender of the monarchy's rights vis-à-vis those of the Church but now he reversed his approach and sought to rebuild his relationships with it. Both can be seen as attempts to rebuild old domestic alliances and support against the renewed threat from across the seas.

The scene for our story is now set. It only needs its main character to enter, though more must be told of the intervening period if the tale of his final triumph is to make sense. The years that were about to follow were some of the harshest in early English history. It was a time of terror emerging from nowhere in the night, of dragon ships creeping unnoticed along the coast, unleashing death and devastation in their wake as sword and fire consumed the land. It was an age when the English were constantly outmanoeuvred and the great men of the country were divided and apparently powerless in the face of the enemy. It was a moment in history when the ultimate overthrow of England and a Viking conquest of it all seemed an inevitability, only for a hero to emerge at the last and lead a fightback that threatened to repeat the amazing change in fortunes brought about by Alfred the Great himself.

What follows is the recreation of a great Viking saga, a tale of war and greed, of statesmanship and political ineptitude, of treachery and heroism. It is full of incident, of Viking longships stealing like wood-framed sea monsters through the mists that shroud the coast to swoop time and again on an unsuspecting prey, of triumph against overwhelming odds, of the snatching of victory from defeat and finally of unrivalled glory. It has pretty much everything: titanic battles between two mighty warriors and their armies, an arch-traitor who in the end got his just deserts, a woman who was the ultimate survivor and became queen to two different husbands, a Viking war-chief with the name of Forkbeard and, at the heart of it all, a man who was not born as the heir to even one kingdom but later in his life became effectively an emperor with three. In classic Viking tradition there are massacres, the martyrdom of archbishops and the ruthless extermination of enemies. And this saga has one particular virtue to commend it: all the above actually happened.

Yet this is only half the story for the man at its heart, Cnut the Great, was very different from the stereotypical Viking warrior who celebrated his successes in drunken orgies. There was no doubting his ruthlessness for sure; any rivals, even innocent ones, were despatched without compunction (though there were one or two exceptions to the general rule). He was a capable warrior too, though he had tasted the bitterness of defeat and the humiliation of flight in his time. But there were other qualities to bring into the equation too.

The epic nature of the history of this period in general has led more than one modern historian to compare it in passing to

Tolkien's *Lord of the Rings*, a not unreasonable comparison to make when one considers that he was much influenced by Norse sagas, definite shades of which come through in his works. The age of the Vikings as a whole is a remarkable epoch, yet it has been rightly said that their power, influence and contacts probably peaked either side of the year 1000,[37] the age of Cnut. This is a story not just of England, then, but of much of Europe too.

Yet Cnut is hard to place in all this as he is a crossover character, a link between an old and a new world. No pagan Viking this, no fanatical worshipper of Odin or Thor, for Cnut was a strong supporter of the Church. Not only would he rub shoulders with Viking warrior-chiefs or fellow kings, he would also do so with popes and emperors. He was first and foremost a remarkably successful statesman, capable of vision allied to crucial human qualities such as perseverance and tact. He would become king of not only England but also of Denmark and Norway, a veritable Empire of the North. His influence extended not just to the lands he ruled but across a wider continental sphere from Poland to Italy, making him a man of truly European significance. Yet at the same time he retained elements of his Scandinavian origins. He loved the praise of the poets who extolled their heroes in the sagas as much as the next man.

Cnut's greatness was made possible by the conquest of England. Mention such a conquest and most Englishmen and women will think at once of 1066 with the Roman invasion of AD 44 a distant second in the memory. But England also fell into 'foreign' hands in 1016, fifty years before William the Conqueror's triumph, which overshadows Cnut's earlier success. Yet the Conquest of 1066 is not a perfect comparison, for its ultimate outcome was crucially decided by one battle at Hastings. By contrast, the fall of England in 1016 came at the end of a final campaign that had lasted for two years and followed bitter raids and frequent pitched battles between the two adversaries for well over a decade before. Cnut's ultimate triumph in 1016 came as much as anything because his rivals were collapsing – sometimes literally – from exhaustion. The denouement for England was a long time in coming and at one time it appeared that it would not come at all.

1

England: The Long Road to Conquest (991–1002)

The year of Maldon, 991, also saw an important change in direction for King Æthelred. According to several different versions of the *Anglo-Saxon Chronicles*, this was the first year during his reign in which it was decided to buy the Vikings off with what we might now call protection money or at least a bribe to be left alone. It was apparently Sigeric 'the Serious', Archbishop of Canterbury, who suggested this move. This first payment was for £10,000 but it was to be the first of many as, sensing weakness, the Viking raiders would be back for more. It was also a policy that contrasted rather shamefully with the proud defiance of Byrhtnoth at Maldon when he refused to pay any tribute to the Viking aggressor. This protection money would be given its own specific name: 'Danegeld' (although this name was not contemporary with the period and appeared subsequently – the word *gafol* or 'tribute' was more likely to be used at the time).

The title suggests that this was money to pay off the 'Danes' but it is too much to suggest that the raids were part of a concerted national Danish effort or indeed were exclusively Danish at all; the campaign which culminated at Maldon had after all specifically included Norwegians and was led by Olaf Tryggvason, whose interests lay in Norway. The succession of raids from Scandinavia, it has been said, 'are unlikely to have been organised and commanded solely by Danish kings, did not consist entirely of Danes, and frequently appear to have been motivated mainly by a desire for booty'.[1] These were opportunistic attacks and many of the participants were effectively mercenaries with swords (and axes, spears and bows) for hire. Given such motivations, regional origins were often an irrelevance.

The raiders were certainly as happy to be paid off as they were fighting for their gains. Viking raiding parties relied on creating a climate of fear with which to pressurise their opponents into submission. Evidence from surviving rune-stones in Scandinavia shows that some raiders went on a number of raids under different leaders. This was not, then, a process that involved formalised and inflexible war bands but raiding parties that were assembled specifically for one-off expeditions. When later the process changed to one of attempted conquest rather than raids, it is probable that the composition of such groups changed. After all, not every warrior would have wanted to give up his raiding lifestyle and put down roots as a landowner, trader or farmer. But there would still be plenty of opportunities for raiders who did not plan to settle down in England after any conquest.

It would be wrong to assume that the concept of 'Danegeld' was new or even something unique to England. Viking raiders had been paid off in Francia in the ninth century. Even the great Alfred had probably bought the Danes off in 871/872 as Mercia did at around the same time. The raiders were motivated by opportunities to make a profit and men who had been bought off once were very likely to be back for more in the future. In all likelihood the price would go up on each occasion. A rather nasty form of inflation was then likely to ensue and the cost of avoiding conflict would escalate, putting great strain on the economic resources of a country. If a king was forced to rely on such measures it was hardly likely to add to his popularity as it was his people who were forced to pay up the large amounts involved.

At this stage the Viking attacks that had been experienced during Æthelred's reign had not been part of a concerted plan of conquest and were driven more by a desire for short-term profit. Æthelred suspected that the Vikings would return and that the payment made would only bring a temporary halt to the raids. And sure enough, in the following year they were indeed back. Æthelred attempted to prepare for them this time. He gathered together all the ships that he could in London and planned to catch the enemy in a pre-arranged trap. But then there was a most unwelcome turn of events. At the last moment Ælfric, the ealdorman of Hampshire, crept away and warned the raiding Vikings of what was in store for them.

Treachery; it was already hinted at in the Battle of Maldon and now here it was again. The nightmare of the raids had in reality only just begun. The following year the Vikings were back once more. This time they struck much further north. They attacked Bamburgh. Nowadays this is the site of a magnificent medieval castle; according to Thomas Malory it was once Lancelot's Joyeuse Garde. However, Bamburgh was old even in the tenth century. It had been attacked and taken by an earlier group of raiders, the Angles, back in 547, one of their earliest victories in the north-east, and it was a place of great significance to the people of Northumbria. Now the Vikings ransacked it totally, helping themselves to a great deal of booty in the process.

Nor was this the end of it. The raiding party then sailed on down to the Humber where they did great damage. An army was sent to meet them but the commanders of this force, Fraena, Godwin and Frithugist, fled rather than fight. It was suggested by the early twelfth-century chronicler 'Florence' of Worcester that the men who ran away were in fact Danes and this is by no means impossible as two of the names (Godwin being the exception) appear to be of Danish origin.[2] It is an early reminder that to see the upcoming wars as a battle between Danes on one side and English on the other is a huge over-simplification.

One of the problems for the English king was that many of the inhabitants in the Danelaw in the East Midlands of England were of Scandinavian descent, which potentially gave them divided loyalties, though over time their loyalty to their Scandinavian origins may have become much diminished. Neither were the Anglo-Saxons united, as the disputed succession of Æthelred had evidenced. In some regions of the country affiliations were not strong towards the king; this would be especially so in East Anglia for example. The relative youth of England as a nation, and the lack of unity that this led to, would be an ongoing problem throughout his reign.

Yet these elements should not be overplayed. The inhabitants of the Danelaw had found a good life in England. They had given up their piratical activities and settled as farmers and traders. When

Norwegian raiders had beset England in the tenth century, these settlers measured the benefits of an even-handed English overlord who let them retain their own customs and laws against the Viking hordes who threatened their adopted kingdom; they may have been surprised to discover that they much preferred the first option. This was by no means a latent fifth column in the country for Æthelred to worry about. This also reflected what happened in other regions too. Scandinavian settlers showed a marked flair for integrating into and assimilating with local populations, not just in England but also in Normandy and Russia too for example.

Nevertheless, there were a number of internal tensions to be dealt with by the king. This was demonstrated when Æthelred soon after had Ælfgar, son of the unreliable Ælfric, blinded. Yet whatever the reasons behind this violent act, the untrustworthy ealdorman was not removed from office, meaning that he remained in a position of power, ready to prove his unreliability again in the future. This evidence collectively suggests that England as a country was not at peace with itself, let alone with the Viking raiders. This seriously hampered the king's capacity to organise a robust defence of his kingdom.

The raids continued to hit home, creating more misery for the English people. In 995, on the Nativity of St Mary (8 September), nearly 100 Viking ships bore down on London. This brought the king directly into the front line. Two leaders of this force were mentioned in particular. One was Olaf Tryggvason, the victor of Maldon. The other was a ferocious warrior by the name of Sweyn Forkbeard, whom some historians believe may also have taken part in the Maldon campaign though he is not actually named by the sources of the time.[3] It was an alliance of Norwegian and Dane, forged by little more than mutual self-interest. It was not a precursor for long-term collaboration between these two strong men, as we shall see.

The irony of these incursions was that the Anglo-Saxons and the Vikings shared to some extent a common origin. So too did the Jutes, who originally came from Jutland in Denmark during migrations probably in the fifth century but were eventually subsumed by the Saxons in England. Cultural connections between the Scandinavian peoples and Anglo-Saxons are not hard to find. For example, the famous seventh-century Sutton Hoo ship burial artefacts bear a marked resemblance to items from Sweden. And the great epic *Beowulf* is not set in England at all but betrays its Scandinavian roots by taking place in Denmark and Sweden.[4] A number of linguistic similarities can also be observed to reinforce the connection. From a cultural perspective, Anglo-Saxons and Vikings can be thought of as cousins.

However, over time the closeness of that relationship had lessened to some extent. One major reason for this was the introduction of Christianity. It took hold in Anglo-Saxon England several centuries before it did in Scandinavia and this weakened the cultural ties. A similar situation may be observed in Francia where the Franks, also originally Germanic in origin, adopted the new religion very early on with the great Merovingian king Clovis in the late fifth century.

Both Olaf Tryggvason and Sweyn Forkbeard were formidable raiders. In common with many great personalities of the time (the tenth-century Viking king and warrior Erik Bloodaxe would be another fine example), even the name Sweyn Forkbeard conjures up vivid pictures (though wearing a beard forked was not uncommon amongst the Vikings).[5] But firm facts about Sweyn are in relatively short supply. He was the son of Harald Bluetooth, who was important as one of the first Scandinavian kings known to have adopted Christianity. There had been several earlier ninth-century rulers in Scandinavia who converted to the religion, particularly due to the efforts of St Ansgar, 'the Apostle of the North'. However, the religion did not begin to establish a firm hold until Harald's time.

Harald Bluetooth's dynastic Viking pedigree was notable, causing one near-contemporary writer to remark that 'he derived his descent from a most noble source, a thing of foremost importance amongst men';[6] where a man came from mattered greatly back then. He was likely to have adopted Christianity in large part because of pressure from the Holy Roman Emperor Otto, his powerful and pushy neighbour to the south. He certainly does not appear to have had everything his own way in the process of Christianising his country; the later saga-writer Snorri Sturluson suggests that he had to resort to 'making use of force and chastisement' in an attempt to make the change stick.[7] At first glance this might seem surprising: the Scandinavian peoples, after all, were polytheists. Not only were there Odin, Thor and Frey, there were a host of other gods and goddesses too, Baldr the Beautiful and the trickster Loki for example. What difference should one more make? But the Christian God was a jealous deity who would not share his position with any other.

There were several reasons why Christianity was attractive to kings of the time, Viking ones included. By building a close association with the powerful institution that was the Church, an alliance could be formed which would allow the king's power to grow, though this relationship would always be in a state of delicate equilibrium. In an age when kings were attempting to build centralised power at the expense of strongly self-sufficient local nobles, an alliance with the Church and the creation of what we would now call an 'establishment' to run the country could be a significant weapon for a secular ruler. By adopting a state religion both the Church and the ruler would benefit – one reason, probably, why the Roman Emperor Constantine had adopted Christianity in the fourth century. An added attraction for rulers like Harald Bluetooth was that it would help to break the power of the local aristocracy who were important in the practice of older pagan religions. There was much mutual self-interest between Church and king in such collaboration.

Like many new recruits to the Christian religion during these years (and the Anglo-Saxons a few centuries earlier were similar in this respect), it may be that some of the Danes openly adopted Christianity whilst at the same time retaining vestiges of paganism, hedging their bets in a spiritual sense. This maybe explains why some near-contemporary commentators such as Adam of Bremen accuse Sweyn of being an out-and-out pagan even though there is also evidence that he sponsored several new churches in Denmark during his life. It was also true that Sweyn was no political friend of the Archbishopric of Hamburg-Bremen either, which would certainly have helped to poison Adam's pen against him.

There was a close link between Church and State in Western Christendom at this time. The Church, if actively allied to the king, could strengthen the overall bonds that held a state together. On the other hand, if Church and State were divided then problems could follow. Viking kings trying to forge new kingdoms might well be attracted to the extra bonds of power and social cohesion that such an alliance might bring. In other words, it was probably political pragmatism rather than faith that led to the adoption of Christianity by such men.

The process of conversion from paganism to Christianity did not take root in Scandinavia overnight. Men such as Sweyn Forkbeard were selective in their adoption of Christianity. He was first and foremost an ambitious man who committed some very un-Christian acts to fulfil his ambitions; but he would hardly be the first or the last so-called Christian to allow earthly ambition to take precedence over his religious beliefs.

Despite any misgivings we may have as to his objectivity, it is to Adam of Bremen that we owe much of what we know of the history of Scandinavia at this time. Writing just over fifty years after Cnut died, Adam nevertheless had access to men who had known him, in particular the late king's nephew, Sweyn Estrithsson. His account is a priceless insight into a crucial period in the development of the region when 'the fluid Scandinavian empires based on overlordship and tribute-taking, which had characterised the period between 850 and 1050, were consolidating into Western European-style kingdoms supported by bishoprics, administrative institutions and taxation.'[8] Cnut would later be one of the men most responsible for this transition.

Cnut's grandfather Harald Bluetooth was another and in many ways set the scene for him during the three decades of his rule. Denmark is a relatively small country when defined by geographical area but it is a complicated one. It is a combination of a long peninsula, Jutland, jutting out into the two channels that lead from the Baltic out into the North Sea, the Skagerrak to the west and the Kattegat to the east, and a group of islands off the east coast of the mainland. Power in Denmark had traditionally not been in the hands of one king but had rather been dispersed across a group of warlords, each powerful landowners in their own region. They still to a large extent acted as independent chiefs (or 'sea kings' might be a better description), much as in more recent times clan leaders in the Highlands of Scotland still controlled the loyalty of their people whilst paying nominal allegiance to a king with central authority.

The Viking sagas, composed mainly in Iceland several centuries after the events they claim to describe, suggest that these sea kings were adept at playing one powerful figure against another. Mention of the sagas is important to the story of the Vikings. Whilst these tales undoubtedly exaggerated the greatness and the deeds of the Vikings and their leaders, and threw in a large dose of supernaturalism to boot, they also suggest what was expected of a great warrior of the age: bravery, generosity, charisma, cunning and skill in battle. Such heroic figures shaped strong fellowships around them, though ironically the sagas also suggest they could not rely on unbreakable loyalty forever as the supporters of such men often switched sides.

The Danish landowning classes remained unpredictable and very protective of their independence. This situation remained into Cnut's time and well beyond it. It meant that a Danish king could not rule with absolute authority, ignoring the wishes of the powerful earls around him. He was instead forced to strike a difficult balance whereby he set the overall direction for his policy and that of the lands he would rule but only by taking into account the wishes of the independent-minded men who surrounded him. He had to hone and cultivate supporters. As a number of kings of the time would find out the hard way, it was a balance that was difficult to get right. In this respect, Cnut would not prove to be an exception despite his relative success.

Harald Bluetooth, Cnut's grandfather, became a quasi-legendary figure and to an extent remains so in modern Denmark.[9] His line, founded by his father Gorm, became known as the Jelling dynasty after a settlement on the east coast of Jutland. Here Harald erected a standing stone complete with carvings which exists still and gives a powerful insight into Danish art and beliefs at the time. Although the style is very much Norse with flowing, interwoven curves and lines etched on the stones, it is complete with a Christian message in the shape of a Christ with open arms, as if welcoming new converts to his religion.

The stone has been sometimes called 'the birth certificate of Denmark'. It is now much-eroded, but a representation of the carving serves as the front page of the Danish national passport. It acts as a reminder of a remarkable event: the founding of the Danish ruling dynasty. What makes this truly extraordinary is that in modern Europe only in the Scandinavian kingdoms and Britain do there exist such dynasties that can still trace their origins back a thousand years and more in a virtually uninterrupted fashion. From the region of Jelling, Harald built a kingdom that overwhelmed many of the smaller petty kingdoms that still existed on the Jutland peninsula and the islands of Denmark, and established himself as king, though not as firmly as he would have liked as events would prove.

Harald also erected a famous fort at Trelleborg (although by far the best-known, he built others too). A massive circular earth embankment acted as the walls here, topped by a wooden palisade, not too different in design from a Celtic hillfort. A number of large longhouses were also built on the site, giving the appearance of a barracks for about 500 troops. It is still a vastly impressive site.

It is worth remembering, when thinking about these wooden defences, how skilled was Viking carpentry, as evidenced by their shipbuilding excellence. Capable of holding many men, the forts could dominate a local population and be used as a point of assembly for troops. Their design suggests that their main aim was to enable a force to concentrate to repel an enemy, though that might be an external foe or an internal one; it is often suggested that the forts were built by Harald Bluetooth as an assembly point for his men against those of his rebellious son, Sweyn Forkbeard. It is interesting that in their campaigns in England the Vikings would sometimes assemble near old Celtic hillforts (as would indeed the English), somewhere that they would probably have felt very much at home.

To the south, in Jutland, a massive earthen wall, the Danevirke, had acted as a barrier against invading forces from Germany since the eighth century. It was from this direction that the Danes of the time perceived the greatest threat and a Danish king would always keep one eye on developments in the south if he wished to hang on to his throne. Regional geopolitics also involved the kings of Poland to the east, who sometimes sought alliances against the Danes. So political relationships between neighbouring peoples could be complicated and this was a very unsettled region with complicated border relationships to manage.

The size of the forts constructed by Harald suggests several things. First of all, as they must have taken a significant amount of time and effort to construct, they hint at access to substantial levels of resource and strong centralised control by Harald; the emergence of Hedeby as a major market town in the region at around this time also suggests this. Secondly they suggest a king who was no longer prepared to be merely a first amongst equals but who wished to be a dominant power in the region. This was a good thing in terms of laying the foundations of a nation state, yet it would not have been universally popular amongst many of the leading men of the country who found their opportunities for self-aggrandisement and profit curtailed as a result; consequently, they looked for chances elsewhere, in overseas raids, to make up for what they had lost in Denmark.

Harald had a fierce and ambitious son in Sweyn Forkbeard. Some accounts suggest that Sweyn may well have been baptised along with his father but there was little evidence of Christian love in what was to follow, which may be due to suggestions that Sweyn was not in fact a legitimate son of the king. In the 980s (probably 985 or 986) Sweyn revolted against his father; interestingly this seems to coincide exactly with the time that Trelleborg was constructed. In another striking connection, Trelleborg seems only to have been occupied for a short time and was seemingly abandoned again by around 990, when the civil war was over.

The writer of the work known as the *Encomium Emmae Reginae* suggests that Harald had a deep-rooted hatred of his son and blamed him for the uprising.[10] Taking a completely opposite view, Adam of Bremen is blunt in his statement of what happened: 'Sweyn Otto [Forkbeard], the son of the great Harald, king of the Danes, set on foot many plots against his father, taking counsel also with those whom his father had against their will compelled to embrace Christianity, to see how he might deprive him of the throne now that he was advanced in years and less strong.'[11]

This contradiction is a good example of the problems of reading too much into the words of chroniclers with a vested interest. Yet whilst this poses a risk, in the absence of many other sources of evidence it would be remarkably short-sighted to ignore these accounts altogether. The suggestion that there were a number of people who were forced to accept Christianity amongst the Danes and that they did not all feel comfortable with these events is completely logical. It is not difficult to accept that giving up belief systems that had existed since time immemorial did not come easily for those who had little choice but to publicly follow the decision of their 'chief' (or in this case king). Many might privately have retained their old religious affiliations in such circumstances. This is human nature, as the precedent to be found in the adoption of Christianity by the Roman Empire half a millennium previously also evidences.

Sweyn Forkbeard lived during a period of transition in Scandinavia. Again it is completely logical that a man of some perception as well as military ability saw that affiliations to the 'old religion' could be exploited whilst contrary pressures to accept the dictates of a new creed also existed. There is no doubting Sweyn's ambition or his ruthlessness, and so it is certainly plausible that he set himself up as a protector of old traditions for his own personal advantage, especially when his father was ageing. Adam paints a picture of Sweyn, the rebellious son who overthrew his saintly father and, he claims, in the process took advantage of lingering pagan superstition to overthrow Christianity; the chronicler referred back to the Biblical precedent of Absalom rebelling against his father David in his criticism.[12]

As a result of Sweyn's plotting, open war broke out between father and son. Subsequently, Harald lost his throne and was forced to leave Denmark, finding refuge amongst the Slavs. He died there of his wounds though his body was later brought back to Denmark, possibly being entombed in the church of the Holy Trinity that had been recently built in Roskilde.[13] Here it was said miraculous cures soon followed for some of the diseased pilgrims who visited his shrine.

So Sweyn seized the throne of Denmark but he was soon facing enormous challenges. Adam goes on to describe how King Erik of Sweden met Sweyn's Danish fleet in 'many' sea-battles and eventually put them to flight. Sweyn was forced to leave Denmark, which then fell into the hands of Erik. Sweyn then made his way to Norway and from there to England, where perhaps he was understandably not well received, and finally on to Scotland where he found a refuge for a time. His orbit shifted from Scandinavia to the British Isles and here he would play a major part in the story that is about to unfold. He was every bit a warrior and Snorri Sturluson suggested that it was not long after he became king that he was busily engaged in raiding, not only in England but also in 'Saxland' (the Saxon lands in Germany) and 'Frisland' (Frisia on the North Sea coast of what is now the Netherlands, stretching up to cover small parts of what is now Germany and Denmark).[14]

The writer of the *Encomium* suggests that in time Sweyn became a diligent warrior and, when his men were not fighting, did everything he could to make sure that they stayed alert. He went out of his way to ensure that his men would not 'be softened by inactivity'.[15] As Sweyn matured he became a formidable warrior but also, in some ways at least, almost a reincarnation of an old-time Viking raider.

These were the days which also saw the zenith of a semi-legendary group of Viking mercenaries known as the Jomsvikings. The deeds of these men were recorded in a great saga. If the saga is to be believed (not everyone agrees that the Jomsvikings even existed), they were fiercely pagan and available for hire to anyone who was prepared to suitably recompense them. Historians suggest that they were based around Wolin on the south shores of the Baltic (on an island now off the coast of Poland). They were, according to later saga, formed by Harald Bluetooth after his exile from Denmark. These were times of great turmoil in Scandinavia.

Not all historians are convinced that Adam's account of Sweyn's movements is reliable and at some stage Sweyn certainly reclaimed the crown of Denmark. As king he proved to be not just an out-and-out warrior, though his qualities in the field of warfare need not be doubted. For example, some of the earliest coins yet found from Viking-age Denmark with a king's name on them date from the time of Sweyn's reign, though those so far discovered are not great in number. It is indicative of rather close international links that they were crafted by an English moneyer named Godwin and that they were modelled on coins of Æthelred, King of England.[16] If Sweyn would prove adept at extorting money out of England, he would not be slow to take ideas from her too.

There is much uncertainty about the birth and early life of Sweyn's son, Cnut. For one thing, it is not clear when exactly he was born. Dates of around 985 or 995 have been suggested – a wide range indeed, though support now tends to gravitate towards the later date. The court poet Ottar the Black says of Cnut that he was strikingly young when he became a conqueror, which would support a birth year of 995.

Neither is it agreed by all chroniclers who his mother was, though most accounts suggest that she was Gundhild, daughter of Boleslaw, King of Wendland (the land of the Wends, a Slavic people who lived on the southern shores of the Baltic Sea); this is certainly the case according to Snorri Sturluson, the later great saga-writer from Iceland. A probable point of origin for his mother in the region of modern Poland is suggested by a rather garbled later entry in the records of the New Minster in Winchester. It mentions an otherwise unknown sister of Cnut with the unusual name of 'Santslaue'. It has been plausibly suggested that the nearest possible equivalent to this is 'Świętosława', which is a Polish name. This is a reminder that Cnut had a good deal of Slavic blood in his family tree.

Gundhild had been married before to Erik the Victorious, King of Sweden, the man whom Adam credits for depriving Sweyn of Denmark. She would later be rejected by Sweyn after giving him three children, a not uncommon process in the period, particularly amongst Germanic peoples and one that Cnut himself emulated. For a time, she went into exile into the kingdom of the Slavs in the region of modern Poland before being recalled after Sweyn's death (this is one account, but Snorri Sturluson suggests that Gundhild died and Sweyn remarried Sigrid the Haughty soon after).[17]

The connection with the Wends is interesting. In some ways a marital alliance between Denmark and Wendland made sense as their frontiers were close to each other. But the Wends were also still largely pagan at the time. Various expeditions had been launched to bring them to heel; they were a warlike people and they did not take kindly to the Christian missions that were sent to convert them. In fact, not until centuries later would the Wends finally be Christianised, well into the time of the Crusades – one of the last groups in the whole of Europe to convert.

Cnut was not the eldest child; his elder brother Harald was crown prince of Denmark. There was also a sister, Estrith (who later took the Christian name of Margaret), and a half-sister from another relationship of Sweyn's named Gytha. In these uncertain times the fact that he was not the eldest son did not necessarily debar Cnut completely from a claim to the country when his father died though it did put Harald in pole position.

The writer of the *Encomium* is in isolation in claiming that Cnut was in fact the eldest son. This is not strongly supported by the facts of the situation. First of all, Sweyn left Harald in charge of Denmark when he later launched an invasion of England and it was common practice at the time for such a task to be deputed to the eldest son. Secondly, there is a clue in the name. Despite ultimately being overthrown by his son Sweyn, before that Harald Bluetooth had been an iconic figure in Denmark and it was common practice for a father to give his eldest son the name of a prestigious ancestor, especially his own father.

Whilst Sweyn was king of Denmark, he also saw great opportunities in England, first for profit through raiding activities and later for conquest. The victory at Maldon and the large 'Danegeld' payment that followed did not buy the Vikings off but instead whetted their appetite for more. As raids had been going on for a number of years now, England was starting to feel the strain of fighting them off and coping with the consequences.

One Viking threat at least disappeared from England at around this time. The victor of Maldon, Olaf Tryggvason, was bought off by Æthelred in 994, an example of one occasion when the payment of 'Danegeld' actually worked and a reminder that it was not always the useless, self-defeating exercise that later historians painted it to be. If in the end the policy was a disaster, at the beginning it was not always so. The conditions of the treaty stipulated that not only should Olaf's men desist from raiding but that they were required to help the English against other Vikings. Olaf was encouraged to return to Norway and conquer the country for himself. This was a smart move as it would distract Sweyn from raiding England as he sought to deflect the claims of Olaf further north. Adam of Bremen suggests that Olaf was followed by English missionaries, including one only known rather vaguely as 'John', who proceeded assiduously with their task of trying to convert the Norwegians to their religion.[18]

The success enjoyed by Æthelred in getting rid of the unwelcome attentions of Olaf Tryggvason is somewhat at odds with his reputation as an incompetent, bungling monarch. Those perceptions are fuelled by hostile accounts in the *Anglo-Saxon Chronicles* which were composed after his death and must therefore attract some doubt as to their neutrality. Æthelred convinced Olaf to become a Christian and stood as his sponsor at his baptism at Andover, a repeat of the situation when King Alfred had done the same with the Danish raider Guthrum in the latter part of the ninth century. It was a remarkably successful initiative and Olaf would not return. However, plenty of other Viking raiders would appear to take his place.

The story of Olaf Tryggvason is told by the later saga-writer Snorri Sturluson. Of course a saga is likely to have a number of embellishments but that does not mean that every detail is wrong. Snorri's tale is of a young babe-in-arms who is taken into exile by his mother when her husband, the King of Norway, is killed. He then grows up in several foreign lands such as Estonia and the kingdom of the Rus, the Norse lands in what is now the west of Russia.

Later Olaf became the archetypal Viking raider and got to know the British Isles well. His raids took him to Scotland and Northumbria, to the Isle of Man and Cumbria and to Wales and Ireland. According to Snorri he was resting up in the Scilly Isles when he came across a Christian soothsayer who managed to convince him of the merits of Christianity, though this contradicts the story that it was Æthelred who was responsible for his baptism.

Olaf would become a fierce supporter of Christianity; 'fierce' is an apt description if the accounts of Snorri Sturluson are accurate. He gives many examples in his saga of the violent measures that Olaf adopted, threatening stubborn peasants who were too attached to the old religion with a choice between battle (and probable death) and conversion. It is a tale of pagan temples being burned down and of serious disgruntlement on the part of many who disagreed with Olaf's policies. Hostages were taken to ensure that the adherents to the new faith did not subsequently backslide. In one of the more gruesome (and less believable) stories, one man who obstinately refused to convert had a live adder forced down his throat.[19]

Inevitably given the thought patterns of the time, the appearance of a comet in 995 was feared to herald more troubled times for England. There were eleven comets recorded in the *Anglo-Saxon Chronicles* as appearing between AD 679 and 1114 – such astronomical phenomena touched a particular nerve with the chroniclers who did their work in that more superstitious age.[20] Most famously the appearance of Halley's Comet in 1066 coincided rather neatly with the Norman Conquest of England that year, but references from other years often associate such astronomical phenomena with natural disasters such as famines (Halley's Comet had last appeared over England in 989). However, apart from the death of Archbishop Sigeric and his replacement by Ælfric there were no great disasters in 995, though a period of great instability was close at hand.

In fact, the raids on England that were launched by Sweyn in 995 did not achieve much. There is evidence that when the Danes were beaten off from their attacks in England in that year they searched further afield for a suitable target. The Welsh *Annales Cambriae* record that Sweyn and the Viking fleet moved into the Irish Sea and fell on the Isle of Man. Although the surviving evidence does not definitively prove that the man responsible for this was indeed Sweyn Forkbeard, it would certainly make a suitable consolation prize for his fleet.[21]

Sweyn operated over a wide area and his position in Scandinavia was probably helped by the death of Erik the Victorious in around 994 or 995. He would involve himself in the affairs of Normandy and also quite probably with those of Viking settlements in Ireland such as Dublin, Wexford, Waterford, Cork and Limerick (though much of Ireland remained a land of forest, mountains and bogs ruled by independent chiefs outside of these Viking strongholds).[22]

As a result of the difficulties of subduing the wild areas of Ireland outside their port bases, and indeed the limited economic benefits of doing so, the Norse in Ireland instead looked out across the Irish Sea for opportunities to both raid and trade (for in all times the incidence of piracy has been linked with areas that are attractive for mercantile reasons). The problem for England was that she was surrounded by enemy bases from which maritime assaults could be launched by the skilled Norse seafarers from a variety of different directions. Given their mobility, this was very hard to resist at a national level and defence therefore relied on the local fyrd assembling quickly when in the path of a Viking raid.

England's long coastline was very difficult to protect along its complete length and therefore she was very vulnerable to Viking attacks. Part of her shores lay opposite Flanders and this was a region with which she seems in the main to have enjoyed good relations. However, the best that could be expected from Flanders was a form of neutrality and that was probably what England had to settle for.

More problematic were relations between England and Normandy. The Vikings had settled the duchy not too long before in the early decades of the tenth century (Duke Richard I was only two generations removed from Rollo, who had founded the Viking land there) and therefore it was only to be expected that the Normans would be well-disposed towards the Viking raiders. Guarding a long coastline against piratical raids was not easy; even the Romans had found this out when they had constructed their formidable fixed defences known as the Forts of the Saxon Shore, ironically against the ancestors of the very people who were now struggling to defend themselves. The French crown had guarded against more Viking incursions by granting land to Rollo in return for his protection.

There are references in papal correspondence to a treaty brokered between Normandy and England in 991, the gist of which was that neither side would shelter the other's enemies. This desirable outcome was negotiated by the papal envoy Leo, Bishop of Trevi, who arrived at the English court on Christmas Day 990 having been given his orders by Pope John XV. The peace treaty was signed in Rouen in the following March.

In its way, this suggests some good proactive diplomacy on the part of the English, who stood to be the main beneficiaries of this arrangement: another plus point for Æthelred's strategy. This was useful but when Duke Richard I of Normandy died in 996, it was unlikely that his son and heir Richard II felt himself honour-bound to continue with the terms of this particular arrangement.[23] Indeed, the later eleventh-century chronicler William of Jumièges wrote of an English fleet launching an attack on the duchy at some time and although he does not give dates and no other chronicle mentions these events, we cannot exclude the possibility that some kind of pre-emptive strike against Vikings taking refuge there was launched at some point in this period.

By 997 the Viking raiders were back in England. This time they sailed around the south-west peninsula of the country and up into the Severn. Even if they did not come from Normandy, there were plenty of other Viking bases in Ireland, the Isle of Man and the Western Isles that they could have set out from. They raided widely, which they were able to do due to the mobility given them by their longships. Cornwall, Devon and Wales were all hit by attacks. There was also a bloody confrontation at Watchet in Somerset. They then sailed south-west again, past Land's End and up into the Tamar. The shallow draft of their ships meant they were able to sail upriver, like an arrow into the heart of the region, and they sacked Lydford and destroyed the monastery at Tavistock. If these Vikings had indeed been Christianised, they were not showing much charity towards their co-religionists.

The destruction of Tavistock Abbey struck right at the heart of the English monarchy. It had been developed recently by Ordwulf, the brother of Elfrida, mother of King Æthelred; it is very possible that she had grown up close by. Much wealth and effort had been put into its recent development and now it was all wasted. Ordwulf had become one of the king's main counsellors by 993 and was a prominent landowner in Devon and Cornwall. Another man, Æthelmaer, was also a major supporter of the king and held lands especially in Dorset, such as Cerne, Minterne, Winterbourne Abbas and Little and Long Bredy. It is notable too that this was another area under frequent attack from Viking raids.

Elfrida, now back at court after a number of years in internal exile, must have been devastated by this news. The Vikings did not attack Tavistock, some miles inland, by chance. They must have known of it, possibly from trading activities. Alternatively, they may have had some inside information to alert them to the prizes they would find in the abbey. In this respect, it is interesting to note the words of Snorri Sturluson, who said of a late tenth-century Scandinavian, Lodin (the foster-father of Olaf Tryggvason), that 'often fared he as a merchant, but upon occasion as a viking', in other words a man who could quite comfortably co-exist in more than one world.[24] It is likely that he was far from unique in this chameleon-like behaviour.

Several years of intensive raiding followed. Dorset, Hampshire, the Isle of Wight and Sussex all fell victim to raids in 998. The next year, the Vikings sailed to Rochester via the Thames and the Medway. This time an army was ready for them and a tough fight followed. But in the end the English were unable to drive them back and the Vikings held possession of the 'place of slaughter' – as the *Anglo-Saxon Chronicles* calls many battlefields of the time. The Vikings' sea power allowed them great mobility and made it difficult for the English to calculate where they were likely to make a landing, so the raiders were always in a position of advantage.

But it was not just ships that were employed by the raiders. After their triumph near Rochester, the raiders helped themselves to horses and made their way into West Kent, a standard Viking tactic which also allowed them great mobility on land as well as the sea. Æthelred assembled two forces in response, one a land force and the other a ship-army, to fight off the raids. However good this strategy was in theory, it proved impossible to implement in practice as the two forces could not be properly coordinated. The ship army was a white elephant, an expensive waste of money, as the men on board the ships sat around idly waiting for something to happen – and nothing did in any way whereby they could intervene. The helplessness of the English defence only served to embolden the raiders even more.

Despite this, 1000 saw something of a respite. The raiders took up temporary residence with their close cousins who had set up home in Normandy, showing well enough where the Norman Duke Richard II's loyalties currently lay. Relieved by this short-term inactivity, Æthelred led his army on a pillaging expedition into Cumbria (possibly in retaliation for Viking raids launched from the area, which was then subject to strong Norse influence)[25] whilst his fleet raided the Isle of Man, then a Viking-held territory. Perhaps the ship-army served some useful purpose after all, though it was again noticeable that the efforts of the land force and the fleet could not be easily coordinated. These activities in the west of the British Isles are a reminder that many Viking attacks did not come from Scandinavia but rather from the opposite direction and this was presumably the English king fighting back against them.

There were good reasons for the Vikings to be quiet around this time as Sweyn had distractions elsewhere to occupy him. Matters were moving to a head in the long-running conflict for the possession of Norway with Olaf Tryggvason. This was a region that had been coveted by Danish kings for a time but was very much disputed territory. There are frequent references in the sagas to Viking raids on lands other than England at this time, including Norway – a major raid on the country by Gudrod, the son of the legendary Erik Bloodaxe, had been crushed by King Olaf.[26] Finally, at the Battle of Svold in 999/1000 a Norwegian fleet led by King

Olaf clashed with one led by Olaf Skötkonung (also known as Olaf Eriksson), King of Sweden, and Erik Hákonarson, the Jarl (Earl) of Lade, in alliance with Sweyn Forkbeard.

The build-up to the battle is told in a somewhat unlikely tale written up by Snorri Sturluson. In his version, Sweyn Forkbeard's sister Tyri was pressurised into a marriage with the much older King Boleslaw, whose paganism was as unattractive to her as his age was. The marriage was every bit as unsatisfactory as she expected it to be and she fled not long after, making her way surreptitiously through Denmark and on to Norway. Here she managed to persuade Olaf Tryggvason to wed her instead. It was said that she bore a bitter grudge against her brother Sweyn Forkbeard from this point on.

In this tale – which would do credit to a soap opera – she then persuaded Olaf to enter into an alliance with Boleslaw, the very man she had cuckolded, against Sweyn. It is an inherently unlikely tale if a colourful one. In any event, war loomed. We read of Olaf's great warship *The Long Serpent* and some of his evocatively named men such as Thorstein Ox-Foot, Thrond Squint-Eye, Lodvir the Long and Ketil the Tall, Griotgard the Quick and Bersi the Strong.

Enter into this complicated domestic entanglement (further complicating it) Sigrid the Haughty, wife of Sweyn Forkbeard and a bitter opponent of Olaf Tryggvason. According to Snorri Sturluson, she had previously planned to marry Olaf but she was a devout pagan and her resistance to her potential husband's chosen religion, Christianity, was so strong that he ended up striking her. The marriage was off and she later became Sweyn's wife instead. Now she incited him to war, citing as a reason the fact that Tyri had married Olaf without his permission. Sweyn was convinced and sought and found allies in the shape of King Olaf of Sweden, the successor to Erik the Victorious, and Earl Erik from Norway. They set up an ambush at sea, and Olaf Tryggvason sailed straight into it.

The later *King Olaf Tryggvason's Saga* gives much detail of the battle, which was effectively a land battle fought at sea. Bitter combat followed – sword and axe thrusting at close quarters, javelins and bows being used for longer-distance missile attack – and the fight was fierce. But Olaf's great ship was surrounded and many men on board her were cut down. Earl Erik and fourteen of his men were able to board amidships from their vessel, the *Iron Beard*, and a hacking match broke out in which Olaf's men were gradually overcome.

A number of chronicles suggest that Olaf Tryggvason's fleet was heavily outnumbered by at least six to one; most of the accounts give Olaf about eleven ships whereas his opponents had, according to the same sources, a minimum of seventy and possibly over 100. Olaf, it was said, fought bravely but the odds against him were hopeless and *The Long Serpent* was overwhelmed. What became of him is a matter of debate. Some saga-writers say that he effectively committed suicide by throwing himself into the water when defeat became an inevitability – in his mail shirt, he sank to the bottom like a stone. Earl Erik's men had surrounded Olaf's ship but they were unable to capture him and he was pulled beneath the waves. He clearly had no intention of being taken alive.

Others suggest a more mysterious end for him. They say that Olaf, a strongly Christian king in a region that was only just emerging from paganism, became a pilgrim and made his way to Jerusalem, living on for several decades more. Snorri Sturluson noted in skaldic fashion that:

> I wot not whether he who stilled the raven's hunger Should of me be praised as of the living or of the dead, Since of a truth his men tell either tale.[27]

Whatever the truth may be, we will probably never know. But one thing is clear: Olaf Tryggvason was effectively removed from the scene. In this case, the end result is probably more important than the details, however interesting they might be.

In the story of the development of the Danish kingdom, and more particularly the remarkable lives of Sweyn Forkbeard and his son Cnut, these were highly significant events. Norway would for a time become part of an extended Danish Empire of the North (or the 'North Sea Empire' as it is sometimes called). It was a very different country to Denmark. Whereas the latter was largely flat and fertile in places, Norway was a place of towering mountains split apart by the finger-like fjords that clawed their way in from the sea.

The highest point in Denmark is just 170 metres above sea level. In Norway it rises to nearly 2,500 metres and there are almost 200 peaks with an elevation of 2,000 metres or more, many of them running like a rocky spine down the country, ensuring that the Norwegian adventurers looked west. Farming land in Norway was in short supply – probably no more than 5 per cent of the Norwegian landmass – and this played a key part in forging the drive and adventurism that saw Norwegian explorers reaching lands far across the Atlantic.

Farming arrived in the north around 4000 BC, much later than in other parts of Europe. At this time barley and wheat appear in the region; there may be a short growing season for these in the far north but the virtually permanent presence of the sun during the height of summer was a partial compensation. Rye and oats did not, however, appear until after AD 1100, part of the benefits of the greater inclusion of Scandinavian society in mainstream Europe. Goats, sheep and pigs were also brought in as stock early on so what had previously been a 'hunter-gatherer' society became more settled. Hunter-gathering Saami always remained in the very far north but elsewhere small villages began to appear. Over time, stock – especially cattle – assumed prominence over crops for practical reasons. Cattle became an important currency and a mark of social status in their own right.

Germanic-speaking settlers arrived in Scandinavia in around 2300 BC. There is some evidence of cultural intermingling suggested by some words that emerged in the Norse vocabulary. 'Dog' for example has no known base word in Indo-European languages and the most likely origin according to experts is that this was taken from existing languages when the Germanic-speaking peoples arrived here. If this is true it suggests a process of assimilation rather than obliteration of existing cultures, a talent that the Scandinavian peoples seem to have retained across thousands of years.

For a maritime power like the Danes, Norway was an attractive proposition even if much of it was wild and largely covered either by mountains or forest. Norway's harbours, if not always particularly accommodating, nevertheless formed a springboard from which sea-borne expeditions, either military or trading in nature, could set out for Scotland and Ireland, for the north of England or further afield in their ships to Iceland and Greenland.

The latter was reached by Erik the Red in around 983/984 and sparsely populated with settlers from Iceland soon after, a journey of 1,000 miles in which seven out of twenty-five ships were lost, a reminder of the perils facing these great adventurers.

The land discovered even further west on the shores of North America was found by accident when a Viking ship became lost whilst looking for Greenland. In around 1000 Leif Erikson, son of Erik the Red, followed up on the chance find. He landed on Baffin Island, then made his way down the Labrador coast and reached Newfoundland. A small settlement followed on the latter which was known as Vinland, some say after the berries that were found there and subsequently made into wine. Archaeology on the northern shores of Newfoundland in the 1960s uncovered a site known as L'Anse aux Meadows that showed definitive Norse traces.

The first attempt at settlement in the region failed after fighting with local natives, *skraelings* as the Norsemen called them, a kind of equivalent of the barbarians known to the Greeks and Romans. A second group of would-be settlers came under heavy attack and, after a difficult winter in 1011/12, the attempted colony was abandoned. A third and final attempt ended when a bitter blood-feud amongst the Scandinavian adventurers decimated most of the party and the last serious attempt at colonisation in the region was over.

Iceland was a particularly interesting example of Scandinavian expansionism that characterised the extraordinary period in which Cnut lived. Populated between 870 and 930, perhaps by independent-minded settlers who had no time for the new-fangled kings who were emerging, by the opening of the eleventh century it was a long-standing part of the Viking world. The settlers fully exploited the local resources – too fully, in fact. The forests of small, stumpy trees that existed in some parts of the island were cut down as timber, which soon ran out and had to be imported from Norway. But this was classic pioneering frontier land. A new settler would throw a wooden beam overboard from his ship and follow it as it was taken by the tides ashore. Wherever it landed, there he would build his house. One such man, Ingolf Arnason, found the beam landed ashore near some warm-water springs. He named the place Reykjavik, 'Bay of Smoke'.

Cattle were shipped in to Iceland with the settlers and they did not take long to decimate the limited grazing land there. Within a few hundred years the farming and building methods brought in with the settlers had created a situation that was little short of an ecological disaster and the scattered settlements that peppered the island were struggling to survive. But this was still in the future. It has been estimated that by 1000, the year that Iceland formally recognised Christianity, there were 70,000 people on the island, spread across the land in farming communities.[28]

This evidences a thirst for land from the settler communities which formed the backdrop to Cnut's era. Yet these were extreme solutions and with land nearer to mainland Europe potentially available, it is understandable that opportunities closer at hand were more attractive. In terms of world geography, it is an interesting fact that Norway, Britain and Denmark all share something in common: very long coastlines in proportion to their total land areas. This may well have contributed to the incidence of Viking raiding success, both by providing plentiful points of origin for raids and varied landing points for them.[29] It also helped to ship would-be settlers to new homes across the sea at a later stage.

Olaf Tryggvason had been an effective block to Danish ambitions in Norway. The country was traditionally fragmented and this led to inherent weaknesses that the Danes could exploit, though not easily on a permanent basis. Olaf had tried to change that with strong centralising policies. His rule had been harsh and far from popular, especially with the independent-minded jarls of Lade in the wild north (in modern times, home to towns such as Trondheim and Narvik). In reality the far north would be hard to hold for any monarch who ruled from the south of Norway.

Sweyn now turned his thoughts back to England. He became the nominal ruler of Norway, though day-to-day government of the country was given to Erik of Lade and his brother Sweyn. Norwegian tradition asserts that Erik was married to Sweyn Forkbeard's daughter Gytha, a likely enough arrangement given conventional marital power-politics of the time. Snorri Sturluson tells us that the brothers Erik and Sweyn were both baptised as Christians but that in practice they left every one of their men to make their own decisions concerning their faith and that they upheld the 'old laws' and customs of the land honourably. In other words, in the lands where they were lords, it is highly likely that many of their people clung on to ancient pagan beliefs.

These events in Norway distracted Sweyn Forkbeard from England for a short while. This was, however, just the calm before a major storm. Raiding had become almost an annual event (1000 excepted) and the English had shown themselves to be weak, being forced to resort to tactics of buying rather than fighting the Vikings off. All this was likely to do in the long term was to suggest that England was a wealthy country but one that was not strong enough to defend herself; a rather dangerous combination. It was highly likely that the Vikings would return to attack the long and vulnerable coastline of England again in the near future. And so it proved.

In 1001, it was the West Country that was again the target. This was a year, according to the Winchester version of the *Anglo-Saxon Chronicles*, of 'great hostility'. There is in fact some confusion in the detail between the Winchester and Peterborough versions of the *Chronicles*. The former says that the Vikings attacked Hampshire first and then moved to Devon whilst the latter does not mention an initial assault on Hampshire. But other details in the two versions broadly support each other.

There was a great battle in Ætheling's Valley right on the borders of Hampshire and Sussex; also known as Dean, this was an important place as it was where Æthelred's children were being brought up.[30] The Hampshire levy came up to do battle and got the worse of it. The king's reeve, Æthelweard, and other important Saxons were killed. The *Chronicles* say that eighty-one men of the Saxon host died and rather more of the Vikings, though the latter held the field at the end of the day. The numbers of the dead are not high in terms of battles in more recent history and give some indication that neither army was large in comparison to later times.

The main Viking target for the year appears to have been Devon. The strong defences of Exeter were assaulted by a raiding party that moved up from the mouth of the Exe but was driven off. It appears to have been a gallant defence and exposed a weakness in the Viking army for siege warfare. However, it was different when they were in the open field. Joined by Pallig Tokeson, Sweyn's brother-in-law and an erstwhile ally of King Æthelred who had deserted the English monarch even though he had received generous gifts from him shortly before, the Vikings ran amok across Devon. Kingsteignton was burned and the host decimated the countryside; everywhere they went, they 'killed and burned'.[31]

An army was gathered by the Saxons to meet them, drawn from the men of Devon and the 'Somerseters'. Led by Kola, Æthelred's high reeve, the English army clashed with their foe at Pinhoe, close by Exeter. It appears to have been a massacre and ended with the English in terrified flight. Nothing could now stop the Viking host, which moved around at will. The estates at Pinhoe and Broad Clyst were burned by the Vikings soon after the battle and they then moved back to Hampshire. They stopped at the Isle of Wight, which now appeared to be completely under their control, and then fell on the estate of Bishop's Waltham on the other side of the Solent, their ships enabling them to move back and forth with impunity.

A hoard of coins uncovered by archaeologists at Shaftesbury appears to have been buried at around this time, hinting at the sense of panic that was developing in the south-west, though the fact that most of the coins were minted in London and the north might suggest that this was a visitor passing through rather than a resident.[32] No English force dared approach them; the Peterborough version of the *Chronicles* noted ominously that 'in every way it was a heavy time, because they never let off their evil'.[33]

Æthelred was both incensed at these raids and bitterly frustrated at his inability to stop them. The following year he came to the conclusion that the only way to rid himself of the Vikings was to buy them off once more. A massive sum of 24,000 pounds was the price – yet more inflation in the amount required – and it was duly paid. But chaos still reigned. The king's negotiations with the Vikings were led by Leofsige, the ealdorman of Essex who had taken the place of the would-be hero Byrhtnoth who had died at Maldon in 991. But soon after, Leofsige was banished for killing Ælfric, the king's high reeve. The king it seemed could trust no one. These were evil days.

Æthelred's regime was stumbling from one crisis to the next with no sign of a long-term solution to England's problems. Nothing it seems could stop the Viking raiders from returning time and time again. That Æthelred was personally struggling to cope with this is hinted at by his reference in a charter granting land to Shaftesbury Abbey at Bradford-on-Avon in around 1001, dedicated to his slain brother Edward as a saint and martyr. A cult around Edward had been growing ever stronger in England and its acceptance by Æthelred suggests that he was giving in to the inevitable. It was followed up in 1008 by a declaration by Æthelred that Edward's anniversary should be declared a saint's day.[34]

Given the perceived association of Æthelred with his brother's murder this was a notable move. It is unlikely that he would have been personally involved in the plot to kill him two decades before but his mother Elfrida (who died around 1000 – the exact date is not known) was right at the heart of events in many people's eyes and he was the main beneficiary. That Æthelred took these steps only really makes sense if there was perceived to be no real alternative to doing so. In order to hang on to already weak support at home, the king was forced to swallow his pride and adopt such measures.

1002 was a seminal year in the life of the king and his kingdom. The first significant event that took place was the marriage of Æthelred to Emma of Normandy. In 1002 Emma was about seventeen years of age. She was the daughter of Richard I, Duke of Normandy, the place where the Vikings had taken up permanent residence under Duke Rollo not so many years before. Emma was herself the great-granddaughter of Rollo and the blood of her Viking ancestors still coursed through her veins. The blood relationship was cemented still further by the fact that her mother was Gunnar, a woman of Danish descent. Gunnar was originally Richard's concubine, though she eventually became his wife in a probable attempt to legitimise their children.

The attribution of concubinage to Emma's mother gives an interesting insight into the mores of the age. It was not uncommon at the time for marriages to be undertaken in traditional (opponents would say pagan) fashion without Christian blessing; they may not then always have been regarded as legitimate from a Christian perspective. Revealingly in the light of our subject, such relationships were called *more danico* – in the Danish way – though the practice was also common in earlier pagan Anglo-Saxon times in England and indeed appeared to have remained so into the more recent Christian epoch in the country. But men engaged in such a relationship would sometimes later take another partner, giving the appearance of polygamy. The men involved would not see a problem with this but the Church would certainly see it as unacceptable. This has great relevance as our story unfolds.

Emma's life was written up in the book known as the *Encomium Emmae Reginae*. This is an incredible survival from the times, giving us an insight into the role played by a formidable woman in what was very much a man's world. We need not expect balance from this book, which was no work of pure factual history. The very word 'Encomium', now a rather archaic one, is Latin and means a work written in praise of a person or thing. Praise-works are unlikely to be very objective in their approach. This is betrayed in this work by the very first line in it: 'May our Lord Jesus Christ preserve you, O Queen, who excel all those of your sex in the admirability of your way of life.'[35]

The survival into our times of the *Encomium* at all is remarkable. What we have now is not the original manuscript but a copy, as so many surviving books from older periods of history are. Only one such copy has survived. It was to be found in St Augustine's, Canterbury, in the fifteenth century. Somehow it escaped the vandalism of Henry VIII when so many other treasures did not during the state-sponsored destruction of the monasteries. But even then it disappeared from public view for a time, only re-emerging in the late nineteenth century.

The marriage to Æthelred was a step up for Emma. Allowing for any perceived personal faults and the extent of the challenges facing him, he was still a king, a man who owed allegiance to no other, unlike the dukes of Normandy, who were vassals of the King of France. This presumably also helped compensate to some extent for the substantial age difference between the young bride and her husband, who already had a large number of children from previous relationships. Their existence made life potentially complicated in terms of succession planning. It seems that right from the off it was decided that any offspring from this match with Emma were to take precedence over those of previous relationships in matters of succession. It is likely that this formed a key part in the negotiations leading up to the marriage.

There is supporting evidence to back this up in charters that appear soon after. Emma appears as a witness to these. It must be highly doubtful that she understood exactly what it was she was signing as her knowledge of Anglo-Saxon England was presumably sparse at this early stage in her queenship. But the fact that she was named there at all was a major development. Æthelred's former wife had never been granted such a privilege so right from the off Emma's status appeared to be altogether higher than hers. Having to deal with former wives as well as the competing interests of the children of the two men she was married to during her long life would prove to be a perpetual headache for Emma for decades.

Other later chroniclers commented on the match, not always favourably. With the precious gift of hindsight and writing from the safe distance of the middle of the twelfth century, the chronicler Henry of Huntingdon saw the marriage as a turning point in English history:

> I mean that on one side the persecution by the Danes was raging, and on the other the connection with the Normans was growing, so that even if they were to escape the obvious lightning fire of the Danes, valour would not help them to escape the insidious danger from the Normans. This became apparent from subsequent events, since from this union of the English king with the daughter of the Norman duke, the Normans were justified according to the law of peoples, in both claiming and gaining possession of England.[36]

This owes everything to hindsight and given the circumstances of the times the match was a good one for Æthelred. It gave him the opportunity to cement an alliance with a powerful warlord from across the Channel who was potentially a crucial supporter of Viking raiders. The deal was duly struck and some of Æthelred's senior advisers made the crossing to Normandy to escort Emma back to their country, which was to be home for most of the rest of her days. She was crowned Queen of England soon after arriving, a coronation of a queen in those days being a rare event (though Elfrida, the king's mother, had also had one). Henry of Huntingdon goes on to suggest that the marriage merely served to fuel the king's pride with disastrous results.

It is quite possible that the marriage went ahead now precisely because Elfrida had died shortly before. With his domineering matriarch removed from the scene, Æthelred now felt confident enough to take steps that he might have demurred at if she had been still alive. Yet he was in the event only exchanging one driven woman for another. Emma has been described appropriately enough as 'the most notoriously determined, manipulative and forceful woman in western Europe'.[37] It was a description that fitted Elfrida well too. If ever this was a case of out of the frying pan and into the fire, for Æthelred this was it.

Emma was given the Saxon name Ælfgifu (which means 'noble gift') on her arrival in England (though we will call her Emma as this is how she is best remembered and, with other women called 'Ælfgifu' involved in the story, this avoids confusion). She was granted properties in Oxfordshire, Rutland, Suffolk and Devon as well as ownership of Exeter and Winchester.[38]

Æthelred's previous marriage was not an uncommon situation; in those uncertain days it was far from unusual for a king to have more than one wife or a queen more than one husband in their lives. Duplicate wives for members of the ruling classes, both English and Danish, were so commonplace as to almost be the rule rather than the exception. From his first marriage to another Ælfgifu, probably the daughter of Thored, Earl of Northumbria, Æthelred already had children. Thored disappears from view soon after 992, probably after Viking raids in the region for whose defence he was responsible were so successful that even the mighty Bamburgh fell.

It was said that the leaders of this earlier defence fought without enthusiasm because some of them were themselves of Scandinavian origin through their fathers. Thored's daughter is a shadowy figure almost to the point of being invisible and indeed we do not even know her name from contemporary sources as she is only referred to in later accounts.[39] Thored was replaced as ealdorman by Ælfhelm, who originated in the north of Mercia. His part in the story is not yet over.

There were children from this previous union including Edmund, in his early teens at the time of his father's marriage to Emma, and his older brother Æthelstan. The marriage to Emma had serious repercussions for them. Æthelred's children from his previous relationship with Ælfgifu appear to have been subsequently kept out of the immediate line of succession, with any issue from the marriage of Æthelred and Emma taking precedence over them. In addition, the government of England was also affected as some who had formerly been the king's principal advisers now lost their influence. These included the successors of the great Æthelstan Half-king in East Anglia.[40]

So there were changes amongst those who governed as a result of the match. Æthelred's alleged inability to pick out a counsellor who could be trusted earned him the nickname 'Unready' – not for the apparently obvious reason that he was poorly prepared but actually from the Old English *'unraed'* or 'ill-advised' though in truth if we blindly accept the arguments of some chroniclers either interpretation would seem appropriate.[41] That said, there was plenty of evidence of the difficulties involved in trusting his councillors.

The homilist Ælfric pointedly stated that the king's council should speak boldly and not in whispers, this written sometime around 1000 and suggesting that at the time they were renowned for doing rather too much of the latter. But the lack of trust in just about anyone else was epitomised by a draconian action taken by Æthelred in 1002. The Danes had been a permanent presence in England since the days of Alfred the Great a century and a half before. The king suspected that those resident in England were aiding and abetting Sweyn; the treachery of Pallig in the previous year would do nothing to discourage this view.

Terrible events followed as a result of the king's conclusions. A charter issued by Æthelred two years later talks of how 'all the Danes who had sprung up in this island ... [were] sprouting like cockles [weeds] amongst the wheat'. He therefore gave orders that all of them 'were to be destroyed by a most just extermination'.[42] Henry of Huntingdon suggests that the massacre was extremely well coordinated. The chronicler told how he had spoken to very old men in his childhood and got the details from them; as he is believed to have been born in around 1088 they must have indeed have been very old, with remarkable memories, though the events were of course truly memorable. They told him how the king had sent secret letters to each city, ordering them to strike the Danes within their precincts in a great synchronised assault, either slaying them by the sword or burning them alive in their houses.[43]

The blow fell on St Brice's Day, 13 November 1002. It was a Saturday, a day which many of the Danes put aside for bathing, and many were therefore caught off guard. Every Danish man (and it seems some women too) was allegedly put to the sword, though this must be a great exaggeration. This was only possible outside of the Danelaw where the Danes would be too strong and numerous for the English king to strike them down.

Amongst the dead according to some accounts were the untrustworthy Pallig and his wife, Gundhild – Sweyn Forkbeard's sister, it is said (though not everyone agrees that she was so executed and some doubt that she ever existed).[44] Detailed glimpses of the terrible slaughter remain, such as an account that some of the Danes in Oxford sought refuge in St Frideswide's Minster but the church was nevertheless destroyed by the populace with them inside it. The location of Oxford as what was effectively a frontier town is significant and it is certainly possible that those killed were visiting traders rather than residents.

Despite her royal bloodline, Gundhild was beheaded along with the rest of the captive Danes. She faced the prospect of imminent death bravely and did not lose her composure even as the fatal blow was about to fall. Even in death she was said to have retained her beauty. Her fate was made all the worse because she first of all had to watch her husband die and then her son was pierced by four spears before her very eyes.[45]

There have been several recent archaeological discoveries possibly connected to massacred Vikings which bear graphic witness to these harrowing events. One find in Oxford, the site of documented massacres, uncovered the remains of thirty-eight men who had been almost literally hacked to pieces. The skeletal remains were in some cases scorched though the ground around them was not, suggesting that the bodies had been burned after the men had been hacked down and were either dying or dead. Twenty of the skeletons bore puncture marks to vertebrae or pelvic bones, whilst twenty-seven had broken or cracked skulls. Analysis of the bones points to a seafood diet, suggesting that these men were traders (or raiders) rather than resident Danes.[46]

Another recent discovery of beheaded 'Viking' skeletons uncovered during the building of a by-pass near Weymouth, Dorset, is equally grim and intriguing. There were fifty-four skeletons found, all of them probably male; none were categorically female though a small number were not definitively male and could have been of either sex. It appears that all the men killed were naked when they met their end or were at least stripped after it as no clothing has been found in the grave. The large number of decapitations in a mass grave of this size from the period is internationally unprecedented. The similarity of the skeletons suggests this could be the crew of a ship stranded on the coast.

Death was caused in all cases by being hit with a sharp, heavy implement such as a sword. All the victims had been decapitated, from the front rather than the back. The site of the mass grave was on the Dorset Ridgeway, a prominent hill location dotted with much older Bronze Age barrows. It has been pointed out that such hilltop sites are typical of Anglo-Saxon execution cemeteries, and the presence of the mass grave right next to a significant road of the period suggests that this was a determined effort to make an example of the victims.[47] There is evidence of slightly more bodies in the grave than skulls, which might suggest that some of the heads may have been taken elsewhere to be publicly displayed (*heafod stoccan* as it was known in Anglo-Saxon).

Many of the men were between sixteen and twenty-five years of age though some do appear to have been older males. They were probably of Scandinavian descent, although scientific reports on isotope levels mention northern Scandinavia rather than Denmark as their likely point of origin. The teeth of one of the skeletons appear to have been filed, a practice known in Scandinavia at the time and not in England. Radiocarbon dating suggests a year of death between 970 and 1030. Although this period includes the time of the St Brice's Day Massacre, the circumstances maybe suggest that this is more an execution of Viking raiders (possibly men of Norwegian or Swedish origin) rather than resident Danes, perhaps men captured during one of the near-contemporary Viking assaults on Wessex which hit the area so frequently at the time.

However, skeletal evidence suggests that not all the remains were of men in prime physical condition and this could be a stronger indicator of a massacre of some non-warrior Scandinavians such as merchants or a crew from a ship (fifty would be a suitable number for such a body of men). Evidence of mechanical stresses on the spine also supports the contention that the men had been involved

71

in some repetitive and physically demanding exercise for some time. They also lacked evidence of previous wounds which had healed, which one would expect from at least some of them if this was a group of warriors of this size. This could suggest the slaughter of a group of non-warriors seized or even hostages, with some suggestions that if it is the latter they might even date to the time when Cnut was later king. Whatever the truth, it is a powerful and disturbing insight into this traumatic period in English history.[48]

The actions taken during the slaughter ordered by Æthelred became known as the St Brice's Day Massacre but, although this title implies an act of unprovoked aggression, Danish raiders had been massacring Englishmen and women for a number of years beforehand – if the *Anglo-Saxon Chronicles* are to be believed, with the active connivance of some of the Danes who were living in England. We would now no doubt see this as a failed attempt at multiculturalism.

It has also been seen as a move that called down the retribution of the Vikings after the massacre, a night of the long knives that precipitated a terrible revenge. Yet this is difficult to sustain in some respects, for the Danes had already been causing considerable damage for some years before without need of an excuse. If reckless, it was a surprisingly decisive thing for Æthelred to do but in the long run it was ill-advised as it gave Sweyn justification to fall on England once more soon afterwards. As Henry of Huntingdon wrote in vivid terms, the act was 'like a fire that someone had tried to extinguish with fat'.

Whilst there is a risk that too much is read into this one event, there are also tantalising clues that from this time forward Sweyn Forkbeard was a driven man. There would be a progressive ratcheting up of the pressure from this point on. Of course this might merely be as a result of opportunism offered by the gradual disintegration of England in the next few years. Yet it does not seem fanciful to suggest that there was something more in the way of revenge going on here. For Sweyn Forkbeard, it was as if the desire to avenge himself on England now took on something of a more personal aspect. He resolved to strike England once more with a vengeance. A terrible reckoning was at hand.

2

Sweyn Forkbeard: From Raider to King (1002–1014)

No doubt the killing of his sister in the St Brice's Day Massacre (if it actually happened) particularly angered Sweyn but we cannot be sure given past experience that he would not anyway have returned to raid England after being paid off. The later eleventh-century Norman chronicler William of Jumièges paints a graphic picture of the atrocities committed in these terrible events, of mastiffs tearing at the naked breasts of women and of children having their brains dashed out against doorposts.

These are stereotypes but unfortunately this did not mean that such horrific things did not happen; even in modern times atrocities in the Balkans and Rwanda for example provide all too much evidence that they still do, with some of the violence committed during these more recent pogroms chillingly similar. This sounds like what would be called in modern times 'ethnic cleansing' and would give the Scandinavian raiders ample excuse to strike back in retaliation. Sure enough, in 1003 the Vikings returned and in this year and the next the raiding was particularly intense.

Devon was again the first target for Sweyn and the *Anglo-Saxon Chronicles* suggest once more that treacherous influences were at play. This time Exeter fell, with the chroniclers suggesting that the headman that Emma had appointed to protect her interests there, Count Hugh the 'Frenchman', singularly failed in his task. It was a rich prize for the raiders, who fell on the city like 'a plague of locusts' and a great deal of plunder was taken. The destruction was absolute, says Henry of Huntingdon, and all that the Danes left behind them when they departed was a pile of ashes.[1] The city had strong defences and this fact alone must have made it disturbing that it had fallen to the raiders, suggesting that the organisation of resistance was weak and possibly even that treason was indeed the cause of its fall. It would not be the last accusation that treachery was the reason for an English defeat.

The levies of Wiltshire and Hampshire were called out in force to meet the threat if it moved eastwards but although it seems the men were resolute enough, their leader, ealdorman Ælfric, was not. As the two opposing forces drew close to each other, Ælfric conveniently fell ill. He began to vomit violently, the chroniclers suggest as part of an act; they mention that he was putting on 'his old tricks'.[2] This referred to his previous history of unreliability. The rudderless English force lost its will to fight and the Vikings were, in stark contrast, buoyed by the dejection of their foe. They moved into Wiltshire, sacking Wilton and Salisbury before returning to the coast and their 'wave-stallions'.[3] Ælfric's failure was a particularly bad blow for the king as the ealdorman was one of his own appointees and it therefore undermined confidence in Æthelred's judgement. Unfortunately, being an ealdorman did not make an individual a formidable or effective war leader and in those days such a prominent man was expected to be so.

It seems very unlikely that the choice of location for some of these raids was coincidence. By attacking Exeter, part of Æthelred's package of gifts to his wife on their marriage, Sweyn was apparently making a strong point about what he thought of the Anglo-Norman alliance that might be hoped for as a result of the recent match. Wilton too was particularly associated with the Anglo-Saxon royal family as it was the site of the nunnery of Æthelred's half-sister St Edith. The fact that the Vikings were able to raid such places with some precision again suggests a good knowledge of local geography and possibly some inside information. It also suggests a very deliberate attack against the king's interests.

These raids showed how formidable were the military advantages of the Vikings with regard to their ships and the mobility they gave them. Rock carvings from prehistoric times in Scandinavia show that shipbuilding was a very old skill in the north, as do burial sites in the region arranged in the shape of ships. Sometime in the eighth century AD, the addition of keels to ships in Scandinavia marked a significant breakthrough which also allowed for the introduction of a large mast with a considerable sail area and associated manoeuvrability and speed of ships (the word 'keel' is of common Anglo-Saxon and Viking origin). The ships that evolved were a formidable combination of strength and flexibility, allowing the vessels to ride out rough waters and travel long distances.

At some time in the later eleventh century a number of vessels were deliberately sunk off Roskilde in Denmark as a way of hampering access to the port for enemy warships (probably protecting against raids from Norway on the country). Recovered in recent times, they provide a remarkable record of what many ships of the time would look like (they appear to have been constructed in about 1030 before being scuttled some time later) and nowadays provide an extraordinary and unique record of the Viking maritime achievement.

The modern museum at Roskilde provides a unique insight into the world of Viking ships. No other museum has the range of vessels that one can see there, both in terms of the remains of the original craft and also the large number of reconstructions. Experimental archaeology continues on-site: modern craftsmen using copies of Viking age tools work away at building craft in the style of the eleventh century. It is as if the world of Cnut can not only be understood but can be touched and smelt.

One of the ships found scuttled in Roskilde Fjord was a warship, about 92 feet long and 15 feet wide, dating exactly to the time of Cnut. There were other ships found too, including a knarr, a cargo ship of a type which was used for long-distance crossings, even across the Atlantic to Iceland and beyond. Scuttled fishing boats and a smaller warship were also salvaged from the fjord and can now be seen in the museum, with full-scale replicas of all of them moored outside and accessible for anyone who wishes to climb aboard them to do so.

The warships in particular were shallow draft, which meant that they could be beached more or less anywhere. Deep-water ports were not required. They could push up shallow rivers far faster than any land army could travel. They could even be carried across land, 'portage' as it is known, a technique used as far apart as England, France and Russia. In the last of these regions the Vikings (mainly Swedes in this case) were able to access great rivers like the Volga and the Dnieper, allowing them to finally reach the Caspian and Black Seas (though over time the latter became by far the more popular route as it allowed direct access to Constantinople). The arc of the Viking world covered an immense area. The trade possibilities were substantial and items from the steppes of Central Asia would find homes as far away as Dublin and York. In this respect it is certainly true to say that the Vikings were far more than merely raiders.

With large stocks of oak and other timber available in Scandinavia, there was plenty of raw material around to build the ships too. Solid tree trunks would be used for keels, smaller branches for the ribs of the vessel. That said, the Viking shipwrights were knowledgeable and experienced enough to use parts of trees with the right shape to construct different parts of the ship. As well as oak, other woods such as beech, pine, spruce and ash also played a part.

These ships were formidable, fast, fearsome – but they would not have been comfortable to travel in, being largely open to the elements and, for obvious reasons, fires could not be used when the ship was out at sea. The Vikings manning these vessels would have slept on an open deck, normally protected from the weather only by whatever furs and cloaks they had brought with them or possibly sometimes using makeshift awnings.

But the warships in particular were fast. The longship recovered from Roskilde Fjord (the original of which was seemingly constructed in the region of Dublin) was reconstructed and the modern recreation completed a circumnavigation from Roskilde to Ireland round the north of Britain, and then up the English Channel and back to Denmark in 2007. The average speed was about 6 knots but in extreme weather conditions she could travel at over 15. Being capable of carrying nearly 100 warriors, this was a formidable instrument of war.

The awe-inspiring form of the amazingly preserved Gokstad ship (now in Oslo) gives another indication of what these ships would have been like, even though this vessel dates to a time a century or so before Cnut's era. The frame was built of oak (though the decking and some other parts were of pine) and is just over 23 metres long. It is clinker-built with the planks overlapping each other, the standard Viking ship construction style. The sail was carried on a yard about 11 metres long and was made of wool, white with sewn-on red stripes. There were oar-holes cut into the third plank down below the gunwales though these could be plugged when not in use. Oars were probably mainly used in coastal areas though of course they could also play a part further out to sea if the wind was in the wrong direction.

The ship was found complete with other maritime gear such as an anchor and a gangplank. A reproduction was sailed across the Atlantic in 1893 as a timely reminder to the American people that Vikings were there long before Columbus had arrived 401 years before. The skipper remarked that it had handled incredibly well and had often exceeded a speed of ten knots.

The dragon figureheads that made such an impression on those who witnessed them were of a surprisingly ancient vintage. Rock carvings dating back to the first and second centuries AD show that such striking elements were present in vessels from Scandinavia even then. Ships were given names, some of which suggest that not just dragons were used to adorn them, such as *Crane*, *Bison* and *Man's Head*. Curiously there is evidence that these figureheads were removed when ships neared land. Icelandic laws required that this happened so that the figurehead's guardian spirit did not depart when the shore was reached. Even the Bayeux Tapestry shows Norman ships with figureheads when the fleet was at sea but they are no longer visible when depicted off the coast of England.[4]

The next year, 1004, was equally as trying for England as the last had been but the Vikings moved the focus of their attacks, perhaps because frequent raiding in the west had already denuded the region of much of the wealth that was worth taking there and the easy pickings had gone. They therefore moved to the east of England. East Anglia had escaped comparatively unscathed in recent times since the Battle of Maldon but this was about to change. Ulfcetel Snilling – 'The Bold' – was the senior English leader in the area but he and his councillors decided that they too would attempt to buy the raiders off rather than fight them after the Vikings had sailed up to Norwich and sacked it.

A truce was therefore agreed but it did not hold. Under cover of it, the raiders fell on Thetford: complying with the terms of such agreements was not a Viking strength.[5] Understandably Ulfcetel felt that this relieved him too of any responsibilities to keep the peace that he had under the terms of the truce and he and his army planned to fall on the Viking ships. It was an astute strategic move; without their fleet the raiders would be trapped and a stronger force could be assembled by the English with who knew what results.

Unfortunately for Ulfcetel, who at least had some fight in him, he had not managed to assemble all his forces by the time he fell on the fleet and the attack on the Viking ships was beaten off. There was a 'great slaughter'[6] on both sides in the battle that followed but it was the raiders who in the end held the field. But it was said that this was the hardest-fought battle that the raiders had had in recent times. It appears that Ulfcetel was not an ealdorman, which may also have had some impact on his ability to recruit men to face up to the Viking threat. Perhaps with more men in his army, a famous victory might have been won. It shows the inbuilt riskiness of one of the king's policies of the time, which was either not to replace ealdormen at all when a vacancy arose or to decrease the lands they held, which might have impacted on their ability to call out the local fyrd effectively.

By this time, the fyrds were not made up of every available man. In earlier Germanic history every man of fighting age was expected to be available for battle in defence of his lord and his territory. This was probably no longer the case. There is evidence that one man was required from each five hides of land. The rest of the men in that district were required to help pay to equip this warrior and ensure that he turned up for battle with the necessary equipment. The provision of one man from each five hides is remarkably similar to what was required in Carolingian Francia and was therefore quite probably inspired by it.[7]

The strength of resistance on this occasion perhaps explains why the raiders did not return to England during the following year. But it might also have been because the country was then faced with a terrible famine. Whilst weakening the English, this also made it difficult for a raiding army to live off the land as they must have been forced to do during the campaigning season. But it would have done little to make the English feel better about the overall situation; famine was one of the indicators of those events that would presage the end of the world, and in an age that took such millenarian motifs very seriously indeed, this was a disturbing portent.

It is important to say, though, that these were still raids rather than full-scale attempts to conquer England. The Vikings undoubtedly weakened the English with each succeeding attack, but for now it seems that the raiders were content to help themselves to as much as they wanted, faced as they were by a weak and divided English leadership. But for Æthelred the situation was now growing ever more parlous. He was faced, it must be said, by an extraordinarily difficult situation. His country was divided and, in some ways, still in its infancy. There were many elements in England, both Danish and English, that were not well-disposed towards him and men who formed part of them took every opportunity that they could to grasp selfish advantage from every situation.

Militarily, some of his strategic decisions had not been ill-advised. The formation of land and sea armies to meet the raiders was in many ways a throwback to the days of Alfred the Great, who had also built up his military forces to face the overwhelming Viking threat. But it was in the execution that things were going wrong. The English were constantly outwitted by Sweyn and his raiders, who consistently caught them on the hop.

The Vikings were far more flexible both in their movement and their thinking than the English and this, time after time, secured their advantage. Despite significant expenditures in money and effort all the defensive measures adopted by the English seemed to fail and in the context of a warrior society, which in many ways Anglo-Saxon England still was, it was inevitable that the king would be blamed for this, not least by those who were faced with increasingly crippling levels of taxation to pay for the Danegeld. This at least is consistent with the modern world; nothing succeeds like success and when the opposite is true then any aspiring leader is in serious trouble. And taxpayers do not like seeing their hard-earned resources expended to no apparent effect.

Æthelred's political judgement also needs to be called into question. Paying off the Vikings as a short-term expedient was not a completely misguided move provided that Æthelred used the time that this bought to strengthen his own position and that of his realm. But despite his efforts to do so, little changed and the Danegeld that was paid merely served to encourage the raiders to come back for more. Over time their financial demands not only recurred but they also increased in size. There was a vicious kind of inflation as a result with the price of buying the raiders off rising inexorably.

It is for the payment of this Danegeld that Æthelred has often received the greatest criticism and for which it might almost be said he has become notorious. That most famous of Victorian/ Edwardian Imperialist poets, Rudyard Kipling, wrote of Danegeld in the following terms:

> It is always a temptation to a rich and lazy nation,
> To puff and look important and to say:
> Though we know we should defeat you, we have not the time to
> meet you.
> We will therefore pay you cash to go away.
>
> And that is called paying the Dane-geld;
> But we've proved it again and again,
> That if once you have paid him the Dane-geld
> You never get rid of the Dane.

In recent times historians have sometimes suggested that the impact of this so-called 'Danegeld' has been exaggerated and that England, as a relatively wealthy country, could afford it. One suggested that it is possible that 'money may have flowed into England as payment for exports even faster than the Danish host could siphon it off'.[8] The logic of this argument is rather hard to follow. Even if England was earning large amounts of money from exports, citizens were hardly likely to be happy to see much of it flowing straight back out again.

It also ignores the evidence of the time somewhat too easily. When the Archbishop of York later spoke of the 'monstrous taxes [that] have afflicted us greatly' in the years leading up to 1014, he was assuredly writing from the heart. It cannot have been easy in every case to find the funds demanded: in around 1010 Æthelric, Bishop of Sherborne, complained in a letter to ealdorman Æthelmaer that various places in Dorset were failing to come up with what was required of them.[9]

Politically, Æthelred appears to have had dubious judgement and relied more on heavy-handed rather than subtle tactics. His choice of advisers appears to be questionable as some of the more prominent of them had let him down. No doubt incensed by the treachery of some, he could strike with decisive ruthlessness when the mood took him. But was this wise? Would he not for example have been better placed by keeping the leading Danes in England captive rather than striking them down on St Brice's Day?

They could then have been used as hostages, bargaining chips against the raiders when needed; a use of their own tactics against the Vikings. By killing them, the advantage that he might have held was lost and only served to give the raiders further excuse to attack the country repeatedly. He was weak when he should have been strong, and strong when he should have been measured. He seemed incapable of matching his approach to the needs of the moment. And in times of crisis, emotion won out over rational thinking.

The next move on the part of the Vikings was not difficult to predict. The Dane Thorkell 'the Tall', associated with the semi-legendary Jomsvikings, sent messengers to Sweyn inviting him to England, 'telling him that the land was rich and fertile, but the king a driveller; and that wholly given up to wine and women his last thoughts were those of war; that in consequence he was hateful to his own people and contemptible to foreigners; that the commanders were jealous of each other, the people weak, and that they would fly the field the moment thy onset was sounded'.[10]

This invitation from Thorkell – if it actually happened, which must be doubtful in the light of subsequent events – is interesting. It implies a degree of coordination which was not always necessarily the case in practice. Thorkell was a strong and powerful overlord in his own right and not always an easy man for Sweyn and his son Cnut to deal with. He would also show a marked propensity to support whichever man, English or Dane, currently offered him the greatest personal advantage.

But that said, there are hints in the sagas that it was not always this way. It has even been suggested that Thorkell fostered the young Cnut.[11] Fostering was common enough in Scandinavia and this is not impossible, though as these tales come from later sources they might not be accurate. That relationships with Sweyn had previously been good is suggested by Thorkell's presence at the decisive Battle of Svold at the close of the tenth century. But certainly links between Sweyn, Cnut and Thorkell were destined to become extremely complicated.

The raids that were taking place with such frequency were not at this stage part of a coordinated effort led by Sweyn; Viking raiders were very much their own men, more than capable of acting independently and on their own initiative, driven on by their own motivations. One surviving source of evidence, runic inscriptions connected to Ulf of Boresta in Sweden, tells how he received gelds or payments for services from three leaders, Tosti, Thorkell and Cnut.[12] Thorkell and Cnut are of course well-known figures. Tosti we are less sure about though a man of that name was referred to by the later Icelandic saga-writer Snorri Sturluson, who describes someone of this name as being the mightiest and most noble man without formal rank in Sweden at this time and it has been suggested that this is he.[13]

Sweyn, having been in England on a number of occasions now, presumably already knew many of its weaknesses anyway. In any event, after midsummer in 1006 the Danes were back, led once more by Sweyn, who William of Malmesbury tells us was 'naturally cruel, nor did he require much persuasion'. They came to Sandwich on the Kent coast and spread out from there, burning and killing as they went. Æthelred called out all the men he could from the core English regions of Wessex and Mercia. Chasing after the Danes at around harvest time, they were once more unable to bring them to battle. In fact, the Peterborough version of the *Anglo-Saxon Chronicles* bemoaned the fact that both the Viking raiders and the English army put an impossible strain on the resources of the local communities that were in their respective paths, the cry of many a harassed people caught up in wars over the centuries.

Sweyn came, it was said, accompanied by his three great companions: 'plunder, burning and killing'. There was little it seemed that could be done to resist: 'All England lamented and shook like a reed-bed struck by the quivering west wind.' Devastation came in their wake: 'Wherever they passed they ate joyfully what had been prepared, and when they departed they made payment for their keep by murdering their host and setting fire to their lodging-place.'[14]

By Martinmas (11 November) the Danes had returned to their secure base on the Isle of Wight but they did not over-winter there for, as midwinter was approaching, they crossed the Solent and marched through Hampshire, into Berkshire and up to Reading. There was a saying that if ever the Vikings got to a place called 'Cwichelm's Barrow'[15] they would never get back to the sea again. Clearly the Vikings were aware of it, for it seemed like an act of deliberate provocation against the impotence of the English to make such a bold move.

The barrow was a traditional assembly point for the Anglo-Saxons in the area and it had a legendary association with Cwichelm, a former West Saxon king. It could be seen for some miles off along the long and sprawling ridgeway and would have been a familiar landmark. It had something of a sacred aura about it and it was a sign that the Vikings were feeling extremely buoyant that they chose this place to march to.

The Vikings then duly started to make their way back towards the south coast of England from the barrow. An English army was ready for them on the Kennet but it made no difference as they were beaten off. The raiders continued their journey unperturbed, carrying their booty with them. They marched unmolested past the walls of Winchester. It is notable that, despite the seriousness of the raid, Æthelred was busy enjoying the Christmas festivities well away from the action in Shropshire, a suitable commentary on his inability to face up to the undoubtedly enormous challenges that were facing him and his kingdom. Indeed, it has been remarked that this region was well outside normal itineraries, suggesting that the king had his own specific reasons to be there.[16] We will soon see what those reasons probably were.

The proximity of the raiders to Winchester was significant, for this was then the major city in the country. The church of Saints Peter and Paul had been constructed within her walls on the orders of King Cenwalh in 648 and became known as the Old Minster; it was the cathedral of the city. Winchester had been substantially rebuilt on the orders of Alfred the Great in response to the Viking threat in the late tenth century. A nunnery, the Nunnaminster, was built around this time, as was the New Minster. The latter had been the brainchild of Alfred the Great but construction had not begun until after his death.

The Old Minster lived on as the centre of the cult of the ninth-century Saint Swithun, famously linked with weather prediction even in modern times (though the Old Minster itself did not survive the medieval period, being knocked down to make way for the great Norman cathedral in 1093). The New Minster, a Benedictine abbey, housed the body of the late King Alfred and became a centre of pilgrimage. The two minsters were so close to each other that it was said that sometimes the choirs of both were singing in competition with each other, with rather discordant results.

The Old Minster had been substantially rebuilt in the early eleventh century. Under Ælfheah, Bishop of Winchester (formerly Abbot of Bath, later Archbishop of Canterbury), a massive reconstruction effort had been launched. Inside the Minster was an amazing feat of musical engineering, a massive organ with 400 pipes and twenty-six bellows to work it. An incredible seventy fit men were needed to enable it to function, working in relays.[17]

So this was a hugely significant city and the fact that the marauding Vikings could get so close to it unchecked was a hammer blow to the king's credibility. Not that Æthelred was completely blasé about the threat. The Vikings had ravaged with little check across the south for years and the English king discussed earnestly with his councillors what could be done. It was a reversion to a tried and tested (but not noticeably successful) formula that they came up with: buying the raiders off. Æthelred therefore sent out envoys to the raiders to discuss another large payoff. This time it was more substantial than ever before: 30,000 pounds.

It seemed like a never-ending merry-go-round of one failure after another, yet the following year almost unbelievably the situation was about to get even worse and this time it was with the unwitting connivance of the king. In 1007 Eadric Streona was made ealdorman of Mercia; here the clue is in the name for 'Streona' means 'acquisitive' (though this derogatory term did not emerge until the end of the eleventh century). Some might prefer the name given him by early twentieth-century historians – 'Eadric the Grasper'.

Whatever was best for Eadric seemed to be the only valid criterion by which the new ealdorman would judge the success of his actions. The harsh judgement placed on him by history can perhaps be best understood by the fact that a BBC article in

2005 assessed him as one of the top ten 'worst Britons' of the past thousand years, a list that included other perhaps better-known celebrities such as Jack the Ripper and King John.[18]

Eadric's family came from the region of what is now the Welsh borders, and Herefordshire and Shropshire in particular. This was significant given the fact that the latter region is where the king spent Christmas in 1006 when the Viking raids were in full swing across southern England. The early twelfth-century chronicler John of Worcester states that Eadric's father was in attendance at the English court in the late 980s and the family was therefore closely connected to the ruling dynasty.

John was one of the first to give details of Eadric's treacherous streak. In 1006 the ealdorman Ælfhelm, from southern Northumbria, was invited to a great feast at Shrewsbury. Eadric greeted him like a long-lost friend. However, a few days later he took Ælfhelm out hunting. An ambush had been carefully prepared and at the right moment a Shrewsbury butcher, Godwin Porthund ('the town dog'), fell on Ælfhelm and killed him. There was no chance of retribution for Eadric had friends in high places, as was evidenced soon after when Æthelred had the murdered ealdorman's sons, Wulfheah and Ufegeat, blinded at Cookham in Berkshire. But the family did not lose all influence or prestige, as was shown a few years later when Ælfhelm's daughter Ælfgifu was married to Cnut, son of Sweyn Forkbeard, perhaps in an attempt to take advantage of fissures in the English political landscape and gain a measure of revenge for the way that they had been treated.

These events were crucial to the development of factional politics in England at the time. Æthelred seems to have decided to rid himself of some of the old guard and create a new council that he could mould more towards his own perceived best interests. It has well been described as something of a 'palace revolution'.[19] From what happened subsequently we can assume that he saw in Eadric Streona a man who was biddable to his will, though in the long term the king would be disastrously let down by his new favourite. The king would prove to be no more able to keep the lid on domestic politics than he would in fighting off the Viking threat.

The basis of Æthelred's support base now shifted to west Mercia and the lands held by Eadric. On the other hand, other regions of

England in the east and the north found themselves disadvantaged as a result. The nobles of these regions found that their influence was compromised and the violent removal of Ælfhelm and the blinding of his sons set an unhappy precedent. From now on they were on their guard against the king and his court.

But Eadric was not the only man to benefit from this change in direction. In the north of the country, Uhtred of Bamburgh was made ealdorman of all Northumbria and was later married to Æthelred's daughter. This probably reflected the successes that Uhtred had previously won against a Scottish raid across the borders although it was also a way of trying to buy the loyalty of a powerful, ambitious and successful magnate. Uhtred was given a huge area under his control from the Humber to the border with Scotland.

This bringing together of the northern part of Northumbria (the ancient kingdom of Bernicia) and the southern (Deira) was not the norm. During the heyday of Viking occupation in the tenth century the southern half, based around the crucial archbishopric of York, came under Viking control, culminating in the rule of Erik Bloodaxe. Bernicia on the other hand had largely stayed independent. The lords of the northern part of Northumbria were often bitter rivals of those in the south and the natural dividing line of the Tyne had also become something of a political border. Tension in the region was barely concealed beneath the surface. Not everyone would be happy to see Uhtred's dominance. Matters were about to come to a spectacular head a few years later.

We do get odd glimpses of Uhtred from the historical record. He first married the daughter of Styr Ulfsson, a supporter of the king who probably attested certain charters for Æthelred. Styr's name is of Scandinavian origin and a connection with York is suggested. The change in political direction now extended Uhtred's influence in the southern part of Northumbria.[20] He was assuredly a man on the rise.

Eadric Streona's high standing was confirmed when he became the son-in-law of Æthelred when he married his daughter, Eadgyth. The Danes did not return in 1008 and the king did what he could to build up the strength of the kingdom in their absence. A fleet was built up and armour was collected from across the country.

The relative calm of this year allowed an assembly to gather at Enham in Hampshire, close to Andover. It is not a major settlement but for a few days in May 1008 (which that year included the period of Pentecost in the Christian calendar) it became the centre of England. Here a council was held, attended by Archbishop Wulfstan of York, who seems to have been the driving force behind much of the increased activity of this year, and the king. They debated the vexed subject of how to face up to the future and make it altogether more acceptable than the recent past.

The convention was preceded by a meeting of the churchmen present, presumably deciding on tactics and how to ensure that Æthelred and his councillors lived up to their responsibilities. Here the wider discussions were led by Wulfstan, a powerful homilist and orator, who preached with great effect. He exhorted those present to combine against the Danish threat, reject pagan superstition and unite behind the one True God, ostensibly a strange text for a country that was supposedly thoroughly Christianised. But in lecturing the king and his secular advisors in this way, Wulfstan was imitating contemporary clerical approaches on the Continent.[21]

This was not just about politics: it was also in the context of the times an exercise in religion as the two were largely entwined at this period in history. There is no doubt that the troubles that had beset England, both in the form of the Viking raids and some of the natural disasters that had also struck the population, would have been seen by many, certainly the outspoken Wulfstan, as a punishment from God meted out to a sinful, ungrateful people. Not only was good planning necessary to drive back the Vikings, so too was a large amount of repentance.

Nor was Wulfstan the only homilist of the time preaching such themes. In a work called *De Oratione Moysi* ('On the Prayers of Moses'), written in the closing years of the tenth century, Ælfric of Cerne had also called for repentance, as he too saw God's judgement in the Viking raids. During those days it had been suggested that the 'mass against the pagans' should be said in churches every Wednesday.[22]

Ælfric was a prolific writer, the composer of many works in Old English. He was a product of the great monastic reform movement in England in the second half of the tenth century, mentored by the prominent reformer St Æthelwold at Winchester before being sent to the new abbey at Cerne. One prominent twentieth-century Anglo-Saxon historian, Peter Hunter Blair, even compared his works, in both quantity and the quality of mind that they evidenced, with no less a person than Bede.

Wulfstan was of a similar stamp. In his writings, we can almost touch the frustration pouring out from the pages. There was a strong link between Church and State in England at the time. Whilst the Pope was the titular head of the Church, he was a long way from England and the king was in many ways the dominant figure in the land, even regarding religious matters. The Church paid taxes just as any other landholder did (except for lands owned by the king himself). It was also a supporter in principle of the monarchy; they were effectively two different pillars of the same establishment.

But something was expected in return. There were material gifts, grants from the king's store of land and treasure for one thing. Despite some periods of difficulty earlier in his reign, Æthelred had played his part in this respect. But more than even this was required. According to the teachings of the eminent early medieval theologian St Augustine, a ruler was expected to be a 'just king'. There were murmurings that Æthelred had not always been that. He was also expected to protect the peace and stability of the realm and here the king was failing miserably. A blind eye might have been turned to his other faults if the Vikings had been driven back; suspect measures against some of his own people might have been ignored. But there were no such redeeming features present to offset his other failings and Wulfstan was clearly at the end of his tether at the way things were going.

That said, secular measures had certainly not been completely neglected, not the least of the orders issued at this time being that attention be paid to the restoration of the defences of the burhs, suggesting that they had up until now been allowed to deteriorate. Such measures were the responsibility of the local community and it is easy to see how they might have gone into abeyance as a result. But this was a source of great concern. The burhs had been Alfred's tour de force. Situated typically no more than 20 miles from their nearest neighbour, they had been integral to the defence of England against Viking attack. Their decline was a worrying development now that that England was again in danger.

Another important command issued was that any man who deserted the king's army in the field was to forfeit his life and his property.[23] In the light of both recent and future campaigns against Scandinavian armies this was very significant. But these were secondary to the moral dimension of the discussions at Enham and perhaps the most significant of the utterances made at around this time was that of Wulfstan to 'let us loyally support one royal lord, and let each friend support the other with true fidelity'. This reads like a rallying cry to the people of England to stand rock-solid behind their sovereign lord. Wulfstan was still not ready to turn on God's chosen and anointed king despite all the provocation to do so that existed.

It was not long after this meeting that there was a radical change in the currency. Conventional English coins of the time included a representation of the king on them. But now this was changed and a new penny was issued with the image of the Lamb of God, the *agnus dei*, on one side and that of a dove on the other. These were Christian symbols synonymous with peace and mercy and it is tempting to read them as a plea to the Almighty for these very desirable gifts to be granted to the English. It is hard also to overlook the literal translation of the place-name Enham, which means 'the place where lambs are bred'; even this was imbued with symbolism.[24]

If these actions were a plea for mercy from the Almighty, He did not appear to be listening. For when the raiders did return the year after, it seemed as if the Danish strategy had changed with terrifying consequences. The Peterborough version of the *Anglo-Saxon Chronicles* becomes almost verbose as it goes into detail when describing the next few years, as if believing that they were of especial significance, which they undoubtedly were. Reading it, it seems clear that there had been a change in direction from the Vikings, an altogether higher intensity about their actions. This no longer looked like raiding; it was more like an attempt at conquest.

A great Viking army landed at Sandwich, again the point of entry into England and, one would have thought, long overdue now for efforts to improve its defences. It was led by Thorkell the Tall with an army that seemed to be recruited from across Scandinavia. With him were his younger brother Hemingr and another great Viking warrior, Eilífr, who was the brother of Ulf who was married to Sweyn Forkbeard's daughter, Estrith. This marriage produced two sons, another Sweyn ('Sweyn Estrithsson', who would later be king of Denmark) and Bjorn.[25]

It may even be that Æthelred had prior information that such an attempt at conquest was likely to be made. Wulfstan wrote a strong edict for him in September 1009 ordering the English people to engage in three days of prayer and fasting. During this time only bread, herbs and water could be taken. Everyone was to make their way barefoot to church in a collective and national mark of penitence. Even slaves were to join in. A monetary payment was also to be made. Anyone refusing to participate would be punished for their non-observance of the king's commands. Every priest was to sing thirty masses. A particular psalm was to be sung frequently during these days; its words could not have been more appropriate – 'O Lord, how they are multiplied that trouble me.'

As always, the admonishing hand of Wulfstan can be detected, for he was a man who was never slow to see the visitations of the Vikings as a punishment from God. But it can also be seen as an act of panic which would do nothing to lift the national mood. It smacked of desperation, even defeatism. These events, with their frantic prayers for divine intercession, are a sure indicator of the state of morale in the country at the time. They might also seem very much the actions of those that lived in a different world to our own, yet it is worth recalling that in May 1940, after the withdrawal of the British Army from France after Dunkirk, King George VI issued a call for a national day of prayer to be observed after what the serving Prime Minister described as 'the blackest day of all'.

Æthelred also did what he could to organise a defence against this latest attack. A ship was to be supplied from each 310 hides in England, a hide originally being the amount of land that could be ploughed in a year, but by this period it had become a tax assessment tool. In addition, each hide was to provide a hauberk (a shirt of mail) and a helmet.[26] As a result, Æthelred managed to assemble a significant number of ships, according to the *Chronicles* 'more of them then there had ever earlier been in England in the days of any king'.[27]

This was in itself a very expensive expedient. Consideration of the costs of war at this time tends to focus mainly on the very visible expense of collecting Danegeld to pay the Vikings off. Whatever the political demerits of effectively paying 'protection money' – and the fact that the raiders kept returning suggests very strongly that it did not work at all in the long run as far as discouraging Sweyn and his type from coming back for more was concerned – it might often have been cheaper on occasion than organising a defence.

Not only was there the procurement of ships to consider but there was also the issue of arming the army properly for the challenge that faced them. Despite all the criticism that Æthelred receives, he did take measures to ensure that his warriors were better equipped than they were in the past. He arranged for such men to wear byrnies, or hauberks of mail: in 1016 there were said to be 24,000 items of such equipment in London alone, an extraordinarily high number. If true, it has been estimated that the cost of this was £50,000–60,000 in 1008 alone, significantly higher than most Danegeld payments.[28] In other words, the costs of defending the county against attack were enormous.

The assembly of such large amounts of armour requiring such significant sums of money was a drain on the country's resources but the fact that they could be collected at all showed that England, if nothing else, was a realm with a well-organised administrative machine. But such a large-scale armament process intimates that there were serious shortages of armour in England at the time, suggesting that up to this point the country had not been well prepared to face a challenge on such a scale. The country had not been on what we would call a 'war footing'.

Of course, costly measures on their own are not enough; they need to lead to some tangible results. It was therefore important that such huge amounts of expenditure led to some clear improvement in the situation of the English. Expecting that the Kent coast might be vulnerable, the ships had assembled together at Sandwich. So far, so good – but it was only a matter of time before the defensive plan started to unravel once more. Again the English themselves were their own worst enemies. Beorhtric, the brother of the scheming Eadric, suggested to the king that a prominent South Saxon, Wulfnoth, was not to be trusted.

Whatever the exact truths of this perception, what was probably happening here was an internal struggle for control between

Æthelred and his supporters on the one hand and on the other those of the Ætheling Æthelstan, the eldest son of the king, whose primacy in the line of succession was now under threat from the sons of Emma. Wulfnoth was a known associate of Æthelstan and is widely regarded as the father of the famous future earl, Godwin (though this cannot be proved beyond doubt). Wulfnoth's father Æthelmaer had been a powerful ealdorman in his time too but had seen his influence vastly diminished by the rise of Eadric Streona. Perhaps also remembering what had happened to the ealdorman Ælfhelm in 1006 at the hands of the same Eadric, Wulfnoth decided to absent himself from the forces around the king as quickly as possible.

Eadric may have been justified in his assumptions for Wulfnoth did indeed get away, along with twenty ships. Neither was this a purely passive move to take himself off to somewhere safe. With these vessels he proceeded to attack various locations across the South Coast, where the populace was presumably struggling ever more to differentiate friend from foe. This merely served to anger Beorhtric who, along with eighty ships, set out to chastise Wulfnoth. Sadly for him, a violent storm broke out and his ships were battered and thrashed to pieces and forced to put ashore.

Beorhtric's ships were now like beached whales, incapable of movement, stranded on the shore. Wulfnoth, who rode out the storm rather well by the look of it, fell on the ships and burned them. The remainder of Æthelred's fleet lost heart and the king, no doubt frustrated beyond words, took himself off. The fleet then returned to London, having achieved precisely nothing and indeed having lost around 100 ships in the process. If ever one isolated incident summed up all that was wrong in England at the time, then this was it. Confidence in the king on the part of many of his subjects must by now have been plummeting towards rock-bottom. He had invested heavily in terms of both money and credibility in the fleet and all these efforts had been completely wasted.

Confidence in the king was not about to pick up either. The Vikings had not even arrived yet and all was chaos. When they did come back to England led by Thorkell the Tall soon after 1 August (Lammas day), they entered a now deserted harbour at Sandwich. From there they went to the sacred city of Canterbury, which was left alone after the residents begged to be spared; a payment of 3,000 pounds from the people of East Kent presumably helped.

Others were not so lucky. The Vikings made their way towards their favoured base of the Isle of Wight, sacking settlements in Berkshire, Sussex and Hampshire on their way. Æthelred sent out orders that a national army should be assembled as quickly as possible but this did not deter the Vikings one bit and they continued to move around where they wanted, facing virtually no opposition as they did so. When eventually Æthelred managed to catch up with the Vikings, he was deterred from attacking them (so say the *Chronicles*) by the untrustworthy Eadric.

So there was no decisive battle. Instead, in a move that was resonant with threat, the Vikings returned to Kent, where they planned to spend the winter. Moving back in time about a century and a half, this was precisely what Danish armies had done in the ninth century when they started their planned conquest of England (they had also used similar tactics in the Carolingian Empire at around the same period in history). Now they ransacked surrounding areas, Essex in particular, for stores to support them through the winter and even attacked London, though without success.

Winter was no bar to their attacks either; after all, most of them were used to surviving far worse weather back home in Scandinavia than anything they were likely to find in England. They rode up through the Chilterns and fell on Oxford, which they sacked, perhaps as an act of revenge for the St Brice's Day Massacre a few years before. An army was put on alert in London to intercept them as they returned but the Vikings merely bypassed it. They arrived safely back in Kent where they spent the rest of the winter repairing their ships.

This was merely the beginning and barely a taster for what was to happen in the next four years. England was starting down a road which would turn the country on its head. Although 1009 had been an awful year for the English people, things were about to happen that would make it look like mild in comparison to what was to come.

Just after Easter in 1010 the Vikings came bursting north. Bypassing London, they fell on East Anglia, which had escaped their attentions for a few years. They first came to Ipswich, reaching it in May, and then moved on to the place where Ulfcetel 'Mare's Head' was with the English army. It appears that the Vikings were deliberately looking for a fight and a brutal, bruising encounter followed at the Battle of Ringmere.

It was long thought that the battle took place on open heathland at Bridgham though more recently it has been suggested that it may have happened at Rymer Point, 4 miles south of Thetford. The former does, however, have an intuitive attraction as it was the assembly point of six vills, and such places were convenient spots for the fyrds of different areas to meet up. In the fight that followed, there was great loss of life on the English side and amongst the dead were Æthelstan, the son-in-law of King Æthelred, and Oswy, the son-in-law of the ealdorman Byrhtnoth who had died in heroic fashion at Maldon nearly two decades previously.

Ulfcetel fled and East Anglia was left to the far from gentle mercy of the victorious Vikings. Many men fled with him though it was noted that the men of Cambridgeshire fought bravely until broken. For three months after this, the raiders ravaged the region, killing men and cattle, even breaking through the watery frontiers of the Fens. Thetford and Cambridge were both left destroyed in their wake. Flaming churches across the region marked where they had passed. Then, their looting there done, they headed back to London and on to Oxfordshire. They burst into Buckinghamshire, and moved on to Bedford and then Tempsford, burning everything as they went.

The Peterborough chronicler noted drily that when the Vikings were in the east, the English army was in the west and when they were in the north the English were in the south. They ravaged far and near, destroying Northampton on St Andrew's Day (30 November) and then moving many miles to the south-west, into Wessex and Wiltshire in particular. In contrast to previous raids, this was warfare on a far wider scale. At last, at midwinter they headed back to their ships and a temporary halt whilst they recovered their strength. Æthelred, partly through incompetence but partly also through factionalism, seemed completely incapable of fighting off the challenge from the raiders. He was also not a young man by the standards of the time and this must all have sapped his vitality.

The Vikings were winning through a philosophy of 'divide and conquer', one in which they frankly did not have to do very much themselves as the English were undertaking all the hard work for them. So bad were things that the *Anglo-Saxon Chronicles* noted in despair that 'no shire would help the next' after suggesting that 'even if anything was decided, it did not last a month'. These events were painfully exposing the inherent weaknesses of the fyrd system, which was essentially a policy of local defence where allegiances to the relevant ealdorman outweighed wider tactical considerations. Even when a larger army was assembled composed of several fyrds from different shires, it seems likely that each element remained a largely individual entity. This was not conducive to the development of a coherent and coordinated national defence.

Faced by this sorry tale of defeat after defeat, Æthelred reverted to tried and tested (but not necessarily successful) tactics once more; he would buy the raiders off again. The chronicler lamented, not because the king had again been forced to adopt this council of despair but rather because he had taken so long to do it. He gives a long list of the areas that had been overrun: East Anglia, Essex, Middlesex, Oxfordshire, Cambridgeshire, Hertfordshire, Buckinghamshire, Bedfordshire, half of Huntingdonshire, all the Kentish and the South Saxons, the Hastings district, Surrey, Berkshire, Hampshire and much of Wiltshire. Little of the south and east of England or the Midlands had escaped. Even those areas not specifically mentioned by the chronicler seem to have been under threat, as evidenced for example by the removal of the mint at Ilchester in Somerset to the nearby ancient hillfort of South Cadbury or the selling of lands at Corscombe in Dorset because of Viking attacks at around this time.[29]

But despite the taxes, the raiding continued and 'they travelled about everywhere in bands and raided and roped up and killed our wretched people'.[30] The situation was now extremely parlous; England was clearly unable to defend herself against the threat and therefore any truce that might be bought with Danegeld could be ignored with impunity. Sometime between 8 and 29 September 1011, the raiders succeeded in taking Canterbury, which according to the *Anglo-Saxon Chronicles* was betrayed by Abbot Ælfmær, the spiritual head of St Augustine's Abbey in the city – even a churchman it seems could not be trusted (though 'Florence' of Worcester insists that he was not the guilty party, who was instead another man of the same name). When Cnut later became king, Ælfmær became bishop in Sherborne. It has been plausibly suggested that this was some form of payback for services rendered.[31]

Several important prisoners were taken as a result of these developments including Ælfweard, the king's reeve, and Bishop Godwin of Rochester. The reeve played an important role in the local government of England at this time. At the top of the hierarchy next to the king was the ealdorman, a kind of provincial governor. Next to him came the shire-reeve (later called the 'sheriff') who fulfilled a number of important administrative functions at the shire level. The shire-reeves, in theory at least, seem to have reported straight to the king and acted in some ways as a check and balance on the local ealdorman. They brought cases to the local courts for judgement, and ensured that any sentence that followed was duly carried out.[32] Therefore the capture of a reeve, and of course a bishop too, was no small event.

But the greatest prize of all taken at Canterbury was none other than its Archbishop, the foremost prelate in England. His name was Ælfheah (later known as Alphege) and the scene was set for one of the most harrowing scenes in the long history of the Vikings in England. The Vikings under the command of Thorkell the Tall took Ælfheah away with them, accompanied by a number of other ordained priests, monks and nuns.

Henry of Huntingdon paints a vivid and harrowing picture of the scene that resulted from the Vikings' actions at Canterbury:

> And thus the victors returned to their ships. You would have seen a terrible sight: the whole of the ancient and beautiful city reduced to ashes, corpses of the citizens lying packed together in the streets, the ground and the river blackened with blood, the lamenting and wailing of women and children being led into captivity, and the head of the English faith and the source of Christian doctrine [the Archbishop] taken in chains and shamefully dragged away.[33]

Henry is not alone in describing such terrible scenes. 'Florence' of Worcester writes of people being put to the sword, others burned alive and yet more thrown to their deaths from the walls. Men were allegedly hung up by their testicles. Women were dragged by their hair through the streets and thrown into the fire. Infants were either impaled on stakes or crushed under cartwheels.

A panicked king called his council, including the untrustworthy Eadric Streona, to London before Easter 1012 (Easter falling on 13 April that year). Eadric seems to have had other priorities at the time as he launched a raid deep into West Wales at some point during the year. Another 8,000 pounds of Danegeld was found but for the Viking host this was not enough. They still had Ælfheah with them and they sought to extract yet more money by demanding a ransom for their important hostage. But the archbishop was a brave man and he demanded that there should be no negotiations or payment for his release. On the day before Easter, they offered Ælfheah his life if he managed to raise a ransom of 3,000 pounds. The archbishop would have nothing to do with their demands.

His stance infuriated some of the raiders. They hauled him before one of their gatherings (known as a *husting*) on Easter Saturday. Fuelled by large amounts of wine that they had helped themselves to during their successful raiding in southern England, a number of the Vikings in attendance became uncontrollable. They hauled the recalcitrant archbishop out and began to pelt him with ox bones. Whatever his religious beliefs, and however strong his courage, this must have been a terrifying experience, surrounded by the baying Danes, lusting for blood from this stubborn priest.

Then one of the mob, more drunk perhaps than the others, smashed the archbishop on the head with the butt of his axe, often used to crush bones. The archbishop fell to the ground, the life-blood flowing out of him. The fatal blow, says 'Florence' of Worcester, was struck by a man with the memorable name of Thrum, and he had only been confirmed as a Christian the day before, a sacramental act that supposedly bound him closer to the Church. Now, as 'Florence' described it, this man 'with compassionate impiety split his head with an axe and he instantly fell asleep in the Lord'.[34]

Perhaps the Vikings already regretted their actions, in the cold light of day on the following morning, for many of them were – nominally at least – Christians by this stage in their history, and slaughtering such an illustrious cleric was a sacrilegious act.

At any event, the bishops of Dorchester and London were able to reclaim Ælfheah's lifeless body and take it to St Pauls in London for honourable burial where he was received by the citizens with deep reverence. Soon after, it was said that miraculous events took place there and the martyred Ælfheah was already on the road to sainthood.

That lover of tales of divine intervention William of Malmesbury himself told a story that explained why the Vikings, who had so shortly before killed the Archbishop, were now mortified at their actions. Some of those present at this act of butchery saw that dead wood, stained with his blood, miraculously grew green again overnight. They therefore ran to kiss his remains and carried them on their shoulders. Horrified at the execution of such a saintly man, they allowed his corpse to be taken away for an honourable burial.[35]

It has been suggested that the writer of the *Anglo-Saxon Chronicles* felt that the slaying of the head of the Church presaged the demise of the English Crown.[36] It is easy to see why. Just two centuries before, England and Europe had been shaken by the sacking of Lindisfarne amongst other holy places. But these were hit-and-run raids, carried out with speed and difficult to defend against. This was something different. The senior official of the Church in England had been slaughtered in the cold light of day and the English king was powerless to stop it. What made it worse was that he was butchered at Greenwich, on the very doorstep of London, and this merely stressed the impotence of Æthelred to intervene. The symbolism of the slaughter of the figurehead of the English Church whilst a powerless king was just a few miles off was hard to ignore.

It may be that the commander of this particular Viking host, Thorkell the Tall, was personally horrified by such acts for soon after he switched sides and took up a position as an ally of Æthelred. Certainly Thietmar of Merseburg, writing within a few years of these events, wrote that Thorkell did all he could to dissuade the drunken mob from performing this brutal execution. A more cynical interpretation is also possible: he may have merely considered it advantageous to switch sides at this point and therefore it was a change inspired more by opportunism than anything else. He would anyway be a very welcome addition to

Æthelred's party as they sought to resist the Danes. This was at least one beneficial side-effect of the killing of the archbishop. It must have been with a sense of irony that Thorkell attested a charter with Æthelred during the following year, signing after his old adversary Ulfcetel in an award to Bishop Godwin who had been taken prisoner at Canterbury.[37]

The impact of these frequent attacks was now so great that the nature of collecting the Danegeld was changed. Previous amounts had been raised on an ad hoc basis, painful no doubt but at least nominally one-off in nature. Now, though, a land tax was raised, called the *heregeld* or 'army tax', as a regularised feature of taxation policy in the country. It would remain as a tax for nearly four decades, another tacit acceptance that the Viking threat was here to stay and high levels of taxation along with it.[38] This once more did nothing to endear Æthelred to his people but we should note that collection of the tax continued long after he died.

There was also evidence that the purpose of the tax was now something different. Rather than for paying the Vikings to go away, it instead appears to have been money used to entice Thorkell to stay. This was in fact a move with a lot of sense behind it. The English were clearly not up to the task of fighting off one raid after another so, if they had to pay money, they may as well do so to bring real protection on themselves. The Frankish king Charles the Simple had done much the same in the previous century when he gave land to Rollo in Normandy in return for using him as a shield against future Viking raids, a policy that largely worked.

There were a number of signs that Sweyn Forkbeard and Thorkell the Tall did not always see eye to eye but that need not mean that the men personally loathed each other, merely that both men were opportunists and would not hesitate to advance their own interests at all costs; two men of a very similar stamp, in fact. So Thorkell stayed in England along with forty-five ships and their men, his services bought by these expensive measures.

Nevertheless, the fighting continued. 1013 was the year in which the denouement finally seemed imminent. Now with Thorkell on the opposite side, Sweyn Forkbeard returned once more. And now for the first time the *Anglo-Saxon Chronicles* note the presence of his son, Cnut.

The fact that Cnut is not mentioned before suggests that this was his first involvement in a raid on England and perhaps also gives a clue as to his most likely date of birth. If he was born in 995 this would make him eighteen years of age by now, a not unreasonable age to blood him on campaign, whereas if an alternative date of 985 is assumed it would have made him twenty-eight, which seems late for a first involvement in a raid on England given the extended period of time that such actions had been taking place.[39]

Sweyn wisely had one eye on what might happen in Denmark whilst he was gone as Scandinavia was still an unsettled region. He left his son Harald there along with a council to help him to govern. It was in some ways (with the benefit of hindsight) a watershed moment for from this point on Harald was linked with Denmark whilst Cnut's destiny lay, in the short term at least, in England.

It was an impressive sight as the Danish fleet set out on yet another mission of depredation towards the shores of England:

> When at length they were all gathered, they went on board the towered ships, having picked out by observation each man his own leader on the brazen prows. On one side lions moulded in gold were to be seen on the ships, on the other birds on the tops of the masts indicated by their movements of the winds as they blew, or dragons of various kinds poured fire from their nostrils. Here there were glittering men of solid gold or silver nearly comparable to live ones, there bulls with necks raised high and legs outstretched were fashioned roaring and leaping like live ones.[40]

Once more the Vikings made landfall at Sandwich. There was a fight when they landed but they drove the English away and from here pushed on to East Anglia. Then it was further north for the first time for a while, into the mouth of the Humber and along the Trent to Gainsborough. In an act of immense significance Earl Uhtred of Northumbria soon after submitted to Sweyn in a manner that suggests any resistance on his part was token at best.

What made this particularly hurtful to the king was that, just a few years before, Uhtred had taken his third wife: none other than Ælfgifu, daughter of Æthelred himself. Marriages of princesses to non-royals in England at the time were extremely rare, yet Æthelred had arranged such matches for his two daughters: one to Uhtred, the other to Eadric Streona, both men of enormous regional significance in various parts of his kingdom and seemingly a deliberate policy by the king to secure their support. The marriage to Uhtred probably took place in around 1009 for we find him attesting charters regularly after this date. But if Æthelred had hoped to buy loyalty, it was a policy that had clearly failed. We know that Uhtred was in occasional attendance at the king's court during the previous few years as he sometimes attested charters, including one not long before. Now he had submitted to the enemy.

At the time the king's court was not just an entity with honorific functions. In the absence of a proper civil service in the modern sense, it was also the effective government of the realm. The earls like Uhtred were occasional visitors but there were a number of other important men who were effectively close attendants to the king. Some would have personal responsibilities to him but others would have more of a governmental function. There would be men responsible for arranging matters of war, others for finance. Matters of law were often in the hands of clerics as, more obviously, were affairs of religion. This was a close knit community where any lack of loyalty would have been strongly felt. If a king could not trust one of his ealdormen, especially his own son-in-law, then who could he rely on?

Gainsborough was not an obviously important settlement and it might be asked why the Vikings set up their base there. The answer is pragmatism. It was right on the border of the Five Boroughs, those crucial Viking settlements in the Danelaw, and Anglo-Saxon Mercia which was under the control of Eadric Streona. The lack of any serious efforts by many of the English to fight off Sweyn suggests that the increased factionalism of England itself meant that some prominent men at least were actually colluding with the Danes. The will of the north of England to fight seems to have been broken by now and this did not augur well for the future.

Northumbria was somewhat isolated from the heartlands of the newly emerged England with its powerbase further south in Wessex and Mercia. For many years in the not too distant past Northumbria had been cut off from southern England by a Viking kingdom based on York and was less securely integrated into the country than all the other regions. It is interesting to note that fifty years later the Norman conquest of England was preceded by a Viking invasion of the north of England that took place with the full support of Tostig, who was at that time the recently exiled Earl of Northumbria. The region's incorporation into a wider England as yet seemed somewhat loose and the fact that it had been subject to influence from the Viking kingdom centred around York in the recent past and its historic Angle roots probably meant that its identification with the Saxon heartlands in the south of England was to an extent tenuous.

Moving into the Danelaw, Sweyn won support there too, in particular from the key towns known as the Five Boroughs, namely Leicester, Lincoln, Derby, Stamford and Nottingham. He then crossed over the historic Roman road of Watling Street, the official boundary between the Danelaw and southern England as agreed in the peace treaty made between Alfred the Great and the Danish leader Guthrum back in 878. It was said that Sweyn issued a pronouncement as he crossed over Watling Street. He published an order that stated that his troops should 'lay waste the fields, burn the villages, plunder the churches, slay without mercy all the men who fell into their hands, reserving the women to satisfy their lusts, and, in short, do all the mischief they could'.[41]

This is significant. Up until now Sweyn had been on unusually good behaviour, a stance that makes complete sense if he wished to ingratiate himself with the people of the north. Now he was moving into enemy territory and the gloves were well and truly off. His pronouncements that his men should help themselves to what they wanted south of Watling Street create the impression of a stereotypical Viking raid and although we should be careful not to accept everything said by the writer 'Florence' of Worcester at face value, we may nevertheless assume that what followed for the lands impacted was a particularly harsh and terrifying sequence of events.

Cnut was left behind in the north to look after the ships and the hostages; it is highly likely that he was also to watch Sweyn's back against any move from Uhtred just in case. But further south the Danish army moved on relentlessly. Everywhere they went they took hostages – and the shocking fate of Ælfheah, whatever else may be said of it, no doubt encouraged the full cooperation of those affected. Oxford quickly submitted to Sweyn, seemingly without much of a fight, as did Winchester. The citizens of the latter city were terrified by Sweyn and his reputation and handed over all the hostages he demanded with little or no resistance. The surrender of what was the foremost city in Wessex sent an alarming message.

Then Sweyn moved on to London which – with Æthelred inside along with Thorkell – held out against him, and a number of the Viking army were lost whilst trying to cross the Thames without the aid of a bridge or a ford. Thorkell was a Dane by birth and had been one of Sweyn's key commanders but his defection to Æthelred along with forty ships was of much help. Sweyn tried all he knew to take the city; subterfuge and violence were two sides of the same coin to him.

Unable to break through the stubborn walls of the city, Sweyn and his army moved many miles west to Bath, passing through Wallingford first. Here at Bath (another symbolic city where the great Edgar had been crowned), ealdorman Æthelmær came from Devon to submit to Sweyn, and he too left hostages when he departed. Relations between the ealdorman and his king do not appear to have been good in recent years[42] and this probably contributed to the submission. Even London, the most loyal of Æthelred's cities, now lost its belief. Here too the citizens offered hostages; greedy to extract every last drop of wealth that he could, Sweyn demanded that they pay him yet more tax to help pay for the cost of the campaign. The Londoners obligingly paid up all that was asked of them, afraid that if they did not do so they would not only lose all their possessions but also their eyes, hands and feet as threatened.[43] With London lost, Æthelred was on the edge of oblivion.

Thorkell's role in all this was very ambivalent. His actions in siding with Æthelred show that he was not by any means Sweyn's man and indeed the latter may have seen him as a major threat to fulfilling his own ambitions in England. But Thorkell's loyalty was first and foremost to himself and what served his own purposes best. In this he was very much a man of his time, a Scandinavian equivalent of Eadric Streona (and incidentally there is no evidence that Eadric was one of those submitting to Sweyn – if he had, we can be sure that the hostile *Anglo-Saxon Chronicles* would have mentioned it). Such men were won over by what gave them the greatest personal advantage. Their loyalty could perhaps be secured by one of two things: what gave them the greatest benefit, or fear of being eliminated by a strong ruler who had access to greater power than they did.

That Thorkell was a striking figure seems to be in little doubt. Even his name is evocative. He was a prominent member of the aristocracy in Skåne, a very independent-minded part of Denmark (now in the south-west of Sweden). Thorkell was important enough to have praise poetry written for him by the skalds, the poets who played such an important part in establishing and enhancing the reputation of the warlords of the Norse world. Such an honour was given to only a few men, and certainly to none who lacked power.

The position of these poets in those days is hard for us to understand. They inhabited a very different world than ours. Michael Alexander, in his translations of and studies on some of the greatest Anglo-Saxon poems, laments the fact that now poets are fringe figures in a 'literate, half-educated society'. Back then, the poet was 'the keeper of traditions which held the cynn [people] together .... The older a sword was, the older a word was, the more it was valued by the cynn. In a primitive society the poet is historian and priest, and his songs have ritual significance.' He was in other words the man who bound the people together and by praising great men like Thorkell he gave substance to the fabric of society.[44] We may therefore assume that Thorkell was a very influential figure if the skalds were writing about him.

But despite all the taxes and the presence of Thorkell, the raids went on. What, one might ask, had become of Æthelred and his family by this stage? William of Malmesbury suggests that all was not well in the king's marriage; adding another coating to the already thick veneer of unrespectability he generally paints for the king, he tells us that the king had become disloyal to Emma, had shunned her bed and instead frequently sported with harlots. The queen, being of august descent, was unsurprisingly very irritated by all this if we can believe William's account.[45]

With England seemingly falling apart, and with suggestions that her marriage was anyway by now on a rather weak footing, there was little reason for Emma to stay put and allow herself to be captured and held as a hostage. Her husband seemed unable to defend his country anymore so she took herself off to Normandy where she found refuge in the court of her brother Richard II, count of that land, a thoroughly sensible move given the alternative possibilities if she stayed put.

She was accompanied by a few loyal retainers like Ælfsige, Abbot of Peterborough (an unsurprising name to mention perhaps in the Peterborough version of the *Anglo-Saxon Chronicles*, this particular version of the chronicles giving much detail for this period of English history). Ælfhun, Bishop of London, had also taken two young princes (or 'æthelings') off into apparent safety overseas. The fates of those two boys, Edward and Alfred, could not in the end have been more tragically different.

Ælfhun's actions show just how varied and useful a bishop's roles were in those days. They were routinely used by Anglo-Saxon kings as envoys on overseas missions and this journey with the young princes was perhaps not so very different even if it was prompted more by a sense of imminent disaster than any positive diplomatic advantage. Bishops could also be warriors in those very different times, though their duties were more often to organise local defence in areas where they held lands than operating in an offensive capacity.

With Emma, Edward and Alfred gone, it left just Æthelred for Sweyn to worry about. But not for him a glorious martyrdom such as that which had befallen the late Archbishop of Canterbury or St Edmund, King of East Anglia, slaughtered by the Danes one and a half centuries ago. Neither would there be any attempt at a fightback, no 'Athelney moment' when he led his people back from the brink of destruction and on to unbelievable victory.

Instead it was flight, first to the Isle of Wight (showing that it was not yet permanently under Viking control despite its frequent use as a base from which raiders had attacked mainland England) where he spent Christmas and then on to the court of his brother-in-law in Normandy. Thorkell the Tall it seems remained at his side, possibly having burned too many bridges with Sweyn Forkbeard by now.

The king had given up, a suitable end to his calamitous reign – or so at the time it seemed.

No one could doubt the immensity of the challenges that Æthelred had to face but he had failed to face many of them successfully at all. Judged by the benchmark of the horrors that overtook his kingdom during his rule, it is hard to conclude anything other than that he was indeed deserving of much of the disdain that came his way. Measured against the admittedly impossible standards of the reign of Alfred a century before, let alone that of the more recent memories of that of Edgar, his period as king could not be regarded as anything but an abject disaster. Whatever modern historians may say about the over-exaggeration of his faults, a king in these times was judged first and foremost by results.

For Sweyn the opposite held true. He had become, in fact if not yet in name, the first Dane to be King of England. His armies had swatted aside any resistance, piece by piece, year by year, returning time after time, always increasing the pressure and seeking for more until one by one all the great men of England had submitted as if they were nothing but a line of flimsy dominoes forced over by the hurricane winds blown in from Denmark. England was finally swallowed up, one morsel at a time.

What is striking about the events of 1013 is that there was not much in the way of a fight to repel the Danes other than the defence of London. The leading men of Northumbria, eastern Mercia and East Anglia had submitted virtually without a murmur at Gainsborough. The lack of resistance may be put down to two things. Firstly, England was just tired and had no confidence that a fight was to any purpose. Secondly, by his own mismanagement of the internal politics of England, the king had disenfranchised too many powerful men and their supporters.

Sweyn took measures to secure the succession through the time-honoured tradition of an important marriage for Cnut, who was married to the lady Ælfgifu of Northampton. She came from an important noble Mercian family and was the daughter of Ælfhelm, the ealdorman murdered by Eadric Streona back in 1006. A son soon followed, named Sweyn – he would later become the King of Norway. It was a marriage that helped bring the royal family of Denmark and the English nobility closer together, and more pertinently it benefitted the east Mercians particularly against the depredations of Eadric Streona and his supporters. The noose around England's neck was tightened still further.

That was that. All that remained was for Sweyn Forkbeard to be formally accepted as king. Then, based on what happened so far, he would milk England for all it was worth, taxing her people to the hilt no doubt. He would, it seemed, be the stereotypical 'Dark Age' king, a warrior lord who lived for fighting and for personal glory and saw his kingdom only as a source of endless bounty to be bled dry. It was said that he even exacted a huge tribute from Bury St Edmunds, where the English king martyred by an earlier group of Danes had been interred. It had become a sacred place due to its associations and as a result had been exempted from all taxes for some time. Now it was claimed that Sweyn threatened to burn the church down if all the money he demanded from it was not duly paid over.[46]

Sweyn's triumph was total. In contrast, the line of Anglo-Saxon monarchs that stretched back over 500 years had been ejected from the country. The line of Cerdic had at last come to an end. A proud and resilient history was concluded, the ruling English dynasty had breathed its last and a new regime had been born in its place. There was no way back, nothing now for Æthelred to do but live out the rest of his unsuccessful life in lonely isolation in Normandy. England had fallen and the Viking conquest was complete. Or so it seemed.

3

Cnut of Denmark: The Prince without a Land (1014–1015)

The Greeks have a word for it: hubris. We might now say more colloquially that pride comes before a fall. With his triumph complete, Sweyn began to consider how best to make full use of his newly won realm. It was of course possible that in the long term he would become a wise king, respected if not loved by his subjects, though based on what we have seen so far such an outcome seems unlikely. After all, time and again his men had plundered without hesitation across the length and breadth of the land. Truces had been broken, settlements burned, men and women enslaved or killed, archbishops slaughtered. England was first and foremost seen as a source of tribute, now without the need to fight for it.

Of course much of the evidence for Sweyn's actions comes from the scribes who wrote up the *Anglo-Saxon Chronicles*. They were not natural friends of the Danes and therefore any positive features that could be ascribed to Sweyn Forkbeard were unlikely to figure prominently in their words. The *Anglo-Saxon Chronicles* are also incomplete; in their current form they are not original material but later copies and the writers focused more on events in Wessex and Mercia than further north in England, so we only get half a picture. In other words, they should be treated with due caution. But until historians can prove definitively that none of the shocking violence ascribed to the Vikings during the preceding years actually took place – which seems distinctly improbable – then much of England, certainly in the south and east, had been through something close to a hell on earth during the years that led up to Sweyn's triumph.

A great deal more pain still loomed and more years of high taxation and exploitation seemed to lay ahead for the conquered English. After all, in an age of warriors this was what conquest was for, as William, Duke of Normandy, would perfectly illustrate half a century later. There was no pretence that conquest was somehow all in the name of Civilisation or Christianisation (or often a combination of the two) as some more recent colonisers around the world have claimed. Conquest then was not dressed up in hypocritical justifications, explained away by flowery, mealy-mouthed words with little real basis in reality. Conquest was all about helping yourself to what belonged to somebody else.

And what of the conquered? For some perhaps there was a sense of shame that the Anglo-Saxon dynasty had been replaced by one from Denmark. Yet that was probably a minority view. Amongst many of the people there was more likely a fear; not a fear of the unknown, more a fear of what had become known only too well. There was probably therefore also desperation – a hopelessness born of an impotence to do anything to change the awful harshness of their lot.

But just now, when Sweyn's conquest seemed complete, total, unanswerable, there was a miracle. From out of nowhere a lightning bolt struck the earth, as if flung down from the skies by Thor himself, the great Norse deity seemingly determined to not yet be completely replaced by the Christian God. On 2 February, Candlemas 1014, without warning Sweyn Forkbeard died. He probably expired at Gainsborough and some say he was later buried at York, though after this his remains would be returned to Denmark. He may on his death-bed have hoped to be heading for Heaven rather than Valhalla, but he was in many ways a man every bit in the tradition of the great Viking leaders.

Some men who had no time for Sweyn and saw him as nothing but a savage brute claimed that divine intervention was behind his death. It was said that he had often disparaged the merits of the Anglo-Saxon martyr-king Edmund and that whilst holding court at Gainsborough he continued to denigrate him. One night Sweyn was feasting with his men. Suddenly his mood changed from one of cocksure bravado to one of terror. Although he was surrounded by a crowd, he alone saw a terrible figure striding towards him, an angel of death in the form of no less a person than the much-maligned St Edmund himself.

In this version of his end, Sweyn cried out in horror, asking his comrades to save him from the man he had been so quick to criticise, who even now was coming at him with a spear. They looked at him in amazement as they saw nothing. Sweyn's pleas for help or mercy did no good. The invisible saint ran him through with his weapon and Sweyn slumped to the ground from the warhorse on which he was mounted. He suffered terrible torments for the rest of that day, eventually dying in agony.[1]

This is a good story, though we would now consider it unlikely to be true. Whatever the cause of Sweyn's demise, it seems that the reaction of the Danes in England to these developments was prompt and unequivocal and their collective intention was that Cnut should take over from his father. However, this did not apply in Denmark, where Cnut's elder brother succeeded, helped no end by the fact that he was already present on the ground in the country. It is interesting to speculate what might have happened if the roles had been reversed and Harald had been in England and Cnut in Denmark.

Sweyn may in actuality have known that he was dying and before he did so he may have designated Cnut as his heir in England. Sweyn had left orders that his body should be taken back to Denmark after his death; he was under no illusions as to what the English thought of him and deemed it prudent to remove his mortal remains as far away from them as it was possible to do.

But there was a problem in terms of the inheritance of the crown of England. Sweyn had not been crowned; he had quite probably not even been accepted as the legitimate king yet by the *witan* who were required to elect him.[2] This weakened the claims of his dynasty to rule the country. It has been said that there were four elements involved in a legal claim to kingship in the country at the time. These were that the claimant was eligible by birth, had been designated by the late king, elected or recognised by the secular authorities and consecrated by the Church.[3] Not one of these conditions had been met by Sweyn, whose only claim was based on conquest.

This sudden and unexpected turn of events was not the only miracle for the English people. Relieved of the fearsome Sweyn's attentions and perhaps thinking that Cnut was as yet inexperienced and untried and therefore beatable, a number of the leading Englishmen who had not fled the country determined to ask the exiled Æthelred to return. We must assume that the formidable Archbishop Wulfstan was prominent amongst them for he is known to have been nearby, consecrating Ælfwig as Bishop of London less than two weeks after Sweyn's death.

Wulfstan also wrote an extraordinary diatribe at around this time. It was known as *Sermo Lupi ad Anglos* or the *Sermon of the Wolf to the English* (the 'wolf' element of the title being a deliberate play on the first part of his name). In it Wulfstan had castigated the English for their lack of moral discipline, which he felt had led to their punishment in the form of the Danes. It was an extraordinary work, almost ferocious in its vocabulary and written, it would seem, with deliberate intent to shock the English nation out of its lethargy. It was apocalyptic in its tone, set by some of its opening words – 'this world is in haste and the end approaches'.

It was a lengthy haranguing of the English people, accusing them of a catalogue of sins. They (or too many of them) were allegedly murderers and priest-killers, perjurers, child-killers, adulterers, whores, robbers, witches and wizards. He bitterly lamented that English thegns had stood idly by whilst their wives were raped by up to a dozen Vikings. He cursed the English for their cowardice, which allowed large crowds to watch on whilst two or three Viking guards drove dozens of slaves aboard ship and into a life where in many cases their fate would be worse than death itself. He also castigated them for their abandonment of their king. Here was a man that one would not like to be on the wrong side of. But then yet one more miracle followed: Æthelred did something decisive and – most miraculous of all perhaps – ultimately successful.

Æthelred did not return first of all to England on the death of Sweyn but instead he sent his son Edward as his envoy in advance, perhaps to test the water, not entirely confident of what kind of a reception he might receive in person. This action in itself was not as decisive as it could have been, though undoubtedly prudent given the accusations and counter-accusations of treachery that had dogged the king's last years in England. Edward essentially set out his father's manifesto to the English people for him: he would strive to be a good lord and would try to 'improve each of the things that they all hated'.[4] He would forgive all past misdemeanours as long as any offenders truly repented and resolved to serve him faithfully from now on.

However, this was very much a process of negotiation. There were clearly many things that Æthelred's former subjects were unhappy about that had occurred during his previous reign. The Danish incursions, latterly invasions, were of course a major issue but that was not all. The English people were seemingly fed up with the injustices that had been meted out to them previously by men of their own blood as much as by foreign invaders.

Corruption is a constant theme amongst the criticisms dealt out by homilists of the time such as Archbishop Wulfstan of York and Ælfric of Cerne (and later Eynsham). Ecclesiastics of the period had a pessimistic view of the world, fostered perhaps by the closeness of the time to the millennium of Christ's birth and the supposed end of the world. And it certainly seemed that the English people had had plenty to be miserable about.

In recent times, historians have tended to turn somewhat sniffy about supposed perceptions that the world was due to end in 1000. They say that 'Millenarianism', an obsession about that particular year and the end of the world, is an invention of eighteenth-century romantic Enlightenment historians. But Wulfstan certainly believed that something strange was happening in these times. He wrote that 'a thousand years and more is now gone since Christ was among men in a human family, and Antichrist's time is now at hand'. He for one thought that something both sinister and supernatural was not far off.

The pendulum of historical opinion has tended to swing from one extreme to the other on this issue. The most realistic assessment is that at this stage of our understanding we do not know whether people believed that these were the end of times or not. And it is important to be clear what the 'end of the world' was. It was not necessarily the physical obliteration of the world; rather it was the conquest of evil on earth by the forces of righteousness (or, in theological terms, the replacement of the rule of Satan by that of God). In this context people would rather have looked forward to the 'end of the world' in its existing form as opposed to being afraid of it.

Rather than seeing the year 1000 as a key millenarian moment – for few people would have paid too much attention to the passage of time in these terms, or even known about it – we should see this age as one of great social changes and a deepening sense of spirituality when people started to think more generally about the end of the physical world and a coming of the glorious age when Christ and his saints were triumphant. So when Æthelred (or rather the clerks who drafted it) referred in a grant to Sherborne Abbey of 998 to 'we ... upon whom the ends of worlds have come' we should be careful not to read into this that the year 1000 is the key reason for using such terminology.[5]

The discussions in England concerning the king's possible return were not without challenges. This was no open-ended agreement with Æthelred, who would be expected to mend his ways if he was allowed back. Once the negotiations were satisfactorily completed his former subjects welcomed his return. They swore allegiance and resolved that never again would there be a Danish King of England. Seemingly confident of their support now, Æthelred came home in the spring and all, it seems, was turned on its head. It was as close to an 'Athelney moment' as Æthelred would ever get.

The return of the king came at a price though. The implication of this negotiation process was that a ruler could forfeit his right to govern by acting unjustly. The divine covenant with God that the crowning of a medieval king symbolised could be broken if the king did not keep his side of the bargain. It was in the context of the times a remarkable and revolutionary concept and an important part of the constitutional development of the monarchy. In its own way it heralded further tensions in the far distant future when monarchs as varied as King John and Charles I would struggle so desperately to retain their rights against those of their subjects to be ruled fairly. But at the time Æthelred was not really in much of a position to argue. It was this negotiated return or nothing.

Of course the discussions that took place involving Æthelred were not with the people as a whole but rather with the nobility of the kingdom, or those of them who were in London. The city proved one of the more difficult places to access as there was still a large Danish force in the vicinity. They occupied the bridge between London and Southwark on the south bank of the Thames. It was a strong defensive position and it had to be bypassed.

But Æthelred's Norwegian ally, Olaf Haraldsson (also known as Olaf the Stout), who had recently converted to Christianity in Normandy, reputedly in Rouen under the sponsorship of Duke Richard II, had the answer. He got his men to approach the bridge by rowing up the river, lash cables around it and then pull for all they were worth. It was a spectacularly successful stratagem and the bridge duly collapsed, giving rise, some say, to the nursery rhyme 'London Bridge is falling down'.[6] This action emphasised again that the Vikings could be useful allies against their fellow Scandinavians.

London was in a strong defensive position. The original settlement on the site had been Roman but when the Saxons later came they built a new town outside it at Lundenwic. Its defences proved inadequate against the Viking raids of the ninth century and so Alfred had rebuilt it inside what remained of the Roman walls of Londinium and this was where the city was centred by Æthelred's time. The walls were a tough proposition for any invading force to break through. Yet this was a different city to modern London. The population was minuscule by current standards, probably less than 10,000, and there were large areas of open land still inside it.[7]

Æthelred duly re-entered London. For him the decision to marry Emma of Normandy had paid significant dividends. The marital alliance had brought with it practical help from Normandy, as the duchy had served as a place of inviolable refuge for him and his family during his recent troubles. Perhaps the Duke of Normandy even gave further assistance in the form of military support though this is not specifically mentioned in the *Anglo-Saxon Chronicles*.

If there was any military help from Normandy then this was quite a turnaround from just a decade or so before, when the Vikings had been the ones gaining protection from the safe shores of Normandy whilst they were resting up from their raids on England. But the new relationship was not without its complexities. Already the fate of England and Normandy was starting to become intertwined and over succeeding decades it would become ever more so until their affairs were completely enmeshed. The first steps towards a definitive conclusion of the Anglo-Norman situation had been taken; and what a conclusion it would be.

However, we should not be over-confident that Normandy was indeed such a strong, active supporter of Æthelred's return. The policies of Count Richard II were driven more by pragmatism than anything else. Even whilst Æthelred had been resident in Normandy, the count had also been giving sanctuary to two Viking raiders named Olaf and Lacman who had been pillaging Brittany and sacking lands owned by his own kinsman by marriage.[8] Normandy's policy towards England was already decidedly opportunistic, something that pre-empted events of half a century later perfectly. If the count did indeed send troops to help Æthelred, it would only have been to increase his own influence in the affairs of England as a result.

Æthelred's marriage to Emma was therefore not without its pitfalls, and it was not just politically that it created complications. It is noteworthy that it was Edward, born from Æthelred's second marriage to Emma, who the king used as his envoy and not the eldest surviving son from his first marriage, Edmund (the Ætheling Æthelstan had died shortly before, on 25 June 1014). What is also intriguing is that there is next to no mention of Edmund in the *Anglo-Saxon Chronicles* up until this point, as if he had been little involved in affairs of state so far. Alternatively, perhaps he was not considered completely legitimate by some of the scribes who penned them.

Edmund's early life is shrouded in mystery. Now he appears, largely as a bolt from the blue, as England's would-be saviour. He was described as being 'a young man in every respect of noble disposition; of great strength both of mind and person, and on this account by the English called "Ironside"'.[9] It was not all that surprising that not much was known about him beforehand; after all, he was not even the king's eldest son from his first marriage. But the recent death of his elder brother Æthelstan had left him the next in line after his father (certainly if his claims were allowed to take precedence over those of Emma's children). Now he was about to emerge from the shadows with significant impact.

We do, however, get the odd glimpse of Edmund in earlier life. At some time (the exact date is unclear but is probably between 1007 and 1011) he was involved in what was essentially the forced purchase of some land at Holcombe Regis in Devon, an act that it seems was not at all popular amongst the locals, as one might assume. This suggests a man who is ambitious and not too bothered who he upsets in fulfilling his desires. But such glimpses are few and far between.

Whatever the reasons for the anonymity of Edmund prior to this date as far as the *Anglo-Saxon Chronicles* are concerned, he was to prove his worth over the next year or so. But so too were the English more generally and even, to an extent, their much-maligned king. There was even a hint of reconciliation with some of those men whose recent support for the king had been so weak; both Uhtred of Northumbria and Æthelmaer from the south-west are found to be attesting charters shortly afterwards.

Cnut was with the Danish army at Gainsborough whilst these events were unfolding in the south of England. The answer to the question of what he did in response to these developments seems to be pretty much nothing. Perhaps he showed his inexperience and maybe hubris was weaving its mesmerising spell over him too; after all, Æthelred had proved a complete nonentity in battle in the past. Why should this time be any different?

Cnut's position as far as the men with him were concerned was clear; after the death of Sweyn '*se flota eall gecuron Cnut to cyninge*' as the *Anglo-Saxon Chronicles* put it – they elected Cnut to be king. Unfortunately for the young Cnut this did not mean much unless the rest of England concurred with the decision of the men who were at his side in his army. He seems to have been largely oblivious to what was happening elsewhere and unprepared for any kind of meaningful response from the Anglo-Saxon royal dynasty now that Sweyn had departed the scene. Perhaps after Æthelred's hurried exit from England shortly before, it appeared to Cnut that all the fight had gone out of him and his accession to the throne was a formality.

The reality was that Sweyn had been in the de facto role of King of England far too briefly for his son to merely take over from him across the country without a murmur. Yet Cnut was confident; he apparently had dies made to mint coins which proclaimed that he was king of both England and Denmark, which gives a strong indication as to his mindset.[10] But it did not match the reality. There is an English maxim that says that possession is nine-tenths of the law and although it is of doubtful legal validity it has the virtue of pragmatism about it. The people of England did not want a young, untried Dane as their ruler and he was not in a good position to enforce his claim. And back in Denmark there was an older brother, Harald, on the spot and ready to assume the kingship for himself after the death of Sweyn. Cnut might soon find himself a prince without a land, in the wrong place at the wrong time. Certainly England was far from being his at the moment.

Cnut did at least assemble a number of horses from the people of Lindsey, in whose territory he was staying, and from this we can presume that he meant to go on the offensive later in the spring; it was said that locals would even accompany him on a large raid, evidencing the divided loyalties now present in England, especially in the Danelaw.[11] But this was indeed a year of miracles, for the English army was this time one step ahead of him. Rather like King Harold II did with Harald Hardrada at Stamford Bridge fifty-one years later, the English fell on the Vikings at Gainsborough like a pack of hungry hounds on an unsuspecting prey and decimated them. It is noticeable that the English had never managed to catch the wily Sweyn off his guard but now his novice son was found completely off balance. It is also likely, though not certain, that amongst those falling on Cnut were the men of Thorkell the Tall.

The fight was quickly over and Cnut scarcely escaped an ignominious end to his career before it had even begun. A terrible retribution was exacted by the triumphant English, who had so often tasted the bitter cup of defeat. This time it was they who were burning and slaying and, savage though this no doubt was, it must also have been gratifying after so many years of hurt. All that Cnut could do was make his way to safety as well as he could. He got aboard a longship and so escaped the vengeful hands of the English. At least he survived to fight another day. Many of the people of Lindsey were not as lucky, as Æthelred's army ruthlessly punished them for their support of Cnut.

Cnut did not go unaccompanied. With him were some of the hostages that the Vikings had taken during their recent triumphs. They had failed in their purpose to keep the English in check and accepting of the new regime. So now instead they served another use. They were put ashore at Sandwich before Cnut made his way away from England. They were first mutilated by having their hands and noses cut off (or in some versions their nostrils split) as a clear and unambiguous signal of what would happen to anyone who was foolish enough to resist Danish rule, a long-term reminder of the costs of resistance much more salutary than just killing the hostages would be. He might be young and inexperienced, but Cnut was showing early signs of a ruthless and violent streak.

Cnut also had a wife, Ælfgifu, to worry about. She and her young son were left behind with her family in England. They, probably very wisely, feared for her safety at the hands of Æthelred, and she was sent to Denmark along with her child and the late Sweyn Forkbeard's body shortly afterwards. She arrived there safely and was not long after pregnant again, giving birth to another son who would be named Harold, 'Harefoot' as he was also known, a name which some say referred to his speed and skill as a huntsman. Others amongst Harold's later opponents, however – and we shall see why there were so many of them in later times – probably felt that it referred to his general slipperiness and cunning, and his ability to manoeuvre himself into a position of maximum personal advantage with great celerity.

This fairly rapid ejection of Cnut from England shows that Danish rule in the country was not yet firmly rooted. The *Anglo-Saxon Chronicles*, in describing the various successes of Sweyn in the previous year, refer regularly to the people in various parts of England 'bowing' to him in an act that is forced upon them rather than something done of their own volition. It has been said that 'in this way, the annalist implies that in yielding to the Danes, the Anglo-Saxons are conquered, as opposed to being integrated into a new kingdom or a new people'. And that is correct. The Anglo-Saxons had been effectively powerless to resist any longer, or at least their will to fight had been crushed out of them.[12] But submission only works for as long as the conqueror holds, or is believed to hold, crushing power in his hands.

The hostile Vikings had gone for now, but England's troubles were far from over. There was a great flood on 28 September 1014 which claimed a 'countless number of human beings' and wiped many settlements off the map. God was seemingly not prepared to leave England alone even if the Danes might be. This might not resonate much with a twenty-first-century audience but it would have counted for much with the monks who were writing up the chronicles.

No one knew whether or not Cnut would return to England. In contrast to the renowned tenacity of his father, Cnut was as yet an unknown quantity and the English triumph over him at Gainsborough gave some cause to hope that he was not of Sweyn's stamp at all. At any rate, it appeared that the English were fairly sure that Cnut would not be back as they soon after resorted to fighting amongst themselves again.

Why had the campaign gone so badly for Cnut? Friendly chroniclers suggested that it was because he was outnumbered.[13] This seems unlikely in the absence of evidence that many of Sweyn's men had left England after his successful campaigns there just a short time before. What seems much more probable is that the young and inexperienced Cnut had been caught off guard. It remained to be seen whether he would learn the lessons taught or not.

Cnut's subsequent arrival back in Denmark caught his brother Harald unawares. When he landed there it was not clear what was behind his return. It is quite likely that Harald sensed a challenge for the throne from Cnut who, after all, not long before had been thinking of minting coins claiming to be King of Denmark. Soldiers were sent to meet him, ostensibly to welcome him back but much more probably to keep an eye on him. But the two brothers embraced each other when they were soon after reunited and on the surface all appeared to be well between them.

Cnut suggested that the two brothers should divide Denmark between them, which could have been a difficult conversation. But there is some numismatic evidence that the two men did in fact enter into some kind of arrangement whereby they shared power in the country. This might seem unusual from a foreign perspective but there are other examples of this happening in Denmark during this period of history.[14] Certainly Harald helped Cnut to prepare a fleet and an army to make an attempt to recover England. Some writers, such as Thietmar of Merseburg, a contemporary of Cnut's, even suggest that Harald was later in England campaigning with him when he returned to the country.[15]

Denmark was geographically in a complicated position. In some ways it was opportunistically placed. From here it was possible to launch assaults on lands that the kings of Denmark coveted for themselves (Norway and parts of Sweden) after just a short sea crossing. Denmark also controlled the entrance and exit to and from the Baltic, an absolutely vital trade-route. This was all positive. But in other ways the country was under constant threat, for to the south the Holy Roman Empire, that great and acquisitive power, often looked with longing eyes at Denmark, at least those parts of it that were accessible on her frontiers. The relationship between the Empire and Denmark was often uneasy.

Denmark had only recently been Christianised, a move that was driven by the kings of what became known as the Jelling dynasty after a Danish settlement on Jutland where the founding father of the dynasty, Gorm the Old, was buried. During the ninth and early tenth centuries the Jutland peninsula became the focus of growth in Denmark, with Hedeby (close to modern Schleswig) in particular becoming more significant. Even by the beginning of the ninth century there were kings in Denmark, though how much of it they ruled is not clear. One such man was King Godfred, who became a strong opponent of Charlemagne and probably strengthened the great earthwork called the Danevirke that offered a form of protection against the Empire.

Gorm, though, breathed fresh life into Danish kingship, which had gone into decline at the beginning of the tenth century; Danish kings had actually been replaced by monarchs from Sweden for a while. He was described by the chronicler Adam of Bremen as 'a savage worm, I say, and not moderately hostile to the Christian people',[16] a description that speaks eloquently of Gorm's stubborn paganism but also of Adam's Christian bias against him. It was Gorm's son Harald Bluetooth who had played the key role in the adoption of Christianity in the country; though his son Sweyn Forkbeard had picked up the mantle of the supposedly Christian warrior too, there were some (including Adam) who suggested that he was insincere in his affiliations.

Neither could the country be yet considered as one secure, centralised entity. There was still a lot of regionalisation in evidence with many powerful local lords who were often difficult to control. It was also still only in the early stages of urbanisation. On the mainland of what is now modern Denmark there were only three sites that could be considered as towns: Århus, Hedeby and Ribe, though on Zealand Roskilde was also becoming significant. All of these were fortified, with their main function as centres of local trade.

So Denmark was a country in a state of metamorphosis whereas England, whilst also subject to an ongoing process of evolution, had long-established institutions in place. But with England only recently invaded it was still Denmark that marked the seat of

Danish power. It was therefore a prime prize for Cnut to covet. It was after all the ancestral homeland even if the idea of a Denmark as a polity ruled by one overall king was quite recent and only dated back to the days of Harald Bluetooth.

Not all the Danes went back to Denmark with Cnut. Thorkell stayed in England. It was said that he was fond of life in the country and was happy to stay behind and enjoy the opportunities offered, again suggesting an ongoing alliance with Æthelred. On the other hand, it was also suggested that he was secretly still inclined towards Cnut's cause and that his real reason for staying in England was to help him reclaim the crown in the near future.[17] And it was certainly true to say that Thorkell would prove himself to be a very untrustworthy ally for the English cause in the longer run. But perhaps the most likely reason for Thorkell to stay behind was that he saw in England a fantastic opportunity to get rich without too much effort.

Cnut had left England in a hurry and Sweyn's body did not arrive back in the country with him. Instead it was accompanied by 'a certain English matron'[18] (the writer of the *Encomium Emmae Reginae* could not bring himself to mention the name of Cnut's wife Ælfgifu, who this 'matron' probably was; she would become a great rival of Emma of Normandy for reasons that will soon become clear and as such the writer was not well-disposed towards her). Harald and Cnut were informed of the arrival of Sweyn's remains and together led a grieving procession to the Church of the Holy Trinity in Roskilde where the late king had previously arranged a tomb for himself.

Back in England, seemingly relieved of invading Danes, a great assembly was held at Oxford in early 1015 at which many of the most prominent Englishmen assembled. Amongst them were Eadric Streona plus Sigeferth and Morcar, two of the most important nobles from the Seven Boroughs (it is not clear where exactly these were, though it has been suggested that they consisted of the Five Boroughs mentioned earlier plus Torksey in Lincolnshire and York). Present also were relatives of the former ealdorman Ælfhelm of Northumbria, who had been murdered by Eadric Streona in 1006.[19] They had made their way to Oxford, freely as far as we can tell, and they were therefore covered by the king's pledge that he would forgive all past disloyalties provided that they stayed loyal in the future.

But this safe conduct counted for nothing. Eadric, who was a regional rival of Sigeferth and Morcar in Mercia, lured them into his chamber and then had them cold-bloodedly killed when they had obligingly drunk themselves to excess and made themselves insensible as a result. They had probably backed Sweyn in the previous year, which would not have endeared them to Æthelred and his supporters.[20] The slaughtered men's attendants attempted to fight back but were defeated. They took refuge in the tower of St Frideswide's Church, which was burned down with them inside it.[21] Given its terrible part in the St Brice's Day massacre a few years before, it must have seemed an accursed spot.

This was a reckless and foolish move, unless Sigeferth and Morcar were still in league with the Vikings – and there is no evidence that they were. It came not too long after the country had been split apart over the Viking invasions. What was needed now was reconciliation, as appears to have been the case with Uhtred, who had also been disloyal to the king; instead further division was now virtually inevitable. It is inconceivable that the king did not know what was about to happen and we should assume he ordered it.

Æthelred was quick to seize all the dead men's property, sensing profit in the murders and emphasising his culpability, and ordered Sigeferth's widow Ealdgyth to be locked safely in the monastery of Malmesbury. Except that safety here was more apparent than real, for the sanctuary of the abbey was violated by Æthelred's eldest surviving son Edmund. He broke into the abbey and made off with Sigeferth's widow, a significant prize indeed as she was both important and beautiful. He made her his wife, the key to the lock of a treasure store as he saw it. Later writers would extol Edmund's heroic virtues, but he too was an opportunist.

Edmund's true intentions became apparent soon afterwards when he rode north with his men and made his way to the lands of the late Morcar and Sigeferth and claimed them for himself. This was, it seems, with the cooperation of the local people, who were presumably angered by the murder of their former lords. The region was also one with which Edmund was often associated and was effectively his powerbase.

It was a grubby and inglorious state of affairs and it did no one involved in it much credit at all. Above all, it suggested that relations between Æthelred and Edmund were very strained, unsurprising if the king had been trying to promote Edward, his son from his marriage to Emma, as his principal heir instead of Edmund. Relieved of the Danish threat, England had resorted to internal squabbling once more.

Some historians have carefully sifted the evidence and in the process have developed theories that give other reasons for thinking that all was not well in England in 1015 as far as the monarchy was concerned. It has been pointed out, for example, that Edmund started issuing charters himself in this year, something dangerously close to the assumption of royal authority. And he also started to give himself presumptuous airs and graces, calling himself 'King Edmund Ætheling'.

These events were a distraction from even more serious matters. For one thing Æthelred was now lying seriously ill at Cosham on the edge of Portsmouth Harbour. The king's malady was clearly serious and perhaps all England prepared itself for another debilitating succession crisis. Such times had always been perilous in the Anglo-Saxon age and, for all Æthelred's inadequacies, the deterioration in the king's health could hardly have come at a worse time. For just at this precise moment, with the King of England dangerously ill and his eldest son and possible heir many miles to the north in a self-interested effort to improve his own position, stunning news came in: Cnut and his Vikings were back.

Cnut, it seems, had useful contacts back in England. Shortly before he sailed west to reclaim his lost heritage, nine ships were spotted off the coast of Denmark. They had been sent by Thorkell from England. In fact, he was with this small fleet. The ships had lain offshore awaiting permission to land, which was duly given. Thorkell made his way to Cnut and explained that his reasons for staying in England previously were to help Cnut when the time was right. The reconciliation was not an easy one, with Cnut understandably wary of Thorkell, but matters were eventually patched up. Thorkell stayed with Cnut for a month and explained to him that there were thirty ships with their crews left in England, just waiting the word to help in another invasion.[22] So the forty-odd ships left in England had in fact been a cuckoo in the nest.

Quite why Thorkell had swapped sides again is not clear. Perhaps with the large payments he had received he could see no further prospect of profit from staying on the side of Æthelred and the English; the opportunity to make money had run dry. He was certainly a man for whom the prospect of lucre appeared to be the main motivation. Now that he had got what he could from Æthelred, he would do the same with Cnut. Thorkell too was above all else an opportunist, in every fibre a man of his time. It is also quite probable that he considered that it would be difficult to restore his relationships with the tough old warrior Sweyn Forkbeard, but his young son might be far more amenable to his approaches, particularly as he appeared to be down on his luck.

But other possible reasons occasionally suggest themselves through the enveloping mists of time. There are some accounts that say that the English, when Cnut was ejected from their country, plotted against Thorkell and his Jomsvikings, presumably thinking that the battle was now won and there was no need for these troublesome warriors anymore. In what sounds like a repeat of the St Brice's Day Massacre of a decade or so before, many Danes were killed, including Thorkell's brother Hemingr, though the great warrior himself escaped.[23]

It would certainly give Thorkell ample reason to change sides once more, and as a similar massacre had taken place earlier on in Æthelred's reign there is no reason to doubt the plausibility of it happening again. If this story is true, then the English would later have cause to bitterly regret their violent actions. A familiar name is associated with these events: Ulfcetel of East Anglia, a determined opponent of the raiders as we have seen.

Whatever Cnut's real feelings, Thorkell was a mighty warlord and the would-be king needed his influence and his men. It possibly pushed Cnut to make an early strike to regain England. Soon after, Cnut bade farewell to his mother and probably his brother. He had with him a fleet of 200 ships. The anchors were pulled up and the hawsers untied and the armada once more made its way to the west. The wind was favourable and the crossing was seemingly made without incident. This was a relief for the journey itself could be risky. With the wind in the right direction (from the south-east) this was a three-day voyage. The North Sea was considered to be 'very large and exceedingly dangerous'.[24]

This was a large fleet by the standards of the time. Some of the vessels were 'dragon' (*drekker*) ships with up to 100 men – sixty to row, forty to deal with the cumbersome sail. The skill of the shipwrights who were responsible for building these craft was immense yet they have left no written records. There have been a number of modern attempts to reconstruct these vessels which have helped to confirm their manoeuvrability and durability.

They carried formidable warriors too. Many of them bore swords, some up to 3 feet long. The Vikings were skilled ironworkers though swords from elsewhere, especially of Frankish manufacture, were highly prized. The axe was another valued weapon. Some were throwing axes, others heavier weapons that required great strength to wield: the Vikings had done much to make the axe, which had at one stage virtually gone out of use, fashionable again. The mighty broad-axe (*breidox*) had a hardened, curved edge, crescentic in shape, sometimes measuring 18 inches along the cutting edge. Spears were also of great use. They could catch in an opponent's shield, making it unusable, as well as being capable of striking men down.

Vikings and their Anglo-Saxon foes also had access to body armour which was very useful defensively; battle plans often made use of the defensive tactics of the shield wall and then striking with a determined counter-attack when the enemy was tired and demoralised. The armour was called 'ring-shirt', linked small loops of iron similar to the 'chain' mail famous in the medieval period. It typically reached down to the thighs though there are cases where it went beyond this. This protected the torso and was worn over linen padding (which was often all that was available to less wealthy warriors). This was very necessary; mail might be good at stopping sword-thrusts but the concussive effects of hammering against mail on the wearer must have been substantial without some extra form of protection between armour and body.

Conical helmets were used by Vikings too, though some surviving examples of helmets of 'spectacle-type' nose-eye guard forms have been found (though not that many of them). Shields were available to many men as well. This was little different to the type of armour that their opponents were wearing in battle, certainly if they were Anglo-Saxon or Frankish. Although this armour was quite heavy to wear, the bearers were often fit men, used to working the land, hunting and sailing if Scandinavian. However, the armour was still tiring if worn for a long time and there is some evidence that the Viking warrior would wear it as sparingly as possible: the force that was slaughtered at Stamford Bridge in 1066 was caught without its armour on, having left it behind at their ships because of the heat of the season.

Once more Cnut made landfall at Sandwich, seemingly an Achilles heel in England's defences. From here, this time he made his way west into Wessex, the beating heart of the English kingdom. He sailed to 'the mouth of the Frome', a gently meandering river which spills out into the massive haven now known as Poole Harbour, the second-largest natural harbour in the world. It was familiar territory to the Danes, for they had also moored in the mouth of the river in 998 prior to ravaging the greater part of Dorset.[25] Here he probably fell on the town of Wareham, just a few miles upstream. Wareham had been turned into a strong burh in the time of Alfred the Great – the walls that wrap themselves around the town in a protective embrace, in fact earthen ramparts, still stand for most of their length today – but it was not prepared to stand up against the Danish host and was overrun.

When Alfred had ordered the defences to be built first of all, they were topped with a wooden palisade. During the reign of Æthelred these had been replaced by walls made of Purbeck stone, a hard, durable local rock. But the strong walls seemingly only covered the west, east and north of the town; the south was left comparatively undefended, covered only by the frontage along the River Frome. Given the Vikings' talents and the ability of their shallow-draught ships to penetrate far upriver, it was a remarkable oversight with fatal results. Again, flaws in the English strategy were very apparent.

It was not, though, that there was no strategy, rather that there was poor execution behind it. The refortification of Wareham was not unique. At around this time, there is archaeological evidence of the strengthening of town defences at Cricklade, Christchurch (Twynham) and Hereford too.[26] But the subsequent sacking of at least one of these places (Cricklade) suggests that the policy was far from completely effective.

Wareham was an important prize and opened up other crucial places in Wessex to Cnut. During Alfred's times one of the innovative defensive measures adopted was the creation of fortresses or burhs to be manned by local forces in times of a Viking raid, and to be maintained by local resources at other times. Wareham was one such burh. Nowadays a somewhat sleepy, if attractive, small country town, at the time it was much more important. The Burghal Hidage, a document of the early tenth century listing the taxes assigned for the defences of over thirty burhs across England, had Wareham at third in the list when measured by the acreage or 'hidage' covered; only Winchester and Southwark were larger.[27]

Wareham was symbolically important too. Within the town was the Priory of the Lady Mary, one of the largest churches in Anglo-Saxon England which had also been the last resting place of several rulers of Saxon Wessex. It had also briefly housed the body of the supposedly saintly King Edward before it was removed to Shaftesbury. Now the town was probably sacked, throwing a gauntlet down to the English and stating emphatically that Cnut was not going to go away quietly.

Wareham was also the location for a mint; in those days such institutions were spread around the country. One Ælgar was responsible for the striking of coins here.[28] It was a task with great responsibilities and serious punishment would follow if any malpractice was discovered, a crime for which the criminal could lose his life.[29] But Ælgar clearly was a survivor as he was working the mint both during the reign of Æthelred and through the subsequent rule of Cnut.

The presence of a mint in the town in any event spoke eloquently of its economic importance at the time, something that was hinted at during Æthelred's reign when several such were moved to more secure locations to protect them. This included the transfer of the mint at Wilton to Old Sarum (now just outside Salisbury) and of that in Ilchester to the re-fortified hillfort at South Cadbury.[30] Wareham's loss to Cnut was a major blow for the English cause in Wessex.

The problems posed by Cnut's unexpected attack on Wessex were compounded because the English army's most formidable warrior, Edmund, was far to the north whilst this was happening. He hurried south to join forces with Eadric Streona, an unlikely alliance. But the mistrust between the two men was too great to be overcome despite the scale of the danger. The two forces soon broke apart again and did nothing to stop Cnut's advance. Eadric in fact defected with forty ships and submitted himself and his men to Cnut. Treachery was once again the Danes' most potent weapon.

Cnut had been raiding widely in Dorset after Wareham fell, possibly sacking important churches in Wimborne and Sherborne as well as Cerne Abbey, which had only been founded in 987.[31] After Cnut became king, the Church of St Martin in Wareham, which was founded according to tradition by St Aldhelm in the seventh century and may have been destroyed in an attack on the town, was rebuilt, perhaps by a monarch anxious to right a few wrongs and build a few bridges with the people of the town.

Somerset and Wiltshire were also raided; Cnut was apparently incapable of being stopped. He based himself and his fleet for some time in the great harbour at Poole where he, according to some accounts, rested on Brownsea Island, a naturally safe anchorage in a good harbour but offshore and therefore safe from attack.[32] This makes sense: Vikings often rested up on islands, presumably because their naval superiority gave them security there. Other similar sites used over the centuries include Noirmoutier at the mouth of the Loire in France, Walcheren off the Scheldt and Thanet, Sheppey and the Isle of Wight in England.[33]

The men of Wessex, the traditional heartland of Saxon England, submitted to Cnut and handed over hostages as well as horses; and recent experience showed only too well what could be expected to happen to the former if the English did not do what was expected of them. Cnut set up his midwinter base in Wessex and equipped himself with as many horses as he could in anticipation of wide-ranging raids during the following year. It was a return to the terrifying pillaging of Sweyn Forkbeard. And, in keeping with those bitter times, the English seemed incapable of resisting the renewed Viking invasion.

So Cnut bided his time, staying provocatively in the heart of Wessex, that most powerful and symbolically important of Anglo-Saxon lands. It was as if he was daring Æthelred to come and fight him to the death in an all-or-nothing fight for the throne of England. Cnut was though about to get a harder fight than he possibly expected; but it was not to come from Æthelred at all.

4

Ironsides: Battle to the Death
(1015–1016)

Viking hordes of earlier times had probably numbered in the hundreds rather than the thousands.[1] Now, though, things were very different; it was said that Cnut sailed to England with a fleet of approximately 200 ships, which suggests a sizeable force maybe approaching 10,000 strong if these figures are accurate. With the quisling Eadric now at his side, Cnut moved north with a powerful mounted army and fell on Cricklade in Mercia. His army then made its way into Warwickshire, burning and killing as they went.

It was significant that Cnut's first targets in England were Wessex and then parts of Mercia. These were the most important parts of Anglo-Saxon England other than London. In so doing he was throwing down a gauntlet, threatening the ruling dynasty in its very heartlands. If he succeeded in conquering these areas, there would be few places for the Anglo-Saxon monarchy to run to other than back overseas. Eadric's presence with Cnut was significant as the areas pillaged in Mercia bordered on his own territory, the main base of his closest rivals. Personal advantages beckoned and they clearly took precedence over the national interest.

This time there was no King Æthelred on the scene to cobble together an army to fight against Cnut and instead it was left to his eldest surviving son Edmund to lead the defence. He lost little time in getting an army together in response. But the English would do nothing without the king and they also insisted on the help of the garrison in London.[2] Again the English defensive effort came to nothing and the army that had gathered to face up to the Viking threat stood idle, leaving the invaders to their own devices. Once again, internal divisions threatened to completely emasculate the defence of England.

The situation could not go on like this. Even the English now began to realise that some kind of unified response was vital. Edmund managed to add more men to his army and sent urgent messages to his father in London to come to his assistance with all haste. Soon after, the king gave orders that the army was to reassemble after Epiphany, 6 January. Æthelred made his way from London to join the force but in the end it was all the same as before; this force achieved nothing. Once more treachery in the ranks of the army was suspected. Again Æthelred was betrayed and he returned ignominiously to London which, through many disasters, seems on the whole to have stayed loyal to the ruling Anglo-Saxon dynasty in England.

It was a feeble effort and Edmund took himself off to the north where he joined forces with Earl Uhtred of Northumbria whilst Æthelred stood down his own men. Edmund could clearly not place any reliance on assistance from his father, who was by now probably both ground down by the exertions of a long and troubled life and reign and also physically very ill. There was strong evidence too that relations between father and son were not close either and that neither man trusted each other.

The expectation now was that the forces Edmund and Uhtred would assemble in the north would form a united front against Cnut and his Viking army but instead they made a less direct attack by raiding into Staffordshire, Shrewsbury and Chester as well as Leicestershire as the men of those regions had refused to take up arms against the Danes. It was certainly significant that some of these were lands closely associated with the despised Eadric Streona.

Divided loyalties were again tearing the defences of England apart. The uncertainty of the times was evidenced by Uhtred's changes of allegiance. He had been married into the English royal family and had then sided with Sweyn Forkbeard. But it is quite possible that some of those mutilated by Cnut when he fled England were kinsfolk of Uhtred as it is known that he was forced to hand over hostages at the time of his submission to the Danes. As a result, he was hardly likely to be a friend of Cnut now. Certainly he was attesting charters for Æthelred again in 1014 and 1015. It was hard to tell whose side he was truly on. But as a crucial warlord in the north of England, his support needed to be cultivated as he could still bring important resources to the fight.

Whilst these English attacks in Mercia do not make much sense if the efforts of Edmund and Uhtred are seen as part of a coordinated defence of England, they did not represent any such thing. Edmund and Eadric were bitter rivals, one with interests in the east of Mercia, the other in the west of it. It is striking that Edmund appears to have far stronger ties with the area of the eastern Danelaw, where after all his mother came from, than he did with either Wessex or Anglo-Saxon Mercia.[3] To Edmund the main enemy might well have appeared to be Eadric rather than Cnut; and after all the two were now fighting on the same side. Eadric was perhaps the main personal threat to be dealt with.

But why were there these tensions between the king and Edmund, father and son? To understand that better it is necessary to look further at the earlier lives of both men. Edmund had not been Æthelred's first-born. There had been an elder brother, Æthelstan, who had died shortly before, probably in June 1014. In his will he had left many of his prized possessions to Edmund, including a fabled weapon, the 'sword of King Offa', the famous eighth-century Mercian ruler.

This was a deeply symbolic move, which could easily be read as an injunction to his younger brother to lead the fight against the Viking raiders. The bequests made by Æthelstan evidence a man with strong support in the eastern part of Mercia, in East Anglia and in Sussex, some of them certainly areas that do not appear to have been terribly well-disposed towards King Æthelred. But, in the interests of balance, it must also be pointed out that he spoke fondly of his 'dear father' in his will. Perhaps he was one of those rare men who were able to separate a personal fondness for a close member of his family from his anguish at their inability to make effective decisions. On the other hand, his bequests suggest a man who was very much at odds with Eadric Streona for some of the recipients were strong opponents of the opinion-dividing nobleman.

What these provisions in Æthelstan's will may represent is an appeal to some of the leading men in England to protect the rights of Æthelred's sons from his first marriage against the claims of those who had been produced from his second. The eldest son from the marriage of Æthelred and Emma, Edward, in particular seemed to be benefitting from ever-increasing influence and profile at the expense of both Æthelstan and Edmund. There is indeed a claim in the near-contemporary *Vitae Edwardi Regis* (*Life of King Edward*), written in around 1066, that all the men of England swore to recognise the first-born male from this second marriage as the legitimate heir to the throne, though the author of this work had good reasons to be biased.[4]

It was not unique in English history from this period for a second spouse to take precedence over a first. In such cases offspring from the first relationship were subsequently disadvantaged and Edmund and his elder brother Æthelstan's positions may have been compromised because of this. Yet whilst all this internal squabbling was going on matters in England more generally merely became worse. The situation in England and the plight of the English people demanded concerted action against the external threat but they were certainly not getting it.

The English instead kept themselves occupied by fighting against each other in the West Midlands. Cnut in the meantime took himself away on a roundabout route through Buckinghamshire and Bedfordshire, up through Huntingdonshire and the Fens near Stamford and then across Lincolnshire. Then it was on towards Northumbria, neatly bypassing the main English army by his manoeuvring. Whilst Uhtred was away raiding, the Vikings planned to stab the Earl of Northumbria from behind in his own backyard.

It was enough to force Uhtred to leave off his raiding and hurry back north whilst Edmund made his way to Æthelred in London to see if some kind of peace could be patched up between the competing English factions. When Uhtred reached Northumbria he was faced with no option but to sue for peace with Cnut. The bargain was, as ever, sealed with a deal involving hostages.

But it did Uhtred no good, for he had proved a troublesome pest for Cnut and he was promptly killed, allegedly (according to some writers) on the advice of the treacherous Eadric Streona, who was presumably delighted to remove another potential rival from out of his way. However, more commonly the blame is awarded to a Northumbrian noble called Thurbrand the Hold, a man of possibly Danish descent (connected it has been suggested with the region of Holderness in East Yorkshire). Thurbrand and Uhtred seem to have been long-term rivals and enemies in Northumbria.

The late eleventh/early twelfth-century tract *De Obsessione Dunelmi* ('On the Siege of Durham') paints a vivid picture of the killing. In this account Uhtred travels to pay homage to Cnut. However, when he arrives at the great hall of his rival to do so, he is caught off-guard by Thurbrand who was hiding with his men behind a curtain. Uhtred and his men are quickly overwhelmed and by the end of a brief struggle he and forty of his men lay dead. This is a situation no doubt helped by the fact that in the Anglo-Saxon world a guest to a nobleman's hall was expected to disarm before entering it.[5] This is a single-source account not corroborated by other chroniclers but if it is true it is inconceivable that these events took place without Cnut's explicit sanction and he might well have even been in the room at the time. It was another sign of ruthlessness to add to the mutilation of the hostages when he had fled England after being defeated at Gainsborough.

In any event, the killing of Uhtred started a blood-feud that ran on into Cnut's later reign and indeed far beyond it. There is some contention amongst historians about whether or not this was merely a personal affair or something more political. Some have suggested that these violent events were inspired by ongoing tensions between 'northern Northumbria', Bernicia, which was considered to be pro-Wessex, and 'southern Northumbria', Deira, which was more pro-Scandinavian. But this division should not be thought of as a black-and-white dividing line. Research has shown that in Domesday Book, prepared towards the end of the eleventh century, 40 per cent of the place names in the East Riding of Yorkshire were of Scandinavian origin and 38 per cent in the North Riding; but only between 13 per cent and 19 per cent of those in the West Riding.[6]

Again there is a reminder that England was still a very fragmented polity and this must be considered to be one of the main reasons for the success of the Danish invasions as they were able to exploit this fragmentation rather well. This sense of division and the 'otherness' of Northumbria would only have been reinforced by the fact that there were very few lands attached to the Crown in the region when compared to the heartlands of Wessex and Mercia. In fact, in the long reign of the late King Æthelred he is only known to have visited the north twice: Cumbria in 1000 and York in 1014 and then both for largely military reasons.[7]

But the ongoing blood-feud between Uhtred and Thurbrand's descendants, whatever the reasons for it, was remarkably intense even for those violent times. Uhtred's son, Ealdred, later avenged his father by killing Thurbrand, probably sometime in the mid-1020s. Then in 1038 Ealdred was killed by Thurbrand's son Carl, allegedly when the pair were on pilgrimage to Rome together. Another son of Uhtred's, Eadulf, was killed by the then King Harthacnut in 1041. The final act in this amazing sequence of events did not come until the 1070s when Waltheof, Ealdred's grandson, had most of Carl's surviving sons and grandsons killed. It was a long-lived inter-family vendetta that spoke eloquently of the uncertainties of these troubled times.

It is easy to overlook the fact that not just Uhtred had been removed by these actions in 1016 but also forty of his prominent supporters, leaving Cnut with a much freer hand in Northumbria. In the place of the now dead Uhtred, Cnut established Erik of Lade, son of Hákon, the Earl of Hlathir from the north of Norway, as the next Earl of Northumbria; relatively easy to do as the region appeared to be firmly under his control. Then he headed south again and made his way back to his armada and prepared for his next move. Edmund in the meantime headed for London where he joined forces with his father, matters having been patched up in the interests of national unity, and waited for what was presumably going to be a decisive confrontation. Sure enough, Cnut and his host also made their way towards the city.

But then the rules of the game changed decisively. King Æthelred had clearly been seriously ill some time before and it was therefore no surprise when he died. The date of his death had something of an irony about it: St George's Day, the festival of the man who would later be the patron saint of England.[8] The *Anglo-Saxon Chronicles* told with much understatement how the king finally passed on 'after great toils and difficulties in his life'.[9] His body was interred in what we now call 'old St Pauls' with all due honour and ceremony, a somewhat inappropriate end to one of the most troubled reigns of any English king. It was perhaps fitting that even there his troubles were not over as his tomb was destroyed in the Great Fire of 1666.

Those 'great toils and difficulties' did not just affect him but also the people he claimed to rule. Whether or not the chroniclers exaggerate his failings and make him into some kind of a pantomime villain is a matter that may be debated. What is much harder to argue against is the decline of his nation when comparing the situation at the end of his reign to that at the beginning and by this measurement his rule can only be described as an abject failure.

Whatever one may think of the accuracy of William of Malmesbury as a chronicler, he was certainly capable of turning a biting phrase when the occasion called for it. He said of Æthelred that having first obtained the throne of England he 'occupied it rather than governed for thirty-seven years' and that 'the career of his life is said to have been cruel in the beginning, wretched in the middle and disgraceful in the end'.[10] It was an acidic summary of the king's long reign.

One would not have liked to have got on to the wrong side of the scribe of Malmesbury Abbey. But his objectivity must be in some ways doubted; he castigated Æthelred for his participation in the murder of his step-brother but as he was ten years old at the time, this seems a little harsh to say the least.[11] But we may be confident that William went out of his way to exaggerate all of Æthelred's faults, as did others such as the scribes who produced the *Anglo-Saxon Chronicles*.

William was clearly no friend of the late king. It is revealing to note that the same chronicler, despite writing a fairly long chapter on Æthelred's life, did not write up a blow-by-blow or campaign-by-campaign account of the sufferings of England at the hands of the Danes during his life. Instead he relied mainly on a summary of these actions in the following form, using words that again managed to heap scorn on Æthelred:

Who can tell how often he collected his army? How often he ordered ships to be built? How frequently he called out commanders from all quarters? And yet nothing was ever effected. For the army, destitute of a leader and ignorant of military discipline, either retreated before it came into action, or else was easily overcome. The presence of the leader is of much avail in battle; courage manifested by him avails also; experience, and more especially discipline, avail much; and as I have said the want of these in an army must be an irreparable injury to its countrymen as well as a pitiable object of contempt to an enemy.[12]

Certainly Æthelred did not have far to search for critics from many directions. Adam of Bremen summed up his view of the reign by saying that his death was 'a just judgement of God; for he had befouled the sceptre with blood for thirty-eight years after his brother died a martyr'.[13]

Æthelred has been castigated as one of the worst kings in English history but he had an incredibly difficult set of circumstances to deal with. Accounts of his ineptitude appear to have been exaggerated according to some recent analysts. Modern historians, prominent amongst them Professor Simon Keynes of Trinity College, Cambridge, have critically analysed the *Anglo-Saxon Chronicles* and strongly suggest that they have misrepresented Æthelred and vastly overstated his 'awfulness'.

But there is a danger that historical revisionism had tried to swing the pendulum too far the other way. It is inappropriate to judge Æthelred by modern mores. The writers of the time looked for three traits in particular from their rulers if we are to follow the later words of Snorri Sturluson.[14] These were lineage, wisdom and insight, and boldness and success in battle. The late king definitely had the first quality but the second was far more debatable and it is very difficult indeed to argue for the last, certainly at the end of his career, the ejection of Cnut from England excepted.

Perhaps Æthelred should not be seen in isolation from other English kings of the period. Even strong kings of the time sometimes struggled to keep troublesome subjects under control. But there is something revealing in the tale of a troublesome subject called Wulfbald. Several times during the late king's reign he had been cited for criminality but never successfully brought to book. His lands were declared forfeit but were not in practice surrendered. Even after Wulfbald's death his widow killed the king's thegn and fifteen of his companions who came to take the lands. This does not suggest strong kingship or subjects who were very concerned about the long arm of the law and monarchical power.[15]

There is a risk of course that Æthelred is made something of a scapegoat by chroniclers such as William of Malmesbury and others. This perception is reinforced by William's suggestion that the late king was also tormented by his brother's ghost: the chronicler was clearly a lover of supernatural explanations. But if anything he aims even harsher words at Eadric Streona and blames him in particular for the trials and tribulations that had beset England in his reign, speaking of him in the following terms:

> This fellow was the refuse of mankind, the reproach of the English: an abandoned glutton, a cunning miscreant; who had become opulent, not by nobility, but by specious language and impudence. This artful dissembler, capable of feigning anything, was accustomed, by pretended fidelity, to scent out the king's designs that he might treacherously divulge them. Often, when despatched to the enemy as the mediator of peace, he inflamed them to battle.

William ended ominously by saying that 'his perfidy was sufficiently conspicuous in this king's reign, but much more so in the next'.[16] If he and the other chroniclers of the time are to be believed, he was certainly right.

There was not unanimity in England on what to do regarding a replacement for the now-departed Æthelred. Certain accounts say that some men came to Cnut at Southampton and, wishing to bring an end to the years of fighting, repudiated Æthelred and his successors and offered the Dane the crown of England. But the citizens of London and the nobles who were there instead offered it to Edmund.[17] These accounts of divisions in England cannot be dismissed out of hand; evidence would soon emerge that not everyone in Wessex was behind Edmund.

The various versions of the *Anglo-Saxon Chronicles* make no direct reference to such divisions amongst the English. The

Worcester version skates over them, merely saying that 'all the councillors who were in London, and the garrison chose Edmund for king, and he resolutely defended his kingdom for as long as his time was'. The Canterbury versions are less ambiguous: 'all the councillors of the English race chose Edmund for king' – quite a different insinuation altogether.[18] This is one of those occasions where we may suspect the chronicle skirts around an inconvenient truth and chooses to ignore the fact that its 'hero' Edmund was not the unanimous selection of his people as king. But he was in London when his father died and therefore able to influence the late ruler's council on the spot with positive results for himself.

The reference to 'choosing' a king marks the process of succession out as being crucially different to what is the case in modern Britain. In Anglo-Saxon times, a successor was expected to be an 'Ætheling' or a prince of the royal bloodline but he was not necessarily the eldest son. There were several notable occasions when, on the death of one king, the elder son was passed over, for example when Alfred the Great became ruler of Wessex in 871 and his nephew, who was the eldest son of the late king, was ignored. In times of war in particular, experience and standing counted for much more than where a prince was placed in the royal bloodline.

Though there was an element of choice in the identity of the new king, once it had been made the decision was considered irrevocable. The homilist Ælfric wrote that 'no man can make himself king, but the people has the choice to choose as king who they please; but after he is consecrated as king, he then had dominion over the people, and they cannot shake his yoke from their necks'.[19] Once consecrated, a sacred act, a Rubicon had been crossed and there was no going back without offending God Himself as the king was then His anointed.

The process of election could take some time and this may have been the reason why there was a year's delay before the recently expired Æthelred was made King of England after the assassination of his brother Edward over three decades before. Indeed, that earlier election may have led to some quite radical thinking. The circumstances of Edward's death were responsible for a great deal of debate and according to some historians may even have led to some ground-breaking measures in the form of an attempt to persuade the latter's sister, Edith, then a nun at Wilton, to take his place, a revolutionary concept for the time.[20]

Elections could expose serious divisions amongst the English people. The upshot of this only partially hereditary process of succession was that it was often the man who held the greatest power, or who was in the right place at the right time, who was elected to the throne, a kind of Anglo-Saxon monarchical Darwinism.

The body responsible for the election has traditionally been known as the Witan (or more precisely the Witanagemot). In modern times the word has been slightly sneered at on occasion as an anachronism that was not frequently used and the phrase 'assembly' may be more appropriate. Whatever we call it, it was composed of the leading men of the realm. They had an ongoing role in government, for example to act as witnesses to charters and other important documents. But they became particularly crucial when it was time to elect a king, as he would essentially be their choice. Of course, this could – and did – make for all sorts of political games and it also meant that if the country was divided, then so might the assembly be with disunity the end result: disastrous at a time of national danger.

As remarked, it is not at all clear that Edmund was the unanimous choice of the English as king at first. Presumably those living in the Danelaw would have been happier with the choice of Cnut given their recent support for Sweyn and they were natural potential supporters of his, as the harsh punishment handed out to them at Gainsborough not too long before would suggest. There may have been others in the south too who preferred that one of the late king's sons from Emma of Normandy assume the throne. In any event, it would seem that the selection of Edmund was far from universally popular.

But in many ways the timing of the death of Æthelred was fortuitous. There were a limited number of candidates to take over and it gave the English a chance to unite behind a stronger leader. For despite these difficulties and the danger of believing too much of the hyperbole in the *Anglo-Saxon Chronicles*, Edmund had started to prove that he had greater martial possibilities than his late father and he was chosen in the end by enough of the English at least as his successor as King of England.

With the Danes moving on London, it might have seemed unclear how long he would retain that illustrious title but the news of Edmund's election must nevertheless have disappointed not just Cnut but probably also Æthelred's widow Emma, for it meant that any plans she might have had that one of her natural sons should become king were put on hold – for now at least. There are even some Scandinavian sources that suggest that she directed that her son Edward should join Cnut in the fight against Edmund.[21] Certainly there would have been little stomach in England for making another adolescent king after the troubles of the reigns of Edward the Martyr and Æthelred.

London now became the focus of Cnut's attentions. In early May[22] the attack on it began. The Danish ships arrived at Greenwich and then moved on the city itself. The defences were strong and Viking tactics were not well-adjusted to the requirements of siege warfare but Cnut and his men merely bypassed the walls. The relatively slight longships gave them something of an advantage not possible if their ships were heavier for it meant that they could be flexible given strong land defences and merely skirt around the walls. On occasion the Vikings were even able to drag their ships across country for several miles, 'portage' as it was known.

Now they dug a ditch to the south of the city walls and along this they dragged their ships to the west side of London Bridge so that they could control the Thames, something that would have been difficult if the bridge had not been avoided as it was strongly defended. They then dug ditches and ramparts around the city (much smaller then of course than it is now) to stop the defenders getting out. London was therefore blockaded. But as often as the Danes attacked the walls, they could not breach them. Nevertheless, it was a long and hard-fought siege and one collection of Old Norse poetry included a verse that said that 'every morning the lady on the Thames bank sees the sword dyed in blood'.[23]

The blockade must have been a source of major concern even if the city did not fall. Although there was ample room inside the large acreage enclosed by the walls for market gardens, London was still dependent on the outside world for grain. So, although there were also adequate water supplies to cope, the Londoners started to go hungry as the siege started to bite. With the Danes unable to break into London, a stalemate ensued. It became for a time a battle of attrition.

The siege and the general outlook combined started to take their toll on the English. There is a tantalising hint in the *Encomium Emmae Reginae* that the citizens of London were losing hope by this stage and made overtures to Cnut to surrender to him.[24] However, some of the more prominent men in the city did not agree with this strategy, and instead took themselves off with Edmund who seemingly had no intention of being trapped inside London and got well away. Cnut, it was said, actually entered London at one stage but when he did so he sensed strongly that the war was far from over and he might even find himself in a trap. Instead he took himself and his men off to the Isle of Sheppey, where he planned to spend the winter.

Edmund however was an astute strategist and he realised that the heartland of Anglo-Saxon England was not London, important though it was, but Wessex. He needed to keep the momentum in the war and he could not do so by staying walled up in London. He had therefore ensured that he was not trapped in the city but took himself and his men west before the siege was tightly laid. This meant that he would be able to organise resistance against the Danes. At the very least it would force Cnut to divide his forces and this is indeed exactly what happened. The Danes lifted the siege for a time, giving London a breathing space.

Although seriously harassed, Edmund had then done all that he could to raise the men of Wessex against the Viking threat and in part he succeeded. That he managed to do so after so many years of useless resistance and losses in Æthelred's time says much for his personal qualities as a leader. He managed to get together a decent-sized army and waited for Cnut's men to attack. The first confrontation in this latest bout of activity took place at Penselwood near Gillingham in Dorset.[25]

There may have been particular reasons for the West Saxons to choose this spot, for in the year 658 they had won a great and decisive victory here against the King of Gwynedd (a kingdom in Wales) at the Battle of Peonnum which opened up Somerset to Saxon conquest.[26] It was a fine portent which gave hope that another great Saxon victory might now follow, though in the eyes of some historians this particular fight was probably little more than a skirmish.[27]

Penselwood certainly made a fine spot for a defensive action, a position where perhaps the English could take advantage of the great strength of their shield-walls much as they would try and do at Hastings in 1066. There was the great forest of Selwood nearby and also an Iron Age hillfort, called later Kenwalch's Castle, the type of position that Saxon armies had chosen as a point of assembly and defence in the past.[28] In any event, the *Anglo-Saxon Chronicles* do not tell us of the result of the battle fought there but the slightly later account of 'Florence' of Worcester tells us that the outcome was an English victory with the Danes being put to flight.

Kenwalch's Castle nowadays looks an unlikely spot for such a confrontation. It is a long way from anywhere and a modern minor road bisects it neatly in two, probably along the line of where the original entrances to the ancient fortification were. The interior of the hillfort is overgrown and difficult to get through but the earthen ramparts are steep enough to give an impression of how formidable they would have been 1,000 years ago. It stands atop a steep hill and is now quite thickly wooded. It has a slightly other-worldly aura about it, especially on a misty morning, as if the spirits of a world now long gone are not too far away.

Although we cannot be sure that the battle was fought in or around Kenwalch's 'Castle', it is a likely enough place for the local fyrds of Dorset, Somerset and Wiltshire to meet as it is right on the border of all three shires. Such convenient assembly points were often used as a place for defensive forces to meet up. Just over a mile from here in 879 Alfred the Great had called his men together to lead his magnificent fightback against the Danes, a spot now marked by the Victorian 'Alfred's Tower' which celebrates the achievement. It is strange how this quiet corner of rural England has played such a great part in the country's ancient history.

Assembling the fyrd for battle cannot have been an instant process. Summoning them would take time; it perhaps involved written orders calling them out but more likely beacons were used; certainly an *Anglo-Saxon Chronicles* entry for 1006 says that the Viking raiders used them and there are also references in some

Anglo-Saxon charters to the provision of them.[29] There is indeed strong evidence that Anglo-Saxon England had a sophisticated system of inter-sighted beacons that predated the much more famous network linked to the Spanish Armada by at least 700 years. It was the responsibility of the thegns to oversee the coastal watch network though, at a practical level, peasant freemen (cottars) seem to have been tasked with the donkeywork of operating it. The idea was that they could raise the alarm and the population could make their way to the nearest burh in time. It worked less well, however, if the raiding army was large or the burhs had been poorly maintained.[30]

Once called up, each man would be responsible for making his way to the assembly point, usually fixed from time immemorial, though it is highly likely that men from the same local area would have taken the pragmatic step of travelling together. Frequent mentions of battles at known assembly points suggest that the raiders tried to break up the fyrd before it was fully coordinated. Local settlements would be responsible for providing provisions for the men in the fyrd, who may either have stayed in nearby villages or else in tents, which are frequently mentioned in contemporary sources. As well as conventional road networks, there are strong suggestions of a series of *herepaths* being provided for the movements of the fyrd.[31]

What part Edmund played in the battle at Penselwood we can only speculate for details are scarce. But it is not unlikely that he would have followed the actions of Byrhtnoth in the build-up to the fight as described in the poem of the Battle of Maldon. This has the East Anglian ealdorman arranging his troops in the most effective battle order and riding up and down their ranks and advising them. He gave them tips as to how they should fight and told them to look to their courage. This tactical advice does not mean they were untrained and inexperienced troops but that they were being reminded of the part that their leader expected them to play in fulfilling his battle-plan. This pre-battle exhortation over, 'he dismounted, among the people who loved him best, his own most dear and loyal hearth troop'.

Battles at this time were mostly a close-quarters slogging match. Although both Anglo-Saxons and Vikings were well acquainted with horses for getting to a battle, they did not apparently use them in the fight itself. The Anglo-Saxons liked strong defensive positions where their shield-walls could work effectively; hilltop locations such as Kenwalch's Castle or, more famously, Senlac Hill at Hastings in 1066 seem to have been a favourite.

There are few illustrations suggesting the use of archers in battle though bows were in common use for hunting and the Vikings certainly knew of them too as the shooting to death of King Edmund of East Anglia in the ninth century demonstrates. The bow should however not be overlooked. Whilst the axe, the spear and the sword provided the more glamorous weaponry of the soldiery of the time along with shields normally covered with cattle-hide, the bow was not unimportant. Numerous arrows from the period have been found in excavations in Scandinavia and Norwegian laws of the eleventh century even specify the large numbers of bows that should be carried on-board warships. And it is an interesting fact that the oldest known bow in the world has been dated to 8,000 BC and comes from Denmark.

There were two types of spear used by Anglo-Saxon forces: a lighter weapon, probably for throwing, not dissimilar to the Roman pilum and a broad-bladed form, of more use for thrusting at close quarters. Swords were in much shorter supply and were prized objects. The mythical hero Beowulf was given two of them at various stages of his adventures, one named *Hrunting* (possibly 'roarer') and the other *Naegling*, a name that suggests that it was hard enough to cut through nails. The awarding of names to such weapons shows how valuable they were, and they would only be available to the more senior men with the fyrd.

Both English and Vikings made much use of spears. Although there was some homogeneity in these, there could be wide variations in evidence on occasion. Some Anglo-Saxon spearheads were massive, sometimes 800 mm in length. Archaeological evidence suggests that the length of the shaft could vary from 6 to 11 feet. The difficulty of breaking through a shield-wall protected by a bristling hedge of spears by someone who was carrying a sword and that the attacker had to close with can easily be imagined.

Some spears were lighter and were presumably javelins for throwing rather than thrusting. The Bayeux Tapestry shows some Saxon warriors carrying three such javelins. However, according to various accounts the Vikings had an interesting way of dealing with these. Their more skilled warriors could, it was suggested, catch an enemy spear in flight and hurl it back towards the thrower.[32]

A shield wall was not invulnerable. A man in it had to look out for spear thrusts from his front, his left (shield-side) and his right. Modern re-enactors suggest that spearmen were particularly vulnerable to strikes from their right.[33] There is some fascinating if unlikely corroborating evidence for this. English Grenadiers using the bayonet were instructed to attack the Jacobite clansman to their right in the lines they were charging into at the Battle of Culloden in 1746 for the very reason that it would catch them off guard as they held their targe (shield) on their left side; not so very different in principle to the best way of attacking a shield wall. And once a shield wall was breached, it was vulnerable to quick disintegration soon after as, once the united front was broken, many of the men in it were left unprotected as a result.

Whereas local defence in Anglo-Saxon England was the responsibility of the militias or fyrds, a king or an ealdorman would be accompanied by his 'hearth-troops', a personal bodyguard who had a particular role to protect him. For them, stereotypes of fighting to the death in protection of their lord may often have been true. Yet it would be misleading to see every warrior as being inclined to do the same. Accounts of the time are so full of suggestions of men running away to save themselves or, worse, actively betraying their particular party that there must be some truth in the accusations. Perhaps flight was understandable in the context of the times: there are few reports of many prisoners being taken after a battle.

Here we should distinguish between the 'hearth troops', the *hearthweru* as they were to the Anglo-Saxons, and the men who made up the fyrd. To those who were effectively the bodyguard of their lord or king, desertion in battle was a mark of the deepest dishonour. That is why we see Byrhtnoth's warriors of the *hearthweru* fighting to the death when their lord fell. The men of the fyrd were different. There was no such close bond for them; they had not shared his feasts in his hall and sworn oaths of loyalty. There was little reason for them to hang around and share the fate of a lord who was comparatively distant from them.

It is not clear how the *hearthweru* were drawn up in battle, though most likely they were grouped around their lord as a form of personal protection for him. Striking evidence for this comes from the Bayeux Tapestry, made not long after the Battle of Hastings, a battle for which we have far more evidence than most others in the Anglo-Saxon era. Here we can see the *huscarles* of King Harold's brothers (the Scandinavian-named *huscarles* probably performed a similar function to the Anglo-Saxon *hearthweru*) laying down their lives around their lords. Although it is possible that from time to time some of the *hearthweru* were sprinkled around the ranks of the fyrd to bolster their fighting qualities, they often seemed to have fought apart from them.

At any rate, the fight at Penselwood marked a new phase in the war, though details of the battle are scant. Probably at the outset the Anglo-Saxons let out a great war-cry, for which German tribes had been known in Roman times, when it was named the *baritus* or 'roar'. It may have been Christianised by now but at Hastings the Anglo-Saxons shouted out '*ut*' (out), a laconic but apt proclamation which would have done as well as a taunt to the Danes at Penselwood. Then throwing spears would have been launched and arrows too before the opposing ranks moved towards each other and started to spear and hack at close quarters where brute strength and sheer will were the raw ingredients of success.

Edmund's victory at Penselwood – if it was one – was not decisive though. Rather it was the opening blow in a new campaign. Another battle 'after midsummer' was fought at Sherston. There is a place of that name near Malmesbury in Wiltshire, home of the famous abbey from the illusory security of which Edmund had seized his wife. 'Florence' of Worcester however places the battle in Hwiccia in western Mercia or what would now be known as the West Midlands, around Hereford and Worcester. He also suggests that men from Wiltshire and Hampshire were fighting on the side of the Danes. This time the battle appears to have been very hard-fought with heavy losses on both sides.

The *Encomium Emmae Reginae* suggests that Thorkell, eager to secure his position in Cnut's eyes, led the Viking army at Sherston. Edmund assembled his troops in battle array, his best troops in the front rank, the rest in the rear as reserves. He exhorted them with brave battle-speeches, familiar words that would have been recognised by many generations: appeals to serve their country and protect their children, their family and their homes. Then he ordered his men to advance. As they did so, the Danes moved out to meet them.

Tactics from specific battles of the time are not easy to discern. However, evidence that has survived from some suggests that the normal Anglo-Saxon formation would be linear. The shield-wall was the standard tactic but it was only as good as the men who fought in it (and indeed as their morale). If it was broken, then it could quickly disintegrate and be overwhelmed, as was discovered at Hastings in 1066. For the Vikings, tactics were slightly different. The later Danish writer Saxo Grammaticus speaks of a wedge formation (the '*swinfylking*'), a kind of inverted Christmas tree shape with two men in the front rank, four in the second, eight in the third and so on. Presumably its expanding sides could move in on the ranks of the enemy as they pushed into the recesses between each wedge.[34]

Edmund reportedly fought heroically in the front rank at Sherston, striking many of the enemy dead and proving himself to be a courageous soldier and an able general. It would prove to be a long fight. The first day of the battle was a Monday, and at the end of it all there was no clear winner. As the sun dipped behind the horizon in the west, both sides broke off battle and rested for the night.

The next day, it broke out once more with renewed ferocity. The *Encomium* suggests that the Danes were heavily outnumbered by about two to one. At first the English regained the initiative and it seemed that they must win. But Thorkell told his men that there was no place to run to and they must fight their way out of their predicament or die in the attempt.

Just then, as the climax of the battle arrived and the result rested in the balance, an old enemy raised his head once more. Eadric Streona, seeing that the fight was going the way of the English but showing where his own affections lay (or so 'Florence' would have us believe), suddenly turned on a Saxon warrior near him called Osmær and struck off his head. The particular significance of this was that the decapitated warrior bore a striking resemblance to King Edmund. The death of a leader on the field of battle was a disaster to the armies of the time, one which the forces in support of him rarely survived. The turning point of the Battle of Maldon seems to have been the death of Byrhtnoth and the decisive moment at Hastings in 1066 was the killing of King Harold. With Edmund dead, it was likely that the battle would quickly turn into a decisive Viking victory.

Eadric raised Osmær's head high, shouting to the men around him, specifically named as those of Dorset, Devon and Wiltshire, that their leader was dead and telling them to retreat with all speed. Some indeed started to break but before they ran off, Edmund made himself known to them and their courage was renewed. He took off his helmet to show them he was alive (remarkably similar in fact to the action taken by William of Normandy at Hastings, which might make us a little suspicious about the detail) and was so incensed with Eadric's treachery that he flung a spear at him. It missed but was so powerfully thrown that it completely transfixed one warrior near him, came out of the other side and hit another. The rest of the English returned with enthusiasm to the fight but once again at the day's end there was no clear winner and the men from both armies collapsed exhausted into the soothing arms of sleep.[35]

There are two alternative versions of how the battle at Sherston finally ended. The *Encomium* suggests that, inspired more by desperation than any other quality, the Danes started foot by foot to turn the tide. The writer suggests that in the end it was they who won the day and departed with the spoils.[36] But 'Florence' of Worcester's account suggests that as the third day dawned Edmund was infuriated to see that the Danes had disengaged during the night and had gone off to collect a larger army. Eadric was still on hand, re-ingratiating himself with Edmund, though quite how he managed to do this after his actions on the previous day is not at all clear.[37]

It is also noteworthy that 'Florence' of Worcester suggested that there were some Englishmen fighting against Edmund at Sherston, even naming one of them as Ælfgar, lord of Tewkesbury in Gloucestershire and Cranborne in Dorset. It would appear that support for Edmund was far from unanimous within Wessex and that some men at least believed their interests would be better served by siding with the Danes.

The actions attributed to Eadric Streona during these times almost make a caricature of him. Every negative outcome seems to have been regarded as his fault by the chroniclers. There are some important qualifications to be made about this. One is the standard caveat about the bias of contemporary or near-contemporary writers. Another though concerns the danger of seeing England as a unified land. The concept of a 'one nation' England was very new and far from settled as yet. The country was still dominated to an extent by powerful warlords who sought advantage for their own faction ahead of what we might now call a national interest. When the pressure was on and the power of the central authority of the king was failing it was not altogether surprising that fault-lines soon appeared. England was in danger of quickly reverting to a dis-United Kingdom. The truth is that Edmund Ironside and Eadric Streona probably distrusted each other as much as, if not more, than they did the Vikings.

In all likelihood neither side could claim a definitive victory at Sherston. The Danes disengaged from the fight after two days of fierce though ultimately inconclusive fighting. Cnut at London continued to tighten the siege there once more, perhaps thinking that it would be better to fight on ground of his own choosing. Edmund was proving himself a far tougher nut to crack than his late father had been but he did not just have the Danes to contend with. At the side of Cnut were Englishmen whilst those supposedly supporting him included untrustworthy men such as the arch-traitor Eadric Streona, who had turned coat so many times that even he must have been confused as to whose side he was on. There was another quisling named Ælfmar Darling who was also accused of fighting on 'the other side' at Sherston.

In the aftermath of Sherston the armies licked their wounds. Many men who had survived the battle would have been left with serious wounds from the brutal nature of the fighting. Medical care was basic. There are some surviving sources which suggest that the Anglo-Saxons knew of herbal poultices which would presumably only give the most rudimentary and ineffective relief. It is likely that the surgeons of the time knew how to cauterise wounds but the risk of infection must have been high and life expectancy after a serious trauma must have generally been short.

Inspired by Thorkell's efforts, another prominent Viking, Erik of Lade, soon after set out on a raiding expedition of his own. It was another classic expedition of its type, characterised by looting and pillaging, by fire and sword. Cnut it seems stayed at the siege of London and, on Erik's return, forbade further raiding. This was highly unlikely to be on humanitarian grounds but rather because many of the leading men of England were in London which made it a more lustrous prize than ever. Distracting raids could not be tolerated at this stage as it would dilute Cnut's forces around London, who could themselves be exposed to a counter-attack by Edmund at the head of an English army.

The presence of Erik of Lade was, we may reasonably speculate, crucial to Cnut who was still a young and inexperienced warrior and war-chief. In contrast, Erik was a battle-hardened veteran who had served Sweyn Forkbeard well. His loyalty had been proved on many occasions. His presence with Cnut would have been invaluable. Yet this would come at a cost. Erik's lands in Norway had been left in the hands of his son Hákon but he would be driven out of them by Olaf Haraldsson, who now had a much freer hand there.

This Olaf was an important player. He had previously been part of Thorkell's warband in England but had left in around 1012, spending some time in Normandy. A poem from the time describes how he had then become friendly with Æthelred whilst he was in exile and also raided on the coasts of Francia and Spain. He had played a part in restoring Æthelred to power when the exiled king returned to London.

Subsequently he went back to Norway and staked his own claims to power there. With Erik of Lade and Cnut concentrating on England, he was able to drive Sweyn, Erik's brother, out and set himself up in power. Norway was lost to Cnut, who was of course busy elsewhere for a decade as a result; a useful reminder that the war in England at this time cannot be seen in isolation from wider north European events. Olaf Haraldsson in the process established himself as a long-term opponent of Cnut and his part in the story is far from finished.[38] He did not have it all his own way at first as those who preferred the old ways of religion resisted him – he was something of a warrior Christian evangelist – but they were soon overcome.

Olaf's actions show how complex 'Viking' interrelationships of the time were, as do those of Thorkell the Tall. This was a playing out of Viking power politics on a grand scale. The difficulties of a Danish king holding sway over a sprawling 'Empire of the North' were already being exposed in Norway. In truth it is doubtful that such an entity was ever viable in the long term in the context of the times; when an Emperor's focus was on one part of the territories that he held, there would be trouble elsewhere that he was forced to ignore for a time.

The movement of the Danish army back to London at this time might be seen as bait, an effort to entrap the English in a war of attrition. But it was something that Edmund could not ignore if he wished to maintain his credibility given the crucial status of the city. The *Anglo-Saxon Chronicles* are again frustratingly short on detail but they tell us that Edmund was successful in rescuing the garrison and driving the Danes back to their ships. London was saved, for the time being at least.

Edmund entered London in triumph, accompanied by an army that was described as 'immense'.[39] He was enthusiastically welcomed by the people, who boldly declared that they would much rather have him as their king than Cnut. Edmund also allegedly sent a message to Cnut challenging him to single combat, an offer that was declined.

Just two days after Edmund's entry to London, the armies met again at Brentford, on the Thames to the west of the city. We are told of an English triumph, though one not without its cost. It would seem, reading between the lines, that at the moment of victory the excitement of imminent plunder was too much for some of the English army, who sensed rich pickings and the chance for some material profit from this terrible war; it no doubt seemed much like merely getting back some of the wealth that had been extorted from them by force in the first place.

Details once more are scant but we are told that whilst chasing the Danes, presumably crossing the Thames, a number of the English were drowned. But Cnut and his army were defeated and Edmund savoured the sweet taste of victory at the expense of the raiders. However, this bout of fighting was eating into his resources in terms of men and he now made his way back to Wessex to reinforce his army. This merely left London once more open to a Danish attack. Their army, whilst no doubt depleted, was far from knocked out of the war.

Edmund's repeated efforts to replenish his forces with fresh troops speaks eloquently of the problems facing a general of his day in England. There was no standing army and the primary task of the fyrd was to defend the local area. They cannot really be thought of as professional troops but more as militia, with limited training and a marked reluctance to fight far away from their own locality, especially for any length of time. They had no stomach for an extended campaign.

In contrast the Danes were, if sometimes undisciplined at the strategic level, a more coherent force. Their purpose for being in England was to raid and fight, although their motivations were more complex, including a desire to serve the cause of Cnut and also to seek their own enrichment and advancement (not necessarily mutually exclusive options). They had no homes in England to return to (except for those of their number who were resident in the Danelaw before the attacks on southern England). Therefore, if they were defeated then they could simply move off to another part of the country to raid. The only way to stop the Danish army was to wipe it out or make the cost of victory so high that it seemed to be excessive.

In any event London continued to be resilient against all the efforts of Cnut's army whether by land or sea. He was still not in a position to breach the walls and, seeing that his efforts were no closer to success than before and faced with an attack on his rear by the English under Edmund, there was now a change of tactics or, more accurately, a return to tried and tested methods that had been used so often in the past. The Danes were to go back to the highly mobile mode of warfare that had been their hallmark in the time of Sweyn Forkbeard, one to which they were much better suited.

The army therefore returned to a style of warfare that they were probably much more comfortable with. The Danes took their ships up the River Orwell. The Orwell flows from the North Sea, where Felixstowe is now situated, and up through an estuary by Ipswich into Suffolk. Cnut was again taking advantage of the arterial waterways of England and his ships rode the waters of the

Orwell and then moved deeper into the country and on to Mercia. They burned and slew as they travelled, as had the raiders of old. They plundered too, of course, and once they were satiated they took themselves and their loot back to Kent, suggesting a long and winding journey covering four or five hundred miles.

But Edmund was of an altogether different stamp than Æthelred. In the bad old days, such large-scale Danish raids would have met with an ineffective, uncoordinated response. Nowadays things were different. Edmund gathered what we may assume was a large army from 'the entire English nation'[40] and fell on the Danes.

However, not everything had changed, for Cnut's army was still able in the main to stay one step ahead of Edmund. After a confrontation at the Battle of Otford in Kent in which Edmund's force had rather the better of things, they fled into the Isle of Sheppey on horseback and Edmund's men slew 'as many as he could overtake', which implies that he could not overtake more than a proportion of the Danish army. This impression of a hurried escape to Sheppey found in the *Anglo-Saxon Chronicles* is rather at variance with the account given in the *Encomium Emmae Reginae* referred to above which suggests a much more orderly withdrawal, possibly an example of the slightly hagiographic approach adopted by the writer of the latter though the authors of the *Chronicles* were hardly neutral either.

Edmund's vigorous response was impressing people. Such can be inferred from the decision of the turncoat Eadric Streona to change sides once more. He now affected a reconciliation with Edmund, a sign, given his motivations and ambitions, that he believed that the English were now starting to win the war. The Chronicler noted acidly that 'there was no more unwise decision than this was'[41] and indeed the untrustworthy Eadric had not yet finished with his old tricks. The reunion of Eadric and Edmund in any event took place at Aylesford in Kent. If the chroniclers are to be believed, Edmund would have done better to have finished him off there and then.

Whilst this touching reunion was going on, the raiders were able to move off elsewhere and again fell on Mercia. Defeating the Danes in battle was not proving as much of a challenge as it once was but bringing them to a decisive confrontation where a knockout punch could be landed was proving as elusive for Edmund as ever.

However, events were about to develop further and it seemed that such a fight might soon indeed be possible.

Edmund strove to raise yet another army from across England and, realising that Cnut was inland and away from his ships, he sought to catch them before they could make their way back to the safety of their fleet. And for once Edmund's efforts paid off. The two armies came face to face at Ashingdon (or 'Assandun', the 'Asses' Hill') in Essex.[42] Here there was high ground between the Thames and the Crouch estuary. The land to the east of the village of Ashingdon was the likely location of the camp of the English army. Ashingdon was a tiny place – recorded in the Domesday Book some seventy years later as being 'very small'. But it was about to play a very big part in English history. Interestingly, the tenant-in-chief as late as 1086 was named Sweyn, a name that betrays some obvious Danish antecedents.

Edmund planned to catch Cnut and his force unprepared. However, the Dane got wind that an English army was on its way and he got all the men he could off his ships and ready to fight off the attack. The writer of the *Encomium* relates a tale that the Danes had with them a magical banner made of plain white silk, which appeared to be empty in peacetime but on which, when a battle was imminent, a raven would appear. It would open its beak, flap its wings and hop around on its feet. But if defeat was imminent it would hang its head and stay motionless. It is perhaps no surprise that Odin, one of the greatest of the Norse deities, was known as 'the Raven God'.

Such raven banners had been carried by Viking armies for many years. The *Anglo-Saxon Chronicles* tell of one being captured as far back as 878 though the near-contemporary Olaf Tryggvason had as his standard a serpent on a white background. The raven's close association with Odin shows that this was hardly a Christian symbol. It hung on stubbornly as a totem to be borne as the battle standard of Scandinavian warriors, still recorded as being in use in the reign of King Sverri of Norway (1184–1202) when a saga speaks of a warrior extolling men to 'hew a sacrifice beneath the raven's talons'.[43] Beneath this mystical motif the Danes prepared for battle. Cnut marched his men down slowly to level ground. Edmund had assembled his army into three divisions and in this shape he fell upon the Danes. On 18 October 1016, a ferocious fight, a battle of the heavyweights, followed.

Edmund initially took up position in conventional fashion, between the dragon banner of Wessex on the one side and his own personal standard on the other in a position behind the foremost ranks of his warriors. But when he saw that the battle was in the balance he charged into the midst of the front-line battle. 'He split the line like lightning, brandishing a sword chosen and worthy for the arm of the young Edmund, and tearing into the line he passed through the centre, and left his warriors to overwhelm it.'[44]

But as the day wore on, the losses on the English side started to exceed those of the Danes. It was said that even when night fell the warriors on the battlefield fought on, hammering at each other by the light of the moon. And as the battle carried on into the early stages of the night watch, the confidence of the English diminished. They saw that, despite their superior numbers, the Danes were indefatigable and not minded to quit the field. Instead it was they who began to lose heart and the fight started to ebb out of them.

Ones and twos started to leave the battlefield at first, and then it was dozens, and then hundreds. Edmund was a brave warrior but he was not stupid; there was no point in losing his life in a lost cause – better by far to make his way to safety and live to fight another day (just as Alfred had done before his flight to Athelney). Such indeed was his duty if the Anglo-Saxon cause was to live on. And so he also joined the fleeing English. A fight to the death was only glorious if it could not be avoided.

The battle had again been hard and bloody but this time it was the Danes who triumphed, apparently decisively. It was said, perhaps inevitably, that Eadric Streona was the first to break and flee, showing again how much of a liability he was. Though it might be true that he did so, it also has the ring of something of the pantomime villain in action once more. It was said that when he saw that the Danes were about to break, he shouted above the din of battle '*Flet Engle, Flet Engle, Ded is Edmund*' ('Fly English. Dead is Edmund').[45] With him fled the Magonsæte, whose people formed a small sub-kingdom inside Mercia, centred around where Hereford now stands. This was not far from Eadric's home territory in Shropshire.

In any event, his alleged betrayal opened the way for the Danes to win a crushing victory; and it was suggested by some that this was not fear that caused Eadric's defection but rather a deliberate subterfuge set up with Cnut in advance.[46] Edmund did what he could to stem the tide but it was all to no avail.

There was a long roll-call of the English dead at the end of the battle: Eadnoth, Bishop of Dorchester; Wulfsige, Abbot of Ramsey; Ælfric, the ealdorman of Hampshire, a long-time supporter of the king whose earlier actions had sometimes been questioned but who had now paid the ultimate price for his allegiance; and Godwin, who held the same position in Lindsey. Also slain in the carnage was the renowned Ulfcetel; these men fell along with 'all the chief men of the nation of the English race'. If Ulfcetel had played a prominent part in the killing of Thorkell's brother Hemingr then this was sweet revenge for the Viking warrior.

It was noticeable that the dead included men from the eastern part of Mercia and East Anglia who had clearly attached themselves to Edmund's cause in contrast to their position with regard to Æthelred previously. The monks of Ely suffered a great disaster too; they had carried the shrine containing the relics of St Wendred into battle, where the precious remains, along with a number of the monks, were lost (Cnut awarded the relics later to Canterbury). It was noticeable that the late King Æthelred had been a patron of the abbey. Yet the prominent dead came from other areas too. In many respects this was truly a national army, as the roll-call of the dead suggested. But whilst this contrasted markedly with the composition of earlier forces, the end result had nevertheless been a disaster for the English.

It was past midnight when the battle was deemed to have been won and lost. The Danes scoured the battlefield for plunder, helping themselves to the spoils of war. As the watery light of dawn later started to tint the sky, they wandered the field and gathered up their own dead and started to bury them with all the dignity that could be mustered. Although they took all the possessions worth taking from the English dead, the bodies of their enemies were left to litter the field as food for carrion.

Whilst Christian priests said their prayers for the souls of the dead, maybe some of the Viking warriors still looked for something – or someone – quite different. The great god Odin was said to walk the field of battle, a one-eyed figure wearing a broad hat. Those who died gloriously in battle could look forward to the promise of Valhalla, where they would be carried after the fight. Odin was a sinister deity, a lover of wisdom so much that he had deprived himself of an eye and allowed himself to be hanged in pursuit of it. He was cruel to the point of being sadistic, without pity or compassion, a remote and terrifying being. He was the god of the great lords and kings, as opposed to the much more down-to-earth Thor who was beloved of peasants for his approachability.

Although this was an enormous victory for Cnut it was still not quite total. Edmund managed to escape and fled west to Gloucestershire, defeated perhaps but not without hope, especially as he had allies amongst the Welsh.[47] Cnut came after him, though not straightaway, perhaps with his own men also rather weary after the fierce fight at Ashingdon. He brought his army with him to the west but it seems that the ongoing warfare was exhausting both Englishman and Dane. Rather than meet on the battlefield, Edmund and Cnut came face to face on an island in the Severn near Deerhurst, named Ola's Island, Edmund being rowed over from the west bank and Cnut the east. Henry of Huntingdon even suggested that the two men fought a duel. But in the end the two men agreed to cease their fight and negotiate a compromise.[48]

There was a certain irony in the location. Some decades earlier a young monk had entered the monastery there. After a time, he found its rules too lax for his ascetic principles and went to Bath where he set up as a hermit. He later entered the mainstream of the Church and rose up through the ranks to the highest possible position. His name was Ælfheah and he was to become the Archbishop of Canterbury, the very man slaughtered by the Viking raiders at Greenwich.

There are however in some other sources indications that there was one last battle fought between Dane and Englishman. During the Viking age, poets (known as skálds) played a key role, appearing at court and praising the king. One such skáld was a man named Óttar the Black who crafted a work known as the *Knútsdrápa*. This talks of a final confrontation at a place named *Danaskógar* (*skógr* meaning 'wood' or 'forest' in Old Norse). This it has been suggested was the Forest of Dean, which equates well with a meeting in Gloucestershire.[49]

Whether or not preceded by a battle, at the end of it all instead of continuing as opponents, the two men agreed to become partners and pledged peace to each other. Perhaps the triumph of the Danes really was not quite that overwhelming after all, for although Cnut was to be king of the northern parts of England, Wessex was to continue to be ruled by Edmund, although it seems likely that London went to Cnut. Hostages were exchanged and more Danegeld was paid to Cnut to buy him and his men off again. But in reality England was divided to some extent along natural lines, both Danes and English in the main retaining those territories where their influence was greatest. The defeat of Edmund's army at Ashingdon had been significant; but it was not in the end decisive for he kept his crown and a significant part of England.

The retention of Wessex by Edmund was an important concession. It meant that Wessex stayed in the hands of the bloodline of Cerdic, the semi-mythical founder dating back to the sixth century. Wessex alone had remained constantly in the hands of the family whilst all other regions – East Anglia, Mercia and Northumbria for example – had passed into foreign hands some time previously. The pride of the West Saxons was at least maintained.

This division of England is a timely reminder that the country had only been united for a few decades. It was a reversion then to the old way of things and a sign that in some ways regional loyalties still outweighed national ones. London bought a truce with the Danes now and they brought their ships there for the winter, an unambiguous way of creating pressure on the citizens should they misbehave. The Danes were clearly on top by this stage but could not be certain of final victory in this topsy-turvy war with Edmund still on the scene.

Therefore, it was fortunate – and perhaps not entirely coincidental – for Cnut that Edmund was about to exit stage left. For on 30 November 1016, St Andrew's Day, the resilient (but still young) English king and warrior expired, according to the account of 'Florence' of Worcester in London.[50] He was buried soon after at Glastonbury where his grandfather, the great Edgar, was also interred. This was an establishment of great significance and at the time the richest in England (and so it remained when it was dissolved by Henry VIII's commissioners half a millennium later). Edmund's tomb no longer exists but it certainly survived up until the sixteenth century, when it was noted as being in the presbytery of the abbey near the tomb of King Arthur (a sacred place indeed, except that the resting place of the latter was probably a later medieval fabrication).[51]

Quite why this apparently sudden death occurred is not clear. It might have been wounds from battle though if this was so it is surprising that the *Anglo-Saxon Chronicles* do not mention the fact for this was something akin to the hero's death that such a life seemed to demand. It might alternatively have been through natural causes, exacerbated perhaps through his exertions.

Yet there is a nagging doubt that it might have been something different responsible for his death. There was one man above all others who benefitted from this turn of events: Cnut. The removal of his main rival so soon after the great triumph at Ashingdon was, to say the least, convenient. There is no firm evidence, no what we might now call 'smoking gun' to refer to, but there was a very strong motive indeed for Cnut to remove Edmund. He could be, as we have seen before and will see again, ruthless when the occasion demanded, and to eliminate the troublesome Edmund once and for all made sense.

Certainly the colourful account of William of Malmesbury says that Edmund's death was no accident. Unsurprisingly, it is again Eadric Streona who is implicated. The chronicler says that he paid two close attendants of Edmund to murder him. The method of Edmund's death was strange to say the least; he was murdered by having an iron hook thrust into his posterior, a rather nasty end that seems nevertheless unnecessarily complicated.[52] A more believable version, that of Adam of Bremen, who mistakenly calls Edmund Æthelred's brother rather than his son, suggests rather more prosaically that he was eliminated by means of poison.[53]

The version according to Henry of Huntingdon is slightly different. He says that Edmund was murdered in Oxford. The circumstances were somewhat unusual here too and similar in some ways to William of Malmesbury's version. Whilst using the lavatory during the night he was stabbed by the thrust of a dagger upwards into a rather sensitive part of his body by Eadric Streona's son. Then the assassin fled, leaving the dagger in Edmund's bowels. Eadric, according to this account, then went to Cnut and claimed credit for the deed. In response, the Dane offered to set him above all other men and promptly ordered that Eadric's head be cut off and stuck on a stake on a high tower in London.[54]

The chronicler Geoffrey Gaimar comes up with the most ingenious and painful end of all. He suggests that the killer, who lay somewhat uncomfortably in the lavatory pit, was armed with a type of crossbow. When Edmund sat down to attend to the calls of nature the bolt was fired and proceeded to hit the mark, Edmund's 'fundament', so successfully that it did not stop until it had pierced a lung. It was said that so deeply did the missile penetrate that it was not even possible to see the feathers of the bolt after the deed was done.

The cause and means of death may be argued, but assuredly Edmund was dead, leaving the throne uncontested. The centre of any residual resistance against Cnut bade his farewells to the scene. A man once described as 'an English Viking, passionate, brave, impulsive, but unruly and uncontrollable' was no more.[55]

The writer of the *Encomium* suggested that Edmund's death was the best of all possible outcomes. He argued that a country divided could not stand for long and he may well have been right.[56] Certainly Edmund's death left a clear field and the war now spluttered out. The Anglo-Saxon dynasty was no more, or so it seemed. The Danes were triumphant. Given the way that they had plundered the country for all it was worth, it must have appeared that the days ahead were dark indeed for the English people, who now had a Viking king.

1. The medieval tithe barn at Abbotsbury, Dorset. The abbey was a beneficiary of one of Cnut's retainers, named Ork, and his wife Tovi. (Author's collection)

2. The mighty keep at Bamburgh, stronghold of Uhtred and ravaged by Vikings during the late tenth century. (Author's collection)

3. A rare survival of Anglo-Saxon England, Saxon script on the walls of the eleventh-century church at Breamore, Hampshire. (Author's collection)

4. The powerful edifice of Corfe Castle. At the top of the hill where the later castle now stands was once the hunting lodge where King Edward the Martyr was murdered. (Author's collection)

5. The twin towers of Durham Cathedral, visited by Cnut later in his reign. (Author's collection)

6. A later stained-glass window of Edward the Martyr in the church at Corfe. (Author's collection)

7. A wall picture of Cnut's sister Estrith marking the spot where her remains have rested in Roskilde Cathedral, Denmark, for the last 1,000 years. (Author's collection)

8. The atmospheric site of Glastonbury Abbey, burial place of Edmund Ironside and visited by Cnut. (Author's collection)

9. Relic of a bygone age. 'Guthrum's Street' in Viking Jorvik. (Author's collection)

10. Brooding skies over Lindisfarne, ransacked by Viking raiders in 793. (Author's collection)

11. Looking down on Portland, site of the first Viking raid in England in 789. (Author's collection)

12. The site of the forum in Rome, scene of Cnut's greatest triumph of statesmanship in 1027. (Author's collection)

13. Looking down the nave of Roskilde Cathedral, Denmark. Here, on the site of an earlier wooden 'stave church', Ulf – Cnut's brother-in-law – was murdered on his orders. (Author's collection)

14. Daybreak over Roskilde Fjord, near to Cnut's capital in Denmark. (Author's collection)

15. A reconstruction of a Cnut-era ship in the waters by the Roskilde Ship Museum. (Author's collection)

16. The statue of Alfred looks over the ruins of Shaftesbury Abbey where Cnut died in November 1035. (Author's collection)

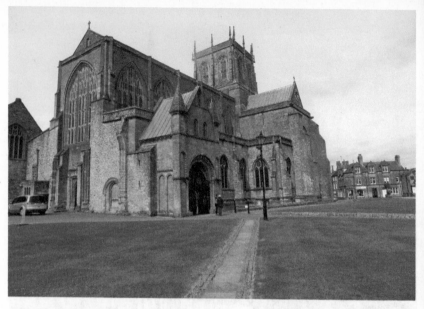

17. Sherborne Abbey with the remains of the Saxon building in the near corner. Cnut and Emma were generous benefactors of the monastic establishment here. (Author's collection)

18. The statue of Cnut's arch-enemy, Olaf of Norway, above the entrance to the church named after him in Jorvik. (Author's collection)

19. 'The Mouth of the Frome' leading up from Poole Harbour to Wareham: launch point for Cnut's seaborne invasion of England in 1015. (Author's collection)

20. Reconstruction of a Viking-era Great Hall at Trelleborg in Denmark. (Author's collection)

21. Looking down on the Frome from the Saxon town walls of Wareham. (Author's collection)

22. The great Norman cathedral at Winchester. The location of the Anglo-Saxon predecessor of the building, where Cnut was originally buried, can be seen traced out in stone on the ground. (Author's collection)

Right: 23. Cnut presenting
a precious cross to the
New Minster in Winchester
alongside his wife Emma.
(Courtesy of Jonathan
Reeve b15p25)

Below: 24. A witan
(or more precisely the
Witanagemot) from an
eleventh-century English
manuscript. (Courtesy of
Jonathan Reeve b60p170t)

25. Viking spearheads found at London Bridge in the 1920s and likely to have been used in one of the many Viking attacks in the early eleventh century at this vital crossing point, the only one across the Thames at the time. (Courtesy of Jonathan Reeve b1000plateXXIleft)

26. Viking battle-axes found at London Bridge in the 1920s. (Courtesy of Jonathan Reeve b1000plateXXIright)

27. Æthelred's pact with Olaf and other Vikings from *Leges Anglo-Saxonicae*. (Courtesy of Jonathan Reeve b12p129)

28. Charter of Cnut witnessed by Æthelnoth, the Archbishop of Canterbury; Ælfgifu (Emma), the queen; Earl Godwine and many bishops, abbots, earls and thegns. (Courtesy of Jonathan Reeve b12p145)

29. Final resting place in Winchester Cathedral of Harthacnut. (Courtesy of Christina Rex)

30. Edward the Confessor from the Bayeux Tapestry. (Courtesy of the Bayeux Tapestry)

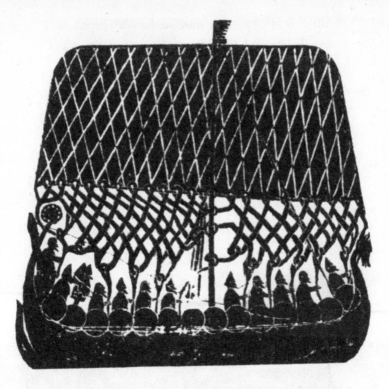

31. Depictions of a Viking ship and Viking warriors from a picture stone in Stenkyrka, Gotland, Sweden. (Courtesy of Jonathan Reeve jr2231b39fp488 and jr2230b39p473)

32. Construction of a burh, one of the ways Alfred protected Wessex from Viking attacks. (Courtesy of Jonathan Reeve b12p165)

33. The Anglo-Saxon church of St Laurence in Bradford on Avon. It was first established in around 700 and is a rare intact survivor. (Courtesy of Jonathan Reeve)

5

King of England: Victory and Kingship (1016–1018)

So now feng Cnut cyning to eall Angelcynnes rice: 'King Cnut succeeded to all the kingdom of England'. 'Cyning' – 'king' – was itself an interesting word. Its root was 'cynn' – 'kin' or 'people' – and the king was their leader, the keeper and protector of their treasure and their defender. It was a position that of course came with great power and wealth but also great responsibility.

Cnut now had the crown of England to himself, with his greatest rival, the resilient Edmund, out of the way permanently. It was suggested by the later chronicler 'Florence' of Worcester that Edmund had said that he wanted the crown to go to Cnut if he were to die in order that his children would be protected,[1] giving the Dane a convenient excuse to take over Wessex as well as the rest of the country. In any event, the very young children of Edmund would not be a threat to Cnut for many years and the Ætheling offspring of Æthelred and Emma, Edward and Alfred, were far removed from the centre of events. Cnut now had no opponents.

It might seem strange that Edmund had declared that Cnut should be his successor if he died but such a deal was not unique. Two decades or so later, Cnut's son and heir Harthacnut would strike a deal with his great rival Magnus of Norway that, whoever died first, the survivor should succeed to all the lands held by the other. Even in later times we find Charles VI of France agreeing with Henry V, the victor of Agincourt, that on his death the English king should succeed to his crown. Such an arrangement was a way for Edmund to hold on to power whilst he lived, and who knew anyway what might have happened before his death?

England was tired of incessant warfare and hardship. The *Anglo-Saxon Chronicles* talk so repeatedly of death and destruction in the three decades leading up to this moment that the reader can become almost blasé about it. However much repetition might make one immune to the horrors of this period, it is important to remind oneself that repetition does not necessarily equate to exaggeration. From what we can gather these were years and decades of terrifying raiding, extortionate taxation and general misery. In all probability some of the English at least were just happy that the fighting was over for a time. But at the same time there must surely have been nervousness now that the throne was in the hands of a Dane.

Much was expected from a king of the times, though he got much back in return. The ideal king was required to deal out justice equitably (as defined by the law) but firmly. He should be a conqueror in battle for if he were not then he had forfeited the favour of God. He should be a protector of the rights of men – and most particularly the Church. In return, the Church would encourage the king's subjects to be loyal to their true lord. If he did his job well, then a king might expect the ultimate reward of an entry into Heaven and a glorious life eternal.

On the other hand, the horrors of hell were laid out loud and clear as a reminder of the alternative, even for a king. In a vivid description of it, 'the place of deathless death, unfailing failure, an end without end', the eleventh-century abbot John of Fécamp told of angels of wrath with heads of dragons, of serpents tearing at the breasts of their victims, of demons gnawing on their bones. It was a message with a strong deterrent effect and it was one that was theoretically aimed as much at a king as at his lowliest subject. Cnut may have been of a time when his ancestors had only been Christians for a generation or two but if he took these threats to heart they would have certainly acted as a powerful guide to his actions as a ruler.

The position of a king in those far-off times has been well-described by a modern historian discussing a near-contemporary ruler in Edward the Confessor. He wrote:

The kingdom was the king's private estate; it was his to manage; and everyone directly under his power or protection owed him tribute. Such a theory was both permissive and restrictive. On the one hand it allowed the king a plenitude of power; the kingdom was his to exploit; and on the other it restrained his arbitrary action by investing him with all the duties of a good lord and, especially, of a good king: his dominions were a trust; he must be a father and protector to his men and, as God's vicar, must exhibit the Christian virtues in the management of his estate. [The king] knew – and sometimes was reminded – that after his death he would have to render to God an account of his stewardship.[2]

At the start of Cnut's reign many would certainly have understood the mention of the king seeing England as his own private estate. Rather fewer would have seen him as a likely candidate for 'God's vicar'. Yet the probably sceptical and nervous majority were, in the latter respect, ultimately in for a surprise.

Quite what the young and new king would make of England is a matter of speculation in the absence of definitive evidence from written sources but some assumptions can be made. Anthropologically Danes and Anglo-Saxons may be regarded as cousins. They had, in historical terms, not too long before lived cheek by jowl and shared many similarities in language, customs and folklore. In recent centuries they had grown apart and the Anglo-Saxons had accepted Christianity as the dominant religion several centuries before the Danes. But there was enough in common for Cnut not to feel that his new lands were totally alien to him.

England offered him a great deal. First of all, it was a wealthy and fertile country compared to Denmark, let alone the rest of Scandinavia. Wealth was a means to wider power and influence. It was also a way for Cnut to secure his position. Generous gifts could be made to those warlords whose support he needed to buy. England also had prestige. She had had some great kings in the past, such as Offa, Alfred, Æthelstan and Edgar, who had been players on the European stage. For a man with ambition this was not an unattractive quality.

England was still a very hierarchical country. Here again there were similarities between Englishman and Dane. So for example the most senior noblemen next to the king were in England the ealdormen. The equivalent in Denmark were the jarls. As a result of some linguistic compromise the English were to end up with earls. At the other end of the scale, there were those on the bottom rung on the ladder, the slaves. These were still widespread in England. It was not uncommon for a man who was destitute to sell himself and his family into slavery. English wills of the period have many examples of the man or woman who dictated them requiring that on their deaths their slaves were given their freedom, manumission as it was technically called.

Similarly, Viking raids treasured slaves as much as gold and precious jewels. The right slave, a powerful young man or beautiful woman, would fetch a good price in the slave markets of Rouen or Dublin (which was the major centre for trade exports from Ireland and parts of Britain, with Islamic Spain a particularly popular ultimate destination). Their life would have been bitter and harsh, deprived of liberty and rights. It would have been a hard existence for most of them and it is difficult from this distance in time to realise exactly how tough it would be.

The English social structure was clearly defined in the law. If a life were to be taken by a criminal act it did not necessarily follow that the perpetrator would die, though capital punishment did exist and was applied commonly enough. Instead *wergild* could be paid, literally a 'man's price'. This could be offered in lieu of capital punishment. The amounts payable ranged enormously. At one end of the scale the king's life carried a wergild of 30,000 thrysmas (a thrysma is thought to have been worth three silver pennies). At the other end of the scale the payment for a peasant was 266 thrysmas with a whole range of payments in between depending on rank. These were amounts stated for men. No specific mention is made of women, though it is often assumed by historians that they carried the same price.[3]

England also had a strong administrative structure, more evolved than was the case with the relatively new kingdom of Denmark. It had a well-developed currency model too which was an important part of the administration of the country. So too in its own particular way was the Church, which not only provided religious leadership but also further bound the social structure together. These were all useful qualities for a new king to try and preserve and indeed even to copy for use back home in Denmark.

It is possibly significant that there is no contemporary reference to a coronation ceremony for Cnut. But later accounts suggest that Cnut was duly crowned in London in the Church of St Pauls, in the same building where the late King Æthelred was buried. Edmund's children were passed over and denied any claim to the crown. His two sons were after all no more than babes in arms. The battle for England was over and it was time to rebuild. As one historian eloquently put it, 'the land was at peace; but the calm was the calm of exhaustion'.[4]

Whilst the crown passed by election rather than automatically going to the eldest son of the late king, it was also normally given to an Ætheling of the Anglo-Saxon royal bloodline and Cnut was assuredly not qualified on those grounds. So this was essentially a right to rule proved by conquest, by sword, spear and axe, rather than the dictates of existing law. Cnut was nevertheless probably formally crowned by the Archbishop of Canterbury, Lyfing. The lack of a contemporary mention of this means that we cannot be certain of our facts here but it is highly likely that Cnut would want a coronation ceremony as part of the process of publicly legitimising his rule.

Formal acceptance by the Church was an important part of establishing Cnut's legitimacy. Lyfing had begun life as Ælfstan and had become abbot of Chertsey Abbey and then Bishop of Wells. He had been appointed as Archbishop of Canterbury in 1013 by Æthelred but had soon after been captured by the Danes. He had managed to survive this experience at least, unlike the martyred Ælfheah. Lyfing had subsequently been released and had taken up his place as the leading prelate in the English Church. In common with other leading clerics such as Archbishop Wulfstan of York, he provided continuity in the new reign and what may have been a comforting symbol that life in England would after all go on despite the regime change. Lyfing soon turned his attentions to restoring Canterbury Cathedral, which was very necessary after the damage it had sustained at the hands of Danish forces not long before.

This continuity of leadership amongst the English Church was a marked contrast to what happened in the country half a century later when William the Conqueror placed his own men in senior positions in the establishment. Partly it was because Cnut had few churchmen of note to replace them with, Denmark being still young in the Christian religion and subject to the influence of German churchmen from the south. But it also helped keep the English people calm when Church leaders whom they knew well stayed in positions of power and influence. Not upsetting the status quo in this area was a sensible strategy with which to begin the reign.

Cnut soon after issued his first coin as the King of England, a quatrefoil penny. Its obverse was marked with his head, a crown prominently placed on it. This contrasted with the standard-issue coins produced during the reign of Æthelred II and as such seemed to be making a very specific symbolic point in an effort to affirm Cnut's legitimacy. It was a throwback to the type of coins minted in the reign of the late, great Edgar, a good precedent to follow. The issue of this coinage was an unmistakable sign that the conquest had been made much more final.

There is also intriguing archaeological evidence of one of Cnut's early moves after becoming king. The burhs had been a core part of England's defensive measures against the Vikings. Now Cnut sought to neutralise these. Evidence has been uncovered that the sites at Cricklade, Lydford, South Cadbury and Wareham were systematically destroyed. The ditches that surrounded them and offered extra protection were filled in.[5] The new king was clearly taking no chances that they could be used in a renewed attack on his position.

Now that England was his, one of Cnut's first moves may seem surprising; in 1017 he split England into four and placed different men at the head of the regions so created. He kept Wessex for himself, a wise decision given the fact that it was the powerhouse of Saxon England and could therefore be expected to be the source of the greatest challenge to his right to rule. Mercia went to the duplicitous Eadric, a reward for his treachery though one that would not benefit him for very long. East Anglia went to Thorkell and Northumbria to the Norwegian Earl Erik of Lade.

The latter, de facto ruler of Norway under Sweyn Forkbeard, had left his brother (also Sweyn) and son Hákon behind in Norway, though the victory of Olaf Haraldsson at the Battle of Nesjar in 1016 in Oslo Fjord led to Sweyn's defeat and Hákon's flight to England. In fact, although Erik did well out of his support for Cnut in England, his territories in Norway were lost to him forever. Northumbria, a portion of which contained one of the most 'Scandinavian' parts of England in the shape of the old kingdom around York, may have been a consolation prize for him, as Cnut was in no position to launch an attack to win Norway back at this particular moment.

The situation in Norway was a major headache for Cnut. The country had only relatively recently been incorporated into the possessions of the Danish Crown and this was a loss to a king who had both England and Denmark to worry about as his main priorities. The harsh country to the north was a distant third in line in terms of priority in all probability but its loss would have been keenly felt nonetheless. Cnut had probably felt confident in being able to hold Norway as Hákon was his nephew, being the son of his half-sister Gytha and Earl Erik. He had either underestimated the strength of Norwegian feeling against being ruled by Danes or overestimated Hákon's ability to defend it, though given greater priorities elsewhere this was a strategic decision that perhaps he had little choice in.

Frustratingly little remains concerning Thorkell's time in charge in East Anglia, which only lasted for a few years. It is not even clear what 'East Anglia' refers to. Rather than thinking of the region narrowly, for example just including Norfolk and Suffolk and their immediate environs, it probably included Essex. Around this period other ealdormen of East Anglia had also held parts of Hertfordshire, Bedfordshire and Buckinghamshire as some of the territory for which they were accountable so this might have been a greatly expanded area for which Thorkell was responsible. But he made little impression on the region, or at least on the records that survive, in which only two mentions of his name have been found.[6]

Erik was likely to have been especially crucial to Cnut at this stage. Eadric's unreliability was approaching legendary status and he was of course English so that on its own was enough to make his loyalty dubious. Thorkell hardly inspired confidence given his past behaviour either. It has been said that 'Erik was the loyal lieutenant and experienced politician and general whom Cnut left in the north to rule it on his behalf'.[7]

But equally his frequent presence at Cnut's side, which can be deduced by his regular attestation of formal documents, meant that he spent a lot of time away from the north and with his king. Indeed, there is also strong evidence that the very far north of

England, the region of Bernicia, was under the control of the late Uhtred's brother Eadwulf Cudel. In such a situation, it is likely that Erik may have been nominally lord of all Northumbria, that land far distant from Cnut's powerbase in the south of England, but that there were a number of local men who still played a key part in everyday life and government in the region.

The death in recent years of Uhtred in Northumbria, who had been a close supporter of the late King Æthelred (sometimes at least), also opened up a vacancy and placing Erik of Lade there might help to buy his ongoing support; the lands of the wild north were not dissimilar in some ways to those of northern Norway, which had always been to an extent semi-autonomous, and that might have been Cnut's plan for this remote part of England too. But there is little doubt that above all it was pragmatism rather than any long-term vision that drove Cnut in his policies in dividing England up at this time. Fast-forward a decade and not one of the men he appointed still held their position.

On reflection there is perhaps nothing very surprising at all in Cnut's policies in splitting England up at this stage (particularly as it seemed that the great King Edgar had done something similar during his reign[8]). He kept Wessex for himself whilst giving other territories to those who had played a key part in the conquest and thus probably hoped to buy their loyalty for a time. The turncoat Eadric was a long-established figure in Mercia and placing him as his representative there merely served to cement a powerful ally in place who had proved his worth whilst paradoxically at the same time proving that he could not be trusted. In many ways the same could be said of Thorkell who was frequently suspected of having divided loyalties – or perhaps more accurately of only having loyalty to whatever his own best interests appeared to be at any given time.

There were no doubt other reasons for the policy of dividing England up.[9] Given the fact that the ruling regime was only very new in post, there was a need to ensure that control was kept locally and that not only was law and order maintained but that taxes were also scrupulously collected. Cnut's central administration was not strong enough to do this in what was still a fragmented country. Cnut at this stage needed strong lieutenants in place to ensure that local policies and tax collections were effectively delivered. However, from what we can gauge of Cnut's personality this would be the policy only so long as it served his purposes and once it no longer did (and he was strong enough to act) he would not be slow to change it.

The fact that Cnut kept the important province of Wessex to himself should not be taken to mean that he was responsible for its day-to-day government. For some time, the comparatively large and certainly significant province had been governed in an administrative sense by two ealdormen. One was responsible for the eastern part covering Hampshire, Berkshire, Sussex and the areas around London. The other, in the west, had responsibilities for Wiltshire, Somerset, Dorset, Devon and Cornwall. Charters from 1018 suggest that there were still two ealdormen in place, Godwin in the east and Æthelweard in the west.

The frequent references made to various charters and other legal documents issued during this period show how important such documents are. Charters, although few in number as far as survivals from Cnut's reign are concerned, are goldmines of information. Such land grants drew up the boundaries of the estates that had been gifted. A further document, a writ, listed the legal and financial benefits attached to it; such rights included that of *infangangenetheof*, largely unpronounceable to the modern tongue, which was the power to hang a thief caught on the property and claim their possessions. The charter also showed the limits of what was expected in return; these would often include military service or the maintenance of bridges or fortifications.

Often, however, this was a two-way bargain. Contracts were given in return to the monarch making the grant; something was normally expected back, either in the shape of a material 'gift' or some form of service. The land granted was still liable to tax. Further, on the grantee's death, a form of succession duty was payable ('inheritance tax' we would call it now; back then it was called a 'heriot'). It was not unusual either for the monarch to expect some of the land to revert back to him in such circumstances though in theory the land could often be passed on as an inheritance to the heirs of the grantee.[10]

These 'heriots' provide interesting details of armour and weaponry expected at the time. During Cnut's reign, a typical expectation for the heriot of an earl was four saddled horses, four unsaddled horses, four helmets, four byrnies (mail shirts), four swords, eight spears and eight shields. This sounds sufficient to equip four fully armed men and four less well-armed retainers. This was what was typically required of an English earl, with less demanded from thegns. In the Danelaw, however, current research suggests that a cash payment was often required instead.[11]

Great men though the earls were, they were not powerful enough on their own to ensure that England was safely held. Cnut was forced to rely on other groups of men too. One group were his *huscarles*, literally 'house servants'. These were paid men and also very often landowners. They owed a personal loyalty to the king in the same way that we think of medieval knights owing such an allegiance to their lord. However, it has been argued that they did not provide a standing army for Cnut or his successors, at least on a permanent basis, even if they might be called upon to act in such a fashion on a temporary basis in times of trouble and might even be asked to provide garrisons occasionally.

They could also be used as administrative officers of the king, effectively his enforcers. We find them being used in this fashion in 1041 during the reign of Cnut's son and ultimate successor Harthacnut when two of them lost their lives in a riot in Worcester after trying to extort high levels of tax from the citizens. Interestingly, in this case we find the *huscarles* also forming a part of the avenging army that was sent to punish the city for their insolence (which indeed they did with great brutality).

The *huscarles* formed essentially a personal retinue of the king and this meant that they were of course involved in warfare when the occasion demanded it, in addition to their non-military functions. But the essential point is that they were tied to the king by bonds of loyalty. That there was money involved too we need not doubt but this was just part of a bigger picture. They served the king and he was expected to look after their interests in return.

Their role can be contrasted with that of what were known as the *lithsmen*. These were to all intents and purposes hired hands who served the king for as long as they were required (and of course for as long as they were paid). These were closer to a standing army though the phrase is perhaps misleading as they were not kept on permanently but only for as long as necessary in any given situation.

In fact, they were in some ways a potential nuisance for the king. They were highly paid and such pay could only be found through taxation, hardly likely to endear them to his subjects who were forced to stump up large amounts of money to recompense them. The trick was to pay them off and get rid of them as quickly as practicable.

But like many mercenaries throughout history, they were also potentially unreliable and liable to change sides should someone come along with a better offer (something for which mercenaries from Normandy, cousins of the Vikings, would become notorious during the eleventh century). Just as they could help to set up a king, they might just as easily bring one down. A ruler such as Cnut might then wish to get rid of the *lithsmen* as soon as they had served their purpose. This may be behind the extraordinarily high levels of taxation that were to be levied in 1018 in an effort to remove a number of warriors from the scene. For many of his English subjects, though, the price must have seemed extortionate and a sign that their worst fears were about to be realised.

The king could not rule alone. The top rank of society below him was the earls but there was also a next rank down of men who were important enough to attest charters. Four names in particular appear prominently in the next few years on a regular basis and interestingly two of them are Scandinavian and two English. The two Scandinavians were Eilifr, who seems to have been given an earldom centred on Gloucestershire (previously part of West Mercia, the province for which Eadric Streona was responsible), and Hrani. Eilifr appears to have been close to Thorkell's brother Hemingr. He was also the brother of the king's brother-in-law Ulf, who was married to Estrith, Cnut's sister. He disappears from English history soon after Thorkell the Tall did in around 1022 and witnesses no charters after 1024, which perhaps suggests that he suffered from association with him.[12]

Hrani was given lands in Herefordshire, which were also part of the west Mercian territories that formed the earldom for which Eadric Streona was responsible. The presence of reliable lieutenants to watch over Eadric is not hard to understand and Hrani seems to have remained in post throughout Cnut's reign though he never rose to prominence and was overshadowed by the Anglo-Saxon Leofric who would later become Earl of Mercia at some time in the

1020s. He would nevertheless still be appearing in various records as late as 1041. He was, it appears, a useful and reliable lieutenant.

Within the kingdom, London was in something of a unique position by this time. Reflecting perhaps both its economic importance and also the possibility that it could become a centre of political dissent given its past support for Æthelred, a Danish garrison was stationed close by the city. It was probably based at Southwark, where there were beaches available that the shallow-draft Viking ships could access and which remained an important anchorage into later medieval times. At some stage it appears likely that two prominent Scandinavian supporters of the king, Osgot Clapa and Tovi the Proud, played important roles in governing the city though they may have been given these slightly later in his reign.[13]

During this period an official called a staller was in place in London. He was a high-ranking official of the king who very closely protected his interests in the area for which he was responsible. It has been suggested that Tovi the Proud was given this responsibility for London,[14] which enabled him to keep a sharp eye on local events and make sure that his sovereign's interests were protected. Cnut seems to have had difficult relations with the city and the placing of a loyal supporter like Tovi makes perfect sense. He could keep an eye on things and react if the king's interests were threatened.

In the aftermath of the conquest there was no one pattern of local government that Cnut imposed across England. Where trouble was possible or indeed where it sometimes actually materialised, Cnut would place his own men in charge or at least in positions of influence. So in western Wessex and many parts of Mercia this is what he did. He had a very particular approach to London which reflected both its importance and its potential volatility. In other areas Englishmen remained prominent. Kent was a particular case where Cnut seems to have been happy to let a clerical force, namely the Archbishop of Canterbury, remain the most significant local power. There was no systematic overhaul of local government in England, rather an approach that was largely contingent on local politics and possible regional loyalties.[15]

It should be pointed out that the Church of the day was not only staffed with what we would consider to be 'career' priests. Bishops and abbots were often nominated by the king and he would therefore wish to appoint men who would protect his interests. Such individuals were often drawn from the lay aristocracy. They were not typically naïve idealists but shrewd operators who were well used to the demands of realpolitik. One modern writer has described it in the following terms: 'The clerical establishment ... constituted the ecclesiastical arm of royal power, counterpart to the secular arm formed by the lay aristocracy.'[16] Given this, it is less surprising than it might be to find churchmen often involved in warfare at the time.

Two particularly important contemporary Englishmen were Æthelweard in the south-west of England and Godwin from Sussex. Æthelweard was possibly the son-in-law of Æthelmaer the Stout (not to be confused with that man's son, who bore the same name – Æthelmaer was a fairly common name in the aristocracy and means 'noble protector') but he was in a part of England that remained loyal to the old Anglo-Saxon regime more determinedly than some others and would suffer for it.

If Cnut was supposed to look after Edmund Ironside's children now that the latter was dead, some chroniclers suggest that he didn't do a very good job. It was said that he decided that he wished to be rid of Edmund's two sons, Edward and Edmund, but not wanting blood on his hands he sent them, Hamlet-like, to the King of Sweden to do the deed. The position of most of Sweden outside Skåne towards Denmark at the time is unclear. Although there are suggestions of a pact between Cnut and his royal 'brother' Olaf in Sweden, there are other hints that the latter was plotting to break away from Danish dominance at the time and indeed most of the country never came under direct rule from Cnut or his dynasty. Olaf was not disposed to kill the princes and they ended up instead in the court of the King of Hungary. Edmund in the course of time died there but Edward married Agatha, niece to the Roman Emperor Henry. From their union, a future player in English history called Edgar 'the Ætheling' would spring.

Edgar the Ætheling would be the last male member of the Saxon royal dynasty in Wessex, the final male representative of the House of Cerdic. Born in 1051, fifteen years later he was declared successor to Harold, the Saxon king who had fallen at Hastings, by the governing council, the Witan, in London. But in the face of the advancing Norman juggernaut this was nothing except an empty gesture and Edgar was unable to enforce his claim and made his way out of England.

Although Cnut acceded to the throne at the end of 1016, England was far from subdued and there is strong evidence of tensions remaining that needed to be dealt with. Soon after, several prominent men were slain on the orders of the king; these included Northman, son of Ealdorman Leofwine of Mercia; Æthelweard, the son (not the son-in-law) of Æthelmaer the Stout, Ealdorman of the Western Provinces (and a bloodline descendant of King Æthelred I); and Beorhtric, son of Ælfheah in Devonshire. Eadwig (or 'Edwy' as he sometimes later appears) 'the Ætheling', brother to Edmund Ironside, was also exiled. The fact that these men were strongly associated with west Mercia and the western part of Wessex suggests that these were centres of resistance against the new regime.

Cnut also had the alleged murderers of Edmund Ironside put to death. But this was not the most noteworthy casualty of the year 1017, for Cnut decided that he could not rely on Eadric Streona for long, and he too was put to death, in London, apparently during the Christmas season, supposed strangled in the king's chamber where the two men had been conversing.[17]

In another version of Eadric's end in the *Encomium*, he approached Cnut for a reward in recognition of his desertion of Edmund in the war that had recently ended. The king responded with grave words: 'Shall you, who has deceived your lord with guile, be capable of being true to me? I will return to you a worthy reward, but I will do so to the end that deception may not subsequently be your pleasure.' Cnut summoned Erik of Lade, now Earl of Northumbria, to him. He told him to pay Eadric what he was owed, at which the Viking lord raised his mighty axe and struck off his head with a fierce blow.

Eadric's body was then thrown over the city walls, carrion for the dogs and wild animals, a suitably inglorious fate, it might be thought, for the arch-traitor. The *Encomium* suggests that this act was inspired by Cnut's disgust at the disloyalty of Eadric against his former lord[18] but it could equally have been just a prudent act on his part, as he realised that such treacherous actions might be repeated in the future with him as the target. In the same sequence of events he also struck down some of Eadric's leading supporters, including perhaps the above-named Northman.

However, Cnut was not striking out blindly. Northman's brother Leofric still eventually became an ealdorman. The chronicles of Evesham Abbey suggest that Leofric was granted lands from Worcestershire to Scotland and was given many of the extensive territories that had been held by Northman, though modern historians express doubts that this happened straightaway. Leofric's father, Leofwine, was still attesting charters in 1023, suggesting that he also survived Cnut's purge intact. The fact that he managed to survive at all says much about Cnut's measured actions and also perhaps the political skills of the ealdorman.

But the record shows that the Norwegian Earl Hákon – now a fugitive from his country – was also an earl in Worcestershire at the same time.[19] He was a young man and he was referred to in glowing terms by Snorri Sturluson, who described him as a handsome man with hair that was 'long and fair like silk'. There is no consensus amongst historians about whether Leofwine was somehow senior to Hákon or whether the two men shared more or less equal responsibilities. Nevertheless, Cnut was, it seems, not taking anything on trust in this part of England in particular.

It has been suggested that the elimination of Eadric Streona was related to a plot to replace Cnut with Eadwig, brother to the late Edmund Ironside. In this version of events, Eadric Streona was again behind the conspiracy and so too were Northman, Æthelweard and Beorhtric. In this interpretation, the plot was centred on the west of Mercia and the west of Wessex. Eadwig appears little in the events of previous years but he was at least of the House of Cerdic and presumably Eadric hoped to manipulate someone who was still young and inexperienced by appealing to natural supporters of the Anglo-Saxon kingly dynasty.

Eadric may already have felt himself compromised by the appointment of Hrani to lands in west Mercia. These included those of the Magonsaete, closely associated with Eadric, and it is very easy to accept the hypothesis that this had been done specifically to keep a close eye on the untrustworthy earl. With the main ringleaders of the plot disposed of, any plans to take the throne nurtured by Eadwig came to nothing.[20] There are some suggestions in the chronicles of the time that Eadwig was not at this stage killed but rather fled, returning in 1020 when he died soon after, either naturally or at the hands of Cnut, and was subsequently buried in Tavistock Abbey, long associated with the Anglo-Saxon dynasty. Eadwig's death, whenever it happened, removed for the time the threat from the House of Cerdic to Cnut's rule.

These were ruthless acts of realpolitik which show that despite his inexperience, Cnut was not to be trifled with. But significant though the killing of Eadric Streona was, it was not the most newsworthy event of the year 1017. Cnut's position with respect to Ælfgifu of Northampton was unclear; she may have been his concubine rather than his wife, or the legal position concerning their marriage may have been ambiguous; certainly Adam of Bremen stated unequivocally that this was the case.[21] Alternatively, they may have been united through the traditional rather than Christian rites known as *more danico* (sometimes called 'hand-fasting').

To give such relationships some context, Adam of Bremen avers that many Swedes had two or three 'wives'. In traditional Germanic and Norse societies children from such relationships would not be debarred from inheriting to titles, William 'the Bastard' of Normandy being a good example. In fact, allegations of 'concubinage' or 'bastardy' against those involved in or springing from such unions came from the direction of the Christian Church and not from wider society.

A possible explanation for the confusion over the precise role of Cnut's first 'wife' is to do with changing definitions of marriage. In the Anglo-Saxon period it was possible to have several different forms of 'marriage'. One form, without the sanction of the Church, was considered to be more a form of concubinage.[22] Children born from such a union could be considered by the Church to be illegitimate and this may have been the case with regard to the issue derived from Cnut's relationship with the now conveniently ignored Ælfgifu of Northampton, or indeed from the earlier case of Edmund Ironside and his brothers.

Naturally the Church struggled to come to terms with this situation. It understandably did not approve of any man, let alone a king, having both a wife and a concubine and indeed specifically debarred priests from ministering to men in such a position. It also forbade any children from a concubine assuming the rights of a legitimate child.²³ But for all that, Ælfgifu seems to have remained in a position of some importance and nearly fifteen years later we find her being sent to Norway as regent along with her son Sweyn who was not yet old enough to rule in his own right. Both king and Church, it seems, could manage to turn a blind eye to such matters when the occasion demanded it.

Whatever the truth of the situation, Cnut now started looking for an alternative eligible partner. Who better than the woman who was already so well acquainted with England and its rule? And so sometime in that summer (before 1 August according to the *Anglo-Saxon Chronicles*) Cnut sent to Normandy with a proposal to marry Emma, widow of the late English king, Æthelred.

If Cnut succeeded in these overtures, it would further strengthen his hold on England. Normandy was a potential source of threat, not least because Æthelred's children, Edward and Alfred, were there and in a good position to potentially stir up trouble as they grew older. If Cnut's marriage proposals proved convincing, then it would do much to neutralise any possible future threat from Normandy. So keen was he said to be on the match that the slightly later chronicler William of Jumièges stated that he offered her weight in gold and silver in return for her hand. Normandy would continue to loom large in Cnut's thinking throughout his reign.

In this context, the presence at the Norman court of Emma's children, Edward and Alfred, was an important consideration. They were not just under the protection of the Duke of Normandy but their presence at his side meant that he was actively in a position to impact on events in England. The two princes appear to have been well-favoured by him. Emma also had a daughter from her marriage to Æthelred by the name of Godgifu and her subsequent marriage to Drogo, Count of the Vexin and a key man in Normandy, was a mark of high approval. The royal offspring were a very useful bargaining chip to the rulers of the duchy. When Edward and Alfred grew to maturity, we find them attesting charters in Normandy, again a sign that they were treated as prominent men in the duchy.

The *Encomium* says that Cnut's marriage with Emma was an arrangement that was only finally entered into after a great deal of searching around, though this is not wholly convincing. Emma is described as 'a lady of the greatest nobility of wealth, but yet the most distinguished of the women of her time for delightful beauty and wisdom, inasmuch as she was a famous queen'. The allusion to her regal status is just about the only hint that she had previously been married; it is otherwise as if Æthelred, her first husband, has been airbrushed from history.

This marriage was complicated, not least because of Cnut's existing relationship with Ælfgifu of Northampton. There were already offspring from the first 'marriage' but in the book later inspired by Emma, the *Encomium Emmae Reginae*, it was said that the children from this second marriage should take precedence over those from the first. Cnut's first wife Ælfgifu was dismissively described as 'some other woman'.[24] This was a situation that would come back to haunt England when Cnut eventually died and also one that echoed a very similar set of circumstances concerning the late King Æthelred's second marriage to Emma when his heirs from his first marriage were displaced. In any event it is likely that either the Duke of Normandy or Emma, or indeed both, were capable of driving a very high price in such circumstances.

There is an interesting counter-story to explain away the marriage of Cnut and Emma. In this version, first told by the near-contemporary Thietmar of Merseburg, Emma was in London with her husband Æthelred when he died. She was subsequently trapped there by the Danish army. She agreed to surrender herself and London's military equipment along with a great ransom in return for her life. This account appears to be wrong in some of its details but that does not mean that there was not a process of negotiation involving Emma first-hand.[25] In this version Cnut later put pressure on the captive Emma to accept him as a husband.

The match was duly made and Emma once more became queen just over a year after flying from the country and it was not long before a son called Harthacnut was born. The father of Gorm the Old, regarded as the founder of Denmark, was also known by this name. The root of the name was the Scandinavian *harde* meaning swift or strong, perhaps hinting at the qualities for which his parents wished him to become known.

Normandy offered great advantages to Cnut if he could only forge an alliance with the duchy. His marriage to Emma was in this respect undoubtedly a vital step forward but it was not the only one. He also at some later stage arranged for his sister Estrith to be married to Robert I, son of Duke Richard II. Yet this was easier said than done. The marriage between the two did not last for long and indeed there was some doubt about whether or not it ever took place at all.

Emma would prove herself to be a formidable partner for Cnut. The nature of her personal relationships with him must be speculative though the *Encomium* suggests they were on very good terms and came to take pleasure in each other's company even though she was probably some years older than him. But she was also a shrewd political operator. Soon after she became Cnut's queen, she persuaded him to hand a small piece of land that Archbishop Lyfing sought over to him. It cost the king little but it helped strengthen his relationships with an important cleric.

With these domestic arrangements in place, Cnut now set himself to the task of maximising the benefits available from his new country. The greatest of them was to be found in the form of tax revenues and in 1018 he raised the princely sum of £10,500 from London and £72,000 from the rest of the country. This was an extraordinary level of taxation. It has been suggested that it equated to £1 for every hide taxable, which was the same amount as the total estimated income for each such unit, in other words a tax rate for that year of approaching 100 per cent. Cnut had a large army to pay off and he clearly had to resort to withering rates of taxation to do so.[26]

Whatever else might be said of Cnut's reign, these were harrowing days for the English. This was the greatest amount of Danegeld yet and to compound matters this time it was not being paid to the Danes to encourage them all to go away. In addition to these vast sums there had been heavy payments extracted by Æthelred in his vain attempts to resist Danish incursions. England was rich but she was not a bottomless pit. Later writers might extol Cnut's virtues as a Christian ruler but it was doubtful that many of his newly acquired subjects would be quite so enthusiastic about him on occasions such as this.

Nevertheless, there is evidence that from early on Cnut appreciated that the relationship between a king and his subjects had to be two-way if it was to thrive or even merely survive. The example of the late Æthelred's reign was still powerfully in the mind and an example of what could go wrong when the relationship had broken down. A king could not rely on his position alone to function effectively; he also had to give something back to his people.

So in 1018 we find that the *Anglo-Saxon Chronicles* say that when the treaty between the English and the Danes was made which brought the war to a final conclusion, the representatives of the former for their part undertook to 'always honour one God and single-mindedly hold one Christian faith, and love king Cnut with due loyalty, and zealously observe the laws of Edgar'. But that is only one side of the story. Two years later we find Cnut writing to his people and announcing that 'to you I will be a loyal lord'. Loyalty in other words was required from both parties to the agreement. The implication, though unstated, was that either party could repudiate the contract between king and people if the required loyalty was not forthcoming, even though practically enforcing a change to the status quo would of course be quite another matter.

Although reference to these mutual relationships between king and people might seem conventional to modern eyes, research suggests that it was rarely referred to in Anglo-Saxon times. Only on six occasions can reference to the concept of the king as a 'loyal lord' be found in surviving prose from the period. Perhaps most significantly the first of them is during the reign of that paragon of contemporary English kingship, Edgar. Three other references are to be found in three different versions of the *Anglo-Saxon Chronicles* relating to the return of Æthelred from exile. This particular reference in Cnut's letter, another of the six occasions discussed, should therefore be seen as very significant and deliberate.[27]

It is likely that the raiding force which accompanied Cnut and helped him win England, although substantially Danish in composition, also included men from elsewhere in Scandinavia. Runic inscriptions from across the region give evidence of widespread involvement in Cnut's raids on England, though in exactly which year is not at all clear. As well as inscriptions in Denmark (though perhaps surprisingly not as many as might be thought), others from Sweden refer specifically to Cnut or more generally to men who had 'killed in England'. An inscription in Norway refers to one Bjor, 'who was killed in the lith when Cnut attacked England'.[28]

Certainly this was a cosmopolitan force and even a number of the Danes would not necessarily feel absolute loyalty to Cnut or would at least wish to return home with the profits of war. Many of the raiding party who had conquered England now returned to Scandinavia, leaving just forty ships with Cnut, a sign that England was now considered to be subdued enough to be thought of as safely secured. Cnut had matters of kingship to attend to: what later times would call a parliament was assembled at Oxford and Danes and English agreed together to adopt the laws of the great English king Edgar.

This was a statesmanlike move by Cnut that strengthened his position with the people of England. It allowed them to keep laws with which they were familiar rather than have foreign law imposed upon them. The law of Edgar was to be the benchmark to be used in defining the legal code to be adopted in the country even though it was now effectively under Danish control. Not only was this something that would be welcomed by many of Cnut's English subjects, it also was a reference back to what now seemed a 'Golden Age' before the alleged tyrannies of the late King Æthelred. Cnut was making a pointed statement that he was offering stability whereas before there had for so long only been chaos. Edgar seemed to be a very good act to follow. In contrast, laws passed in Æthelred's reign – and given its longevity there were many of them – were overlooked.

This meeting effectively marked the final end to the war in England and the completion of the Danish conquest. The results of the discussions certainly have the feel of peace terms about them and the extraordinary amounts of money raised from taxation in the same year marked the very heavy price of such a situation as far as the English people were concerned. Although Cnut demonstrated statesmanship in his dealings, they also evidenced an unequivocal desire to maximise to the full his profit from the wealth of the newly conquered country.

It is also likely, given his inexperience, that the king was being guided in part by Englishmen of standing who knew the country, some of whom probably wished to see it reformed. These were in particular the churchmen such as Lyfing of Canterbury and Wulfstan of York who had served the old regime loyally enough but must have been driven to despair at some of its traumas; we know this to be the case with Wulfstan in particular. Now they had the chance to reshape the country and for the moment the young Cnut was happy enough to go along with them although he clearly had no intention of just being a pliable puppet. He had demanded a heavy price in return.

Cnut had inherited a strong administrative structure in England and this was crucial to his effective government. Ironically, the English now had cause to curse such efficiency as it meant that it was possible to use this powerful tool to ruthlessly extract huge sums of money from the country. The singling out of London for special treatment probably evidences several things: firstly, the wealth of the city meant they were able to pay up a large sum of money, and secondly, they may well have been being punished for their persistent and stubborn resistance against Cnut. It is interesting too that Cnut's main urban efforts in England during his reign were focused in particular on Winchester in what might be seen as an attempt to reinforce the city as the capital of England as opposed to London.

The association with Winchester also linked Cnut to a prominent Saxon saint, Swithun. Most famous now for his weather-forecasting abilities (if it rains on St Swithun's Day there will, according to the legend, be rain for the next forty days and vice-versa) Swithun was in fact Bishop of Winchester in the mid-ninth century, parlous times for Wessex. He was also tutor for a time to Alfred the Great and was extremely energetic in his efforts to drive back the Danish raiders of the time. After his death, his tomb became a place of pilgrimage frequented by thousands every year. Association with a saintly Saxon like Swithun would bring Cnut a good deal of kudos with his subjects and for this reason too Winchester was attractive to the king.

Cnut was careful not to alienate his new kingdom by other actions that were too extreme even though these were heavy levels of taxation. The widespread dispossession of land from English landowners that followed the Norman Conquest half a century later did not occur to the same extent when Cnut conquered England. That there was some degree of dispossession goes without saying and there are some Scandinavian names frequently appearing in records of the time that give hints of who specifically was benefitting, one such name being that of Osgot, who appears on charters of the day.

But the king could not afford to be over-provocative to his new-found subjects and indeed it has been plausibly speculated based on the surviving charters from the time (the list of which unfortunately does not appear to be very complete) that, after becoming king, Cnut may have spent some time travelling around the south-west of England in an attempt to further solidify the strength of his rule in the crucial heartlands of Wessex.[29] Travel was an essential part of a king's role. He would not typically stay in one place for too long but would journey with his court around his lands. Here he would dispense justice and would in the process be seen by his subjects. He would cross-examine the local lords and ensure that they were acting in his interests. It was important that he was seen from time to time by his subjects.

The *Encomium* writer, unsurprisingly given its subject, loads Emma with the credit for much of Cnut's demonstrations of statesmanship. It sees the union of Emma and Cnut as the crowning glory of his reign, a move that brought stability and peace to England. It also created a foundation on which Cnut could build, helping to unite the English and the Danes and thereby building a strength and unity that would serve as a launch-pad for further success, both in England and beyond.

The years between 1016 and 1018 were seminal in the reign of Cnut. Despite his apparent triumph in 1016, this was not an overnight conquest but one that really came about in stages. The decisive military moment was in 1016, a victory that was sealed by the death or removal of Edmund Ironside. 1017 was a year when decisive political measures were taken and, wherever needed, accommodation reached whilst at the same time troublesome elements of the old regime were eliminated. 1018 was the year in which everything finally settled down and Cnut began to feel secure in his role of King of England.

The meeting in Oxford can perhaps be regarded as the moment at which Cnut's reign truly began in a symbolic sense. With the untrustworthy Eadric Streona disposed of and the support (or at least neutrality) of Normandy secured, at least for the time being, the prospects for stability were good. Cnut had also dealt with the problem of paying off those Viking raiders who could not be relied upon even if they were Danish. Now he had the conditions in place to enable him with confidence to put his own stamp on the affairs of England. Despite his relative inexperience, this was the young king seizing control of the situation and laying the foundations for a strong and successful reign.

Not that he was yet completely untroubled in England. He was forced to rely still on the slippery Thorkell the Tall in East Anglia and also depended, probably with much more confidence, on Erik in Northumbria. Of the four leading men in Mercia at this time, three were also of Scandinavian descent, only Leofwine, father of the executed Northman, being of English blood and presumably feeling rather vulnerable. Only in Wessex were Englishmen still at the helm. Cnut would return to this problem later.

Cnut's accession as king also leads to a new form of documentary evidence emerging about him. Much of what we know of Cnut's life comes from chroniclers or saga writers, both groups writing after the event, sometimes centuries later, and neither noted for their quest for accuracy. But now that Cnut was king, charters were produced bearing his name. There are not a huge number of them, about thirty-five in total surviving, but they give an insight into whom the king was giving patronage and give a strong steer as to who were the most important figures in the country.

These charters are grants of land and they range in date from 1018 to 1035, right across the king's effective reign. It is noteworthy that there are no such grants surviving relating to Cnut before 1018, lending further credence to the fact that this was the year when his rule began in practical terms and that in the preceding period he was still finding his feet as king. The grants are either to secular individuals or ecclesiastical figures or establishments. Although not huge in terms of their number, they cover many parts of England. There are grants of land in Sussex, Cambridgeshire, Norfolk, Somerset, Warwickshire, Yorkshire, Kent and Northamptonshire. There are several grants made in each of Dorset, Hampshire and Devon.

There are other charters extant which are now believed to be forgeries; it is not hard to understand why there should be a motivation to forge grants of land, especially after the Norman Conquest and the Domesday Book exercise to see who formally owned what. What is almost as interesting as the grants themselves is which earls attested the charters as this provides evidence of who was in the king's good graces. The positioning of the earls on the list of attestations is also potentially significant as, given the strictly hierarchical world in which they lived, this was an additional indicator of their importance.

Analysis of these charters almost reads like a headline summary of Cnut's reign. Between 1018 and 1019 Thorkell appears at the top of the list on every extant diploma. He then disappears from the list (though no other surviving charter occurs until 1022, by which time Thorkell had been exiled from England). His place is then taken by Earl Erik, who appears at the top of the list in 1022 on three occasions and is also included in most but not all charters surviving from 1018 and 1019.

It is very unlikely that the surviving charters are a complete list and it is rather highly probable that a fair number of key documents have been lost. Some might hopefully turn up in a dusty archive somewhere or other one day but many are likely gone forever, lost or destroyed for example in the Dissolution of the Monasteries centuries later. That said, the list gives an insight into several key features of English government at the time.

There is one name from the surviving charters that stands out above all others. This man appears on all charters between 1018 and 1035 except for one issued at Christ Church, Canterbury, in 1018. He is top of the list in every single surviving charter (eighteen in total) adopted between 1023 and 1035 for which records have been discovered. It is not too much of a stretch to assume therefore that he was probably the most important secular power in the country after the king. There is something of a surprise in his name, for it is assuredly Anglo-Saxon rather than Danish. He was Godwin, Earl of Wessex.

By 1018 Godwin was an earl with his heartlands to be found in Sussex. He was probably the son of that Wulfnoth whose ships had broken away from the fleet of Æthelred in 1009 and caused the king such trouble and, one would imagine, not a little angst. This always made it likely that he would be opposed to Eadric Streona. He was also on good terms with the late Ætheling Æthelstan who appears to have been at odds with his father King Æthelred in the latter years of his life so he may have naturally gravitated to the Danish dynasty that had replaced the House of Cerdic.

It was suggested by some later medieval chroniclers that Godwin came from a humble line of descent but this is highly doubtful.

To achieve the prominence that he did, it is probable that he came from important stock. In fact, some leading historians argue that he was descended from the royal bloodline. They trace his ancestry back to Æthelwulf, King of the West Saxons from 839 to 858. Æthelwulf was the father of no less a man than Alfred the Great, though the Godwin bloodline is believed to have come from Alfred's elder brother, Æthelred I.[30]

The charters are a fertile source of information on the period. These land grants tell us much about who was important, how much wealth the king had at his disposal and even how a monarch wished to be regarded. A good example from the tenth century comes from the reign of King Æthelstan, who presented himself in his charters as *basileus*, the Byzantine term for Emperor, which tells strikingly of how he wished to be seen.[31]

They also give us a glimpse of Cnut's approach to government. On a number of them, the Scandinavian name Thored appears; there were possibly two different men involved, neither of whom had appeared on the witness lists before Cnut's time. It has been suggested that one of them held lands in Surrey and Kent whilst the other did so in the south-west in Wiltshire.[32] Another Scandinavian name that appears is that of Halfdan, along with those of Aslac and Hákon but they only appear comparatively rarely.

Historians who have painstakingly examined the records have concluded that although there was a relatively small number of English 'ministers' who survived from the reign of Æthelred into that of Cnut, they were nevertheless quite significant in their roles.[33] One of them, Ælfgar Maew, had fought on the side of the Danes at Sherston, held lands in Dorset at Cranborne, Wimborne and Dewlish and was connected to Tewkesbury Abbey as well as holding lands in Devon. Another, Ordgar, was the grandson of a man of the same name who was no less a person than the father of the late Queen Elfrida, and there was also a Saxon called Odda seemingly involved.

All of these men came from Wessex, which may suggest that historians who argue that Cnut had support during his battle for England from some men in this region are not too far off the mark. It is also notable that the families of both Ordgar and Odda had suffered at the hands of Eadric Streona's machinations in the last years of Æthelred's reign. Now it was payback time. They all appear to have prospered under Cnut. They acquired large estates and the influence of their descendants lasted on into the 1050s and possibly even beyond.

An overview of the remaining records of the time leads to some potentially surprising revelations. One historian has concluded that 'the large number of Englishmen in Cnut's court is evident and somewhat startling' though they were far from dominating affairs and many Scandinavian names are noticeable too.[34] So, some important Englishmen found a way of reconciling their consciences to working with the new regime. It was perhaps not that difficult to do. King Æthelred was dead, as was his son Edmund Ironside. Before his death Edmund had agreed to the division of England with Cnut. Edmund's children were infants, in those days especially a practical bar to them assuming the kingship. In such circumstances the cooperation of Englishmen with Cnut was pragmatic.

It would be wrong to talk of these men as 'collaborators'. England in 1018 was still very young as a newly united realm and it was an age when the strength and effectiveness of the candidate was the decisive factor in deciding who to support as king. In other words, this was not Vichy France in 1940, a perception well supported by the fact that when the ruling Danish dynasty in England eventually faded out a quarter of a century later, there was little tangible immediate sign of any attempt to seek revenge on the administrators and advisers who had supported them whilst they ruled.

Some of the surviving charters take us back to a world now largely lost to us. Whilst Christ Church Canterbury and Winchester Cathedral (on the site of the Old Minster) resonate still, other names are now only known locally and their histories even less so. Little remains of St Peter's Abbey in Abbotsbury, Dorset, for example, except for an imposing later medieval tithe barn, and virtually nothing of the abbey at Horton in the same county, yet both were beneficiaries of Cnut's largesse or were in some way or other affected by it.

In the east of the country, St Benet Holme in Norfolk had, according to legend, a very direct connection to the Danes through the killing of a Christian hermit named Suneman by Viking raiders in the ninth century. The abbey had been rebuilt by a benefactor named Wulfric and it subsequently benefitted from Cnut's support when he confirmed the lands they held at Horning, Ludham and Neatishead. The abbey subsequently enjoyed considerable success, so much so that a simple church there of humble construction was rebuilt in stone. Cnut's beneficence to a site associated rather more negatively with Viking raiders in the past can hardly be fortuitous; neither, one suspects, can his grant in around 1032 (exact date unclear) to Athelney Abbey, a place so closely associated in Wessex history with Alfred the Great it is as if he is trying to right the wrongs of history.[35]

Cnut now had enough stability in England to rule with some confidence there. Although there were inevitably some underlying tensions to resolve there, his position had been largely secured. However, he also had connections with lands further afield that were at the moment not in his possession. Denmark was still a coveted target, though currently under the rule of his brother Harald, and the Norwegians had reclaimed control of their own affairs. It was very much a case of so far, so good in England but of a great deal of unfinished business elsewhere.

6

King of Denmark: The Years of Consolidation (1018–1027)

The early history of the country that is now Denmark is somewhat obscure. It is not until the middle of the tenth century that a line of kings emerged there on a permanent basis, starting with Gorm the Old who was succeeded by his son, Harald Bluetooth. The influence of this kingdom extended beyond the limits of modern Denmark and it is probable that parts of both Norway and Sweden were included in the territories ruled by the dynasty at various times. Harald and his kingdom were nominally converted to Christianity by a papal missionary named Poppo who allegedly proved his worth, and that of his God, by carrying a bar of hot iron without suffering personal injury as a result.

To the south, Denmark fringed onto Germany, then a part of the Holy Roman Empire, and for a time Harald may have recognised the authority of the Emperor Otto I over him. The River Eider acted as a natural border between Saxons to the south and Danes to the north, eventually flowing out into the North Sea or, as Adam of Bremen called it, the Frisian Sea. But at one stage Harald rebelled against the Germans but was defeated. The Emperor's men then built a defensive fortress on the borders with Denmark but this was burnt to the ground in an uprising in 983. Seeking out alliances, Harald had married a daughter of a Slavic king from the tribes that hugged the coast of the Baltic to the east. Harald later fell out with his son Sweyn (Forkbeard) and fled for sanctuary amongst the Slavs and was with them when he died.[1]

As we have seen, Denmark was in the hands of King Harald II when Cnut had returned there after fleeing from England in 1013 and the two men possibly entered into some kind of joint kingship, a not unusual state of affairs in the Scandinavian world. Then, in around 1018, Harald (whose reign is generally a shadowy one, with very little detail surviving) died, leaving Denmark to Cnut, who was now beginning to enjoy some stability in England. There are surviving hints though that Cnut still had problems in dealing with Viking raiders in England even after he became king. The near-contemporary writer Thietmar of Merseburg told of the king's forces killing the crew of thirty ships who had attacked England in 1018.

Denmark was an important country in its own right. It was a relatively fertile part of Scandinavia but even more useful than that was its geographical situation. In its position astride the entry and exit to and from the Baltic, it almost served as a gatehouse to the region. This allowed whoever owned Denmark to control sea traffic and profit from trade. It also meant that Danish kings were able to secure footholds on the south-western coastline of Sweden, opposite the modern state of Denmark across the very narrow Øresund which a modern ferry crosses in about fifteen minutes. They also often held territory around Oslo Fjord in what is now Norway, from where they could benefit from the iron ore that was obtained from Telemark.

Trading had been key to Scandinavia for many centuries and a shortage of sufficient minerals locally made what iron ore extraction was possible vitally important. This was not just a warrior society; far from it. Even back in the Bronze Age (which lasted here for far longer than elsewhere in Europe) imports of tin and copper, which are difficult to find in Scandinavia, were necessary. In return items like walrus ivory, furs, honey, wood, flax and especially amber, for which the Baltic region is famous, were supplied. There was also a significant trade in slaves, which would give Viking raiders a substantial mercantile incentive to go 'a-viking'. In the case of slaving and raiding there is a natural connection between aggressive attacks and mercantile profit. Many of the markets for these products were in the Near East and the Mediterranean using trade routes across eastern Europe whilst other important trading outlets stretched down the Atlantic seaboard and into Islamic Spain in the west.

When the Vikings raided Britain and Francia, they were not only attacking countries; at first they were even attacking trade routes and trading centres in areas which had enjoyed economic growth in the eighth and ninth centuries, helped by strong rulers like Charlemagne in France and Offa in England. There were improvements in coinage in these countries too during these years, giving fairly standardised units of currency to trade in. Other peoples such as the Frisians had pioneered West European maritime trade and the routes they used were well known. Many of them spread across the Continent via river systems that led down to the Mediterranean. The Vikings were involved in this trade, in particular through the port of Hedeby in Denmark.

Adam of Bremen noted that Denmark was a country composed in part of a number of islands; there are in fact nearly 500 named islands with over seventy inhabited in modern times. But the main geographical bulk of the country, the mainland portion of Denmark, is Jutland. Adam describes Jutland as a region that was largely sterile, a vast wilderness and a salt land which looked like a desert except for places close to rivers. He called it a place where 'the land is avoided because of the scarcity of crops, and the sea because it is invested by pirates. Hardly a cultivated spot is to be found anywhere, scarcely a place fit for human habitation.'[2]

One of the islands, to the west, was Helgoland (now commonly called Heligoland). It was described as being eight miles long and four miles wide and home to an old monastery, its location being perfect for any monks who belonged to that type which valued solitude above other attributes. Adam goes on to say that the place had a fearsome reputation amongst the Vikings for every time that they looted it the perpetrators of such outrages would suffer some kind of divine retribution as a result. Consequently, they were in the habit of paying tribute to the monks there rather than pillaging the monastery. It was renowned as a home for birds and cattle and a place that was good for growing crops. It was, however, treeless and had just one prominent hill.

On the other side of Jutland, that is to the east, was the island of Fyn or Funen. The great city of the region by Adam's time was Odense. There were a number of smaller islands around it, many of them very fertile. Then came the island of Zealand, probably the first home of the people we call the Danes. Fyn was separated from Zealand by seas that could be dangerous both because of the weather and also because of the constant threat of pirates.

Zealand was very important. To the west lay Jutland and the cities of Århus and Aalborg, to the north the Norwegian Strait, to the south Fyn and to the east Scania (or Skåne), the southernmost part of Sweden. Adam describes Zealand as being a place where much gold was to be found due to the presence of many 'pirates'. He says that the people here paid tribute to the King of Denmark, who in return allowed them to plunder at will the unfortunate inhabitants who bordered the Baltic.

He suggests that they abused this privilege to also pillage each other. They even, he alleges, sold their compatriots (including women) from Zealand into slavery. They were a tough breed. Men who were caught committing a crime against their king would rather be beheaded than flogged. It was considered glorious for a man who had been so sentenced to accept his fate joyfully. On Zealand was Roskilde, the contemporary seat of Danish royalty, where Harald Bluetooth had set up a new powerbase in place of Jelling.[3] The new town was the capital of the kingdom. It sat at the base of Roskilde Fjord, a narrow finger of water surrounded by land where a watch could be kept against an approaching enemy (though it was seemingly unprotected by walls). At the time, Zealand was undoubtedly the heartbeat of Danish affairs.

We have some evidence of what these 'Vikings' look like. A remarkable Arab traveller, Ibn Fadlān, journeyed to the steppes of Russia in the tenth century and wrote an astonishing account of his adventures later. Here he met some Vikings, probably Swedish in origin. He wrote of them as magnificent physical specimens, heavily tattooed, and inseparable from their axes, swords and knives. Some of their womenfolk had travelled with them too.

He also told of their disgusting habits, including sharing a bowl of water to wash in, into which they spat and cleared their noses. They also thought nothing of having sex with their slave girls in full view of others. Most remarkably of all, he describes a great Viking ship funeral during which rites of human sacrifice took place delivered by a terrifying old woman known as the 'Angel of Death': dogs, horses, cattle, poultry were all slaughtered in honour of the dead man too. Of course, we would assume that by Cnut's time the Christianised Danes would have abandoned such sacrifices but this is again a useful reminder of just how different the near-contemporary age was compared to our own.[4]

During the early years of Cnut's reign there seem to have been marked changes in the location of the urban centres in Denmark. The towns that had been thriving in the country earlier, namely Århus, Hedeby and Ribe, seem to have gone into steep decline and in some cases were quite possibly completely abandoned. Instead new centres were developing, such as Roskilde and also Viborg in Jutland. There have been some remarkable archaeological finds at the latter. Favourable environmental conditions for the preservation of wood mean that the construction of certain buildings can be dated by dendrochronology virtually to the year. Evidence has been gleaned which dates the building of some parts of the town to 1020, exactly when Cnut is known to have been in the country.

Further evidence shows the addition of other buildings as the 1020s progressed. In perhaps one of the most revealing finds of all, pottery in an English style was found. What is so remarkable about this is that it was made of local clay, suggesting the presence of Englishmen and women in Viborg making pottery in the style with which they were familiar but using materials that were close to hand.

In other words, these items are not imports but were made by English settlers or slaves – the Vikings were not great potters and instead many household implements were made from a soft rock called soapstone. There is other evidence of Anglo-Saxons in the country at the time, particularly in the form of moneyers, of whom a number with English names are known (there are quite a few with German names too). This is strong evidence that Cnut was importing foreign skills into Denmark as a way of developing the country.[5]

Viborg was in a prime location. It was close to the Limfjord, a waterway which back in the Viking Age stretched from the North Sea to the Kattegat. The Limfjord was superb from a maritime perspective; it meant that shipping could avoid the terrors of sailing through the Kattegat and Skagerrak, which were notorious for their dangers. In later times the early thirteenth-century Danish historian Saxo Grammaticus noted that the Limfjord silted up, which must have been a damaging blow to the Danish economy. The North Sea broke through and reopened it again in the nineteenth century.

In the north of mainland Denmark Cnut seems to have adopted similar policies to those that he used in England. Long-established local landowning dynasties were allowed to stay in possession, Cnut presumably reasoning that it would be too difficult to move them. Neither did the old religions die out as quickly as the Church would like and for many years pagan and Christian customs existed side by side. So contemporary Christian burials co-existed with horse-burials, as old a pagan custom as there was.

In Hørning, in the north of Denmark, a Christian church was built as late as 1070 over a pagan burial mound. What was most remarkable about its siting was that the doorway to the church was built exactly over the grave of the woman interred in the mound so that Christian worshipers would have to step over her body to enter. This, as has been pointed out, is very unlikely to be a coincidence and may have been a deliberate move on the part of her descendants, family bloodlines being so critical in Scandinavia.[6]

Roskilde too benefitted from a number of building projects at around this time. Several stone churches had been excavated and date to the period; in one a coin hoard including items dated to 1029 have been found, perfectly timed for Cnut's reign.[7] These were found at the fine church of St Clements (or St Jørgensbjerg), rebuilt in about 1080. There are signs of English craftsmen being involved in its construction. Excavation at another church in the area at St Ibs uncovered a coin from the reign of Æthelred II and another from the reign of Cnut.

Denmark then was different than Denmark now. Skåne was also part of it and would be so for many centuries in the future. It was considered as the fairest of all, 'well provided with men, opulent of crops, rich in merchandise, and now full of churches'. It was twice as large as Zealand and had twice as many churches. It was a land of densely wooded highlands and rolling hills. During Cnut's time the town of Lund also became important. The urbanisation of the region, small scale though it was, helped to build a focal point of control. Viborg, Roskilde and Lund each represented the different points of a triangle delineating an area where Cnut and his officials could take measures to retain control in what was still a relatively new nation.

The fertile nature of Skåne meant that it was very well populated. Its magnificent position, dominating the narrow entrance to and exit from the Baltic, added to its attraction and its wealth. But it was a long way from Cnut's centre of power – especially when he was in England – and not that long before it had been a separate petty kingdom. Its aristocracy was stubbornly independent-minded; Thorkell the Tall had been one of its leading figures. It would be a troublesome region during Cnut's reign.

Cnut's dynasty originated in Jutland so their hold over other parts of Denmark was not necessarily securely established yet. Cnut would have seen urbanisation in England and realised what an important part it played in the administration of the country. He would have seen close at hand what towns like Winchester and London could do, not just in encouraging trade and spurring on wealth creation but also in government. It was something he would certainly have liked to replicate in his Scandinavian lands.

There has been some convincing archaeological evidence found of the growth of Lund in Skåne at around this time. Excavations at a cemetery there show a large number of bodies from the period between 994 and 1048 with a particular peak in the 1020s and 1030s, in other words the time of Cnut's reign. Adam of Bremen stated unequivocally that the aim was to make Lund a rival of London (and the Anglo-Saxon name for London was Lundenburh, which is remarkably similar). There were many mints, a number apparently run by Englishmen with names like Godwin, Ælfwine and Leofwine. There is also evidence of stone churches appearing in Lund at around this time, again a sign of wealth and development.

On the other hand, a nearby settlement called Uppåkra, which had been important in the time of the petty kings who had previously ruled Skåne, from whose bloodline Thorkell the Tall came, appears to have gone into steep decline. There seems to have been little attempt on Cnut's part to assimilate with local nobles once the experiment with Thorkell eventually failed. Lund was an assuredly royal town, and as such it took the place of settlements associated with the old regime, an example as one historian has said of Cnut 'riding roughshod' over the local elite. Other new settlements may also have appeared at around this time, such as Helsingborg, as Cnut sought to put his stamp on Skåne.[8] In contrast to his approach in many other parts of his empire, the policy in Skåne seems to have been one of ruthless suppression of the families who had previously been in control of the region.

But beyond Skåne, most of Sweden was well clear of Danish rule and was inhabited by peoples known as the Goths and the Svear.

The island of Gotland however, on which stood the important city of Visby, was part of Danish territory according to Adam of Bremen though it changed hands with the Swedes with bewildering frequency. It certainly gives strong evidence of being a centre for Viking raiders: no less than 50,000 Anglo-Saxon coins have been recovered there.[9] These were frontier lands, always hard to control by any government. The majority of Sweden as we know it stayed stubbornly out of Cnut's reach throughout his reign. That said, it is important to note that much of both Sweden and Norway was not inhabited by what we might Vikings at the time, with the wild north and remote centre either uninhabited or peopled by nomadic peoples such as the Saami (traditionally known as the Lapps).

The whole Baltic region came late to Christianity and indeed the Wends on its southern shores remained pagan long after most other European peoples had adopted Christianity. Even Denmark was relatively new to the religion and Cnut would strive to be an archetypal Christian monarch. It was a tough job and the later eleventh-century writer Adam of Bremen would still call the Baltic 'the Barbarian Sea'.[10] Its waters were volatile. Sudden squalls, mists and storms could blow up with little warning and in the winter the seas could be covered in ice. But on the other hand it was rich in fish, especially herring, and it allowed traffic to travel, taking the place of roads further south in Europe.

Adam's knowledge of geography is patchy. He describes both Courland and Estland as islands although they are in fact in modern Latvia and Estonia respectively and therefore part of mainland Europe. He describes how both regions clung with tenacity to paganism. In Courland he says that the people were devoted to idolatry. The houses were filled with pagan soothsayers, diviners and necromancers. The oracles there were sought out by people from as far away as Spain and Greece. In Estland, dragons and birds were 'adored' by the inhabitants, who sacrificed human beings to these honoured creatures. But such offerings had to be perfect otherwise they would be rejected.[11]

The priest-chronicler also makes a fascinating reference to the fabled 'island of women' close by Estland. Here the mythical Amazons lived. This is a contrast to classical references who place them around the shores of the Black Sea around Scythia far to the south-east. They were a ferocious breed who became pregnant through various means as diverse as sipping water, holding male concubines for the purpose or breeding with monsters. Such fantastical tales speak eloquently of how unknown the world outside Christian Europe still was. Little less noteworthy were the Alani, who were apparently born with grey hair and who trained dogs to fight in battle for them. This was a remarkable conglomeration of peoples.

The Swedes were regarded as living in a country that was fertile, rich in fruits, honey and cattle. They took little pride according to Adam in material treasures but were instead inspired by sexual prowess. It was nothing for a man to have three wives, and rich men and rulers sometimes had many more. However, any sexual crime was punishable by death. They were very hospitable to guests but were also tremendous warriors.

This strange region, inhabited not only by Amazons but also Cyclopes with one eye, was Cnut's next centre of attention. With England now effectively his, Cnut then sought to protect his position in Denmark. In 1019 he made the crossing across the North Sea back to the country of his birth along with a small fleet of nine ships and over-wintered in the country; the small number of ships suggest that he felt confident in the base of his support there by now. At some time during his reign he attended a council at which Archbishop Unwan of Hamburg-Bremen held negotiations with representatives of the Slavs and this may well have been during this visit. Given the amount of time that he needed to spend in England, Cnut had to ensure that his comparatively brief visits back to Scandinavia were as productive as possible.

This visit to Denmark was the first made by Cnut since the conquest of England and the reason seems clear enough even if details are sparse. Evidently Harald, his elder brother, had died and as a result Cnut had assumed the title of King of Denmark as well as England. There are, however, a few scattered references that suggest that raiding on England from Scandinavia had continued on a smaller scale since Cnut's accession as the allusion already made to killing raiders in 1018 suggests. A letter in the archives at York mentions some unspecified dangers that were troubling England and in it Cnut wrote that 'then I was informed that greater danger was approaching us than we liked at all; and then I went myself with the men who accompanied me to Denmark, from where the greatest injury had come to you, and with God's help I have taken measures so that never henceforth shall hostility reach you from there as long as you support me rightly and my life lasts'.[12]

This is a strongly suggestive quote. It suggests first of all that there was still danger from the direction of Denmark and that Cnut had been forced to go to Denmark and nip trouble in the bud, though as he only took nine ships with him it cannot have been that great a threat that faced him. It hints that Cnut's position in Denmark was not yet fully secure and also acts as a useful reminder that the Viking earls and war-bands were hard to keep in check, even by a king. It is not surprising given recent Scandinavian history that even Denmark was not yet fully under centralised control.

Cnut's own words to the English, enjoining them to continue to support him so that he in turn could provide them with protection, may also suggest that he was not yet fully confident of his position in England and needed to prove himself to his new subjects. Noticeably Thorkell had remained in England and appeared to be the leading secular man in the country at the time now that the king was in Denmark. It suggests that Cnut was either confident enough to leave Thorkell in England whilst he was away or alternatively was not strong enough to force him to come with him.

What measures could Cnut take to strengthen his position in Denmark when he knew that he was unlikely to be spending much time there given the demands on it from the direction of England? Military measures alone are unlikely to have been sufficient. The Vikings were well able to escape temporarily from the clutches of a strong centralised monarchy if they so wished. Their ships would facilitate their getaway and there were plenty of other opportunities open to them outside of Denmark such as service in Russia or even with the fabled Varangian Guard in Constantinople. The latter, known as 'Miklagard' (literally 'the great city'), exerted a magnetic fascination for many Vikings given its great wealth and size, being at least ten times as large as any place in western Europe.

Miklagard became a place of almost fabled wealth and glory for them. It is not hard to see why. The enormous walls that embraced the city in their protective grip had kept all would-be invaders at bay for centuries. At its centre was the awe-inspiring edifice of the

Church of Hagia Sofia, one of the most magnificent buildings in the world at the time (and indeed it remains so). Its scale was, without a hint of hyperbole especially in the context of those times, vast. A princess from the then pagan city of Kiev, Olga, paid one visit to it in the mid-tenth century and decided there and then that if the Christian God could inspire such devotion then it was about time that her country adopted Christianity too. Given the comparatively tiny nature of settlements and the humble churches of the north of Europe at the time, where wooden 'stave' churches were the norm, these must indeed have seemed incredible, even other-worldly, sights to Viking and other visitors.

Yet whilst external links played a critical part in the Viking world, it was still Scandinavia that remained its heart. From this perspective, any military success on the part of Cnut against rebellious elements in Denmark was likely to be a temporary one. What was needed was a permanent powerful counterbalance against such groups that would be able to protect Cnut's interests whilst he was *in absentia*. There are some muted suggestions in surviving evidence, and they are no more than that, that Cnut's response was to cultivate strong relationships with the emerging Church in Denmark as a way of doing so.

Exactly what form these relationships took is the subject of much debate amongst scholars of Cnut's life. Too much can be read into the very scanty evidence that exists, of course, and it is unlikely that resorting to the Church exclusively in the management of Denmark was an option. Instead, appropriate links with the still-young (and therefore not yet that strong) Danish Church were fostered alongside forging alliances with powerful secular lords, much as was Cnut's policy in England. A tempting titbit of supporting evidence is the building of a stone church at Roskilde (though it is believed that his sister Estrith founded it), which would become one of Denmark's most important establishments at around this time. The elevation of Roskilde to the status of a bishopric in 1020 also suggests that the town and its ecclesiastical authorities were becoming a core part of Cnut's strategy in the country.[13]

The need at the same time to strengthen his position in England might also explain one of his first acts when returning there after his visit to Denmark. In memory of the great triumph at Ashingdon, a minster was dedicated there in 1020. Cnut was accompanied by Earl Thorkell the Tall, in whose territory this was, and also Archbishop Wulfstan of York (Lyfing, the Archbishop of Canterbury, had died a few months before and would be replaced by Æthelnoth). A great many other bishops and monks were in attendance at the dedication of this sacred place, built to commemorate the Christian souls lost in the battle nearby, much as a great abbey was built at Battle to mark William of Normandy's triumph at Hastings half a century later.

The presence of Wulfstan is noteworthy as he was also prominent in Æthelred's time. Back then he had been a regular critic of the king and especially his officials for the many injustices he felt were committed in the ostensible name of the law. He wrote books on the subject and preached many a sermon on it too, most especially the famous diatribe known as the *Sermo Lupi ad Anglos*. But he was clearly also a survivor, even capable of impressing a Viking like Cnut. Now here he was, still the Archbishop of York as he had been in the time of Æthelred (whilst simultaneously being Bishop of Worcester until 1016[14]), standing at the side of the Danish conqueror. This flexibility of conscience from a man who was not a lay lord but a strident churchman gives a rather revealing insight into the paradigms of the times.

Wulfstan expressed his views on the role of churchmen in particular in terms that would make the modernising wing of the current Church of England wince. Their role was to preach justice and prevent injustice. They were required to speak out against anything they believed to be wrong: 'if bishops neglect to punish sins and forbid injustice, nor make known God's law, but mumble with their jaws when they ought to speak out, woe to them for that silence'.[15] It is unsurprising to learn that Wulfstan believed that the days of the Last Judgement were not far off and that there were, in his opinion, many signs of the Anti-Christ being active in the world. As time had gone on and the Danish hold on England grew ever stronger, he can only have seen more and more of these in evidence.

Wulfstan was a prominent figure in the reigns of both Æthelred and Cnut. He played a key part in drafting laws for both men and in so doing proved an important point. Separation of Church and state was not a consideration for clerics of the era. The tenth and eleventh centuries saw a battle for supremacy between the two bodies as to who should be the dominant force in secular society. The Papacy in particular sought to increase its power from a relatively low base and a great monastic revival in the tenth century, driven by the reformist monastery of Cluny, reshaped the landscape of Western Christendom considerably. In such an environment the Church could not only be a critical nuisance but also a very valuable ally, particularly given its great landholdings. It has been estimated that the Church at the time held land on an equivalent scale to the king and this brought it both great wealth and power – the two nearly always of course being closely connected.[16]

Cnut had also been on good terms with Lyfing, the Archbishop of Canterbury appointed in 1013 during the reign of Æthelred. Whereas there is scant information on any gifts made to the archbishop during that reign, Cnut made a number of grants for which records survive. These included not just monetary gifts or those of land but slightly more unusual ones such as the arm of St Bartholomew (though it is not certain that this token of favour came from Cnut, there is a distinct possibility that it did[17]). These good relations with both Wulfstan and Lyfing probably stemmed from pragmatism on Cnut's part. They held important positions and, if Cnut could manage to gain the loyalty of both of them, it would help to achieve stability in England and strengthen his position. The payback for this approach may be seen in the law codes developed by Wulfstan which specifically stated that the people of England should 'love King Cnut with due loyalty'.

Lyfing and Wulfstan were not young by the standards of the time; when Cnut became king they were both in their fifties. It was therefore unlikely that they would be around for too long and Cnut could then replace them with men whose appointments he could influence. As it happened Lyfing died in 1020 and Wulfstan in 1023 – not too long a wait.[18] But before his death Lyfing had journeyed to Rome and had returned with word from the Pope that the king should everywhere extol the praise of God, put away injustice, and promote full security and peace. Cnut undertook to do so.[19] He showed much generosity to the Church, even establishments such as Ely that had been associated with the old regime but continued to do well under Cnut (it was also the last resting place of Wulfstan). Although there is a danger that such actions can be taken out of context when we have little background information about why they were made, this at least suggests a young king who was nevertheless showing considerable judgment accompanied by a lack of vindictiveness.

But any such alliance came at a price. If a king wished to have the support of the clerisy, he would have to act to some extent in the way that they desired. This was inevitably a process of negotiation for no king of the time could afford to allow himself to be used as a doormat by the Church. But he could not be too truculent either without losing Church support and in such uncertain times this was to be avoided.

This worked both ways. Wulfstan appears to have become somewhat disillusioned with both Æthelred and Cnut, hence the slightly hectoring tone of some of his writings and preaching, but he must have managed to nevertheless avoid crossing a line where he became an over-active critic of the monarchy.[20] In around 1020 Cnut and his wife Emma may well have presented Wulfstan with the great book now known as the York Gospels as a sign of their affection, real or otherwise. Originally made at Canterbury, it was a precious work. Now, a thousand years later, clerics at York still take their sacred vows clasping the Gospels. It can still be seen at other times in the Undercroft at York Minister.

There were several legal texts issued by the king, given the rather dry labels by historians of I and II Cnut. But what they contained was sometimes far from dry. For example, II Cnut 54.1 forbids the king from keeping another woman in addition to his wife, a rather loaded statement given the fact that Cnut had taken Emma as his wife whilst Ælfgifu of Northampton was still alive. The laws, drawn up by Wulfstan, stated specifically that it was forbidden for a man 'to have more than one [wife], and this is to be his wedded wife as long as she lives – he who wishes to heed God's law aright and to protect his soul from hellfire'.[21] The law further stressed that any man who kept both a wife and a concubine was to be treated as an excommunicate. 'Foreigners' – including, one assumes, Danes – are told to leave the country if they did not regularise their marriages.

I Cnut (clause 2) stresses that the king should be 'a gracious lord', who 'would not fail to support the rights of the Church and just secular law', perhaps by way of contrasting Cnut with Æthelred.

Other rules emphasised the importance of Sunday as the Sabbath. Trading and hunting were specifically forbidden then. Any slave who was forced to work on that day would be declared a free man.

There was, though, a certain skewed approach noticeable in some of the laws. For example, a man was told that committing adultery was a serious offence but no punishment was designated for him if he acted in such a fashion. An adulteress was liable, however, to have her nose and ears cut off. On the other hand, no woman was to be forced to marry a man she did not like and a widow should not be forced into a nunnery too quickly, reflecting the fact that being a nun was a vocation and not a convenient convention. If a criminal committed a second offence, he was liable to lose his hands or his feet – or perhaps both.

There were other references to paganism in the laws. The practice of worshipping heathen gods, the sun or the moon, fire or flood, wells or stones or trees is specifically forbidden, suggesting that it was a problem in the country, one that might well have got far worse with many more Danes in England. Cnut adopted the laws one Christmas at Winchester though whether he meant to practically apply them in all cases to himself with two 'wives', Emma and Ælfgifu, still alive was it seems quite a different matter.[22]

Cnut issued a proclamation to the people of England in 1020, in what was effectively a manifesto for the rest of his reign. This came about as a result of Lyfing's audience with the Pope, we are told. This was around the time that he became King of Denmark and it is as if he had seen that he needed a clear strategy for kingship if he was to successfully rule both his lands. He stated, 'I will be a kind lord and loyal to the rights of the Church and to right secular law.' He commanded his ealdormen to protect the rights of the bishops as well as, of course, his own. He instructed his reeves to 'govern my people justly' and to work closely with the shire bishops.[23]

Nor were the responsibilities of the humbler folk of England forgotten. They were admonished to 'keep the Sunday festival with all their might and observe it from Saturday's noon to Monday's dawning'. No buying or selling was to take place at these times. All men, be they rich or poor, were to seek the Church's forgiveness for their sins and keep to every ordained fast, as well as being careful to honour the Saints, for they were truly the holders of the keys to the gates of heaven. If they did so, they might hope to one day 'share the joys of the heavenly kingdom and dwell with Him who liveth and reigneth forever without end'. It was all a long way from the pagan Viking sea-kings of old.

But Cnut still had some problems in England to contend with. It seemed as if he was surrounded by potential enemies, even amongst his own confidantes, as shown when Earl Thorkell was outlawed at Martinmas (11 November) in 1021. Thorkell was sent into exile from England and returned to Denmark, where he continued to be a powerful influence for some time. Although his ultimate end is uncertain there are suggestions that Cnut had him killed on a visit to Denmark in around 1023 and certainly he fades from the record at this time. Other accounts, though, suggest that the two men were reconciled back in Denmark.

At around this time too Erik of Lade disappears from view, according to Norse sources dying of blood loss following an operation.[24] The earl had apparently been planning a pilgrimage to Rome and according to some saga accounts had actually made one. Cnut's close ties to key Scandinavian allies were fading for one reason or another.

The relationship between Cnut and Thorkell the Tall is a shadowy one. There is ample evidence to suggest that Thorkell could not be always trusted by Danish monarchs, either Sweyn Forkbeard or Cnut. But what may also be implied is that he was too strong to be simply ignored or cast aside. Quite what happened to make Cnut strike out at Thorkell so soon after treating him as his main man in England is not clear. However, a letter to him from the king in 1020 telling him specifically to bring evil-doers to justice might hint that Thorkell had been slow in doing so and may even be a veiled warning to him not to indulge in any evil-doing of his own. But singling him out for a mention also suggests that he was seen as a 'first amongst equals' among the earls of England at the time.

The outlawing of Thorkell in 1021 suggests that Cnut by now felt that he was strong enough to do something about the problems he seems to have had with his foremost earl. Talk of a so-called reconciliation two years later suggests that maybe Cnut had got this wrong. Striking the right balance in this case was difficult for Cnut.

There are some sketchy stories that in Cnut's absence Thorkell had been busy arranging a marriage with the daughter of the former

King Æthelred (possibly the widow of the late East Anglian warrior Ulfcetel). It is an intriguing story that has a certain latent attraction in it. Thorkell had, after all, been a one-time ally of the English king and may have felt that he could appeal to factions both amongst the English and the Danes. The evidence is inconclusive and comes from a later saga source, in which it was stated that Thorkell was sent back to Denmark with his wife. Whilst it cannot be securely accepted as fact, it does not seem a preposterous suggestion that such a marriage actually took place.

There were other hints of problems involving Thorkell and his wife too. In 1020 Cnut had confiscated half the estate at Elsworth in Cambridgeshire and gave it to Thorkell. But then came news of a shocking story that Thorkell's wife had murdered her young son, probably at Elsworth. Thorkell swore to his wife's innocence but was forced to hand back the estate he held there, which was then given to the Bishop of Dorchester. We cannot be sure that this Thorkell is one and the same as Thorkell the Tall but given the location of these events at Elsworth, it is not at all unlikely.[25]

If these stories were true, there was good reason for Cnut to be worried. Thorkell was a leading noble, if not the leading noble, from Skåne, that troublesomely independent part of Denmark. He was vastly experienced and there was no doubting his ambition, his nerve or his fighting skills. Cnut was still young and inexperienced. Yet sending Thorkell off to Denmark was a gamble and it may have been one that did not pay off. The slightly later life of Edward the Confessor, the *Vitae Edwardi Regis*, tells us that there was trouble in Denmark around this time and signs of rebellion.[26] It is not hard to guess who was probably behind them.

In England, Cnut continued to foster good relations with the Church or at least with some of its foremost churchmen. In 1022 Bishop Æthelnoth made a very significant journey to Rome. Here he was greeted with great honour by Pope Benedict VIII. He was consecrated and blessed as archbishop by the Pope himself, the two men then feasting together to celebrate the momentous event. The choice of Æthelnoth as Archbishop of Canterbury in November 1020 was another act that spoke of great statesmanship on the part of Cnut. Æthelnoth was the son of Æthelweard, ealdorman of western Wessex, who had recently lost his position, and brother to that Æthelweard who had been killed on his orders back in 1017. Therefore, this can be seen as an attempt to rebuild bridges with an important leading Anglo-Saxon family which had found itself in the bad books of the king.

Æthelnoth had started his clerical career as a monk in the great abbey of Glastonbury. He had been, it was said, baptised by none other than Saint Dunstan, and so impressed was the baby Æthelnoth with the solemnity of the ceremony that he had, with his infant hands, made the sign of the cross as he was marked with the holy water. Æthelnoth had been Cnut's chaplain before becoming archbishop and he was in the bloodline of the English royal family. It was a remarkable move of appeasement and consolidation by the still young king. But he had also read his man well. Although Æthelnoth cannot always have been in agreement with Cnut, they managed to work well together as far as we can ascertain whilst both men lived.

Cnut held council at Cirencester on his return from Denmark. The holding of the council in the west of the country is a reminder that back then there was no permanent 'parliament' in place and that the king's council was essentially a peripatetic body without a permanent membership, though it is noticeable that certain names appear as attesters of charters on a regular basis so these men apparently followed the king around and must be considered as being in his inner circle.

The meeting at Cirencester took place at Easter 1020, where firm action was taken to secure Cnut's position. Henry of Huntingdon later painted a vivid picture of Cnut as a man who was quick to put his own interests before anyone else's:

Later, the king paid the English a fitting recompense for their villainy. For while he had Wessex in lordship, Eric had Northumbria, Thorkell had East Anglia, and Eadric had Mercia. But King Cnut put Eadric to death, exiled Thorkell, and forced Eric to flee. In addition, he fell upon the leading nobles: he killed Ealdorman Northman: he did away with Eadwig the Ætheling; he cut down Æthelweard; he exiled Eadwig, nicknamed 'king of the peasants'; he took Brihtric's life by the sword. He levied a remarkable tax throughout England, namely £72,000, in addition to £11,000 which the Londoners paid. In this way the just Lord imposed on the English the tax-gatherer they deserved.[27]

This reference is clearly a conflation of different events, many of them not directly connected to the council at Cirencester. The Ætheling Eadwig referred to was the only surviving son of the late King Æthelred. He was first of all sent into exile though it was said that Cnut originally planned to murder him and pressurised the nobleman Æthelweard to do the deed but he to his credit refused, which in turn may have helped to hasten his own demise. However, Eadwig later returned to England with fatal results as he was killed soon after, another a ruthless elimination of a rival by Cnut.

One of the unfortunate confusions of this period is that sometimes the Anglo-Saxons were not very innovative in their names. So for example we have two Æthelweards to contend with, one – the son of Æthelmaer the Stout – executed in 1017 and the other – Æthelmaer's son-in-law – surviving the purge that removed Eadric Streona and some of the other leading Englishmen of the time.

This second Æthelweard was a man of some influence. He is known to have attested a charter of Cnut's in 1018 and came to be regarded as the founder of the well-known Buckfast Abbey in Devon, where he held his lands. He also had interests in Cornwall, as attested by his mention in the Bodmin Gospels. But he was allegedly involved with trouble associated with Eadwig, the 'king of the peasants', and lost his position as a result and disappears from history from this point on.[28] Given Cnut's ruthless streak, one fears for his long-term survival prospects.

However, it was not just England that mattered to Cnut, who was already showing signs that he wished to increase his international standing. Efforts were also made to build up his prestige further afield. Money was sent overseas to Chartres, home of a renowned bishop, Fulbert,[29] though not at that stage adorned with the magnificent Gothic cathedral that would be painstakingly crafted centuries later. The making of this gift in 1020/1021 helped to establish the credibility of the king in the international arena.

The church at Chartres had recently suffered a disastrous fire. One detects the influence of Queen Emma in the making of Cnut's gift. Her brother was buried there, her sister had died there and her mother had made significant donations to it. Fulbert, the recipient of Cnut's gift, wrote back expressing astonishment at the generosity of the gesture. It was a move which, whilst it appears to have caught Fulbert off-guard – he was aware that Cnut ruled pagans as well as Christians – also helped to raise the new king's reputation, not just in Chartres but further afield too.

Soon Cnut was even starting to show a preference for his adopted England over his native Denmark. In 1022, Æthelnoth consecrated a new Bishop of Roskilde in the latter country. The inauguration of Bishop Gerbrand (a German name) by an English archbishop was an affront to the diocese of Hamburg-Bremen, to which such rights had previously belonged, and Cnut was later prevailed upon to concede that in future no such actions would take place without the approval of the metropolitan of Bremen. Adam of Bremen's suggestions that Cnut agreed graciously to this should perhaps be treated with a generous pinch of salt.[30] Further, it is not at all clear that he subsequently went along with the agreement.

With Thorkell removed from the scene in England, Cnut's main secular supporter there for a time appears to have been Earl Erik of Northumbria. But Cnut's position in Scandinavia in the wider sense was increasingly insecure. Olaf Haraldsson had assumed rule in Norway after his victory at Nesjar. In Sweden, King Olaf Skötkonung died in around 1022 and was succeeded by his son Anund Jacob in that year. Soon, ambitious plotting was taking place in the north of Scandinavia. It was only a matter of time before not just Norway but also Denmark might be lost to Cnut.

At some stage in 1022 Cnut took his fleet out to the Isle of Wight. This has been interpreted as being the first step on another journey back to Denmark, perhaps as an attempt to counteract possible trouble from Thorkell from that direction now that he was in exile. It has also been suggested that this interpretation arises from a mistranslation and actually refers to events in Witland in Prussia, where the Vistula spills out into the Baltic.[31]

There were certainly battles to be fought to ensure that Denmark stayed in his hands and Cnut campaigned there with an army of both Danes and English. Amongst his men was Earl Godwin of Wessex. Fighting took place against the troublesome Wends, who may have been in alliance with the problematic Thorkell and needed therefore to be sorted out.[32] In one incident Godwin led a night attack against them without informing Cnut. His initiative, it seems, paid off and the innovative tactics worked.

However, there was a danger of matters going wrong when dawn broke, for when Cnut could not see his English troops he thought that they had fled. He therefore determined to lead his own Danish troops against the enemy but when he arrived at their camp all that was found was bodies, blood and the spoils of war; the English had been there before him. This changed his view of the English forces and from now on he regarded them as highly as men from his own native land.[33] From that point on, it seems that Godwin was in the ascendancy (though he had been attesting charters since 1018, he only becomes first on the list from 1023 onwards). He was given the hand of Gytha in marriage; she was the sister of Ulf, Cnut's brother-in-law, and therefore part of his extended family, a mark of royal favour that is hard to ignore. Their union was blessed with a number of sons, including one called Harold who would play a key role in later English royal history.

At the end of the fighting in Denmark, matters in the country were patched up. Various marriage alliances were presumably designed to help cement loyalties. Godwin's match with Ulf's sister was probably to strengthen links against Thorkell. Ulf certainly seems to have assumed prominence at this time, though the position with regards to Thorkell remains confused. There is even an account in the saga known as the *Heimskringla* that hostages were exchanged between Cnut and Thorkell involving their sons. The exact identity of Cnut's son is unclear. Some suggest that it was no less a personage than Harthacnut although one of Cnut's other ('more expendable') sons such as Sweyn might appear more likely. It is difficult to believe that this was a case of hostage exchange as it would suggest that Thorkell's power must have still been quite undiminished if such a prominent figure was indeed handed over as collateral.

Whatever the identity of the hostage, Harthacnut was in Denmark not too much later, appointed it would seem as a boy-king of the country. It seems most likely that the young Harthacnut was given some kind of figurehead role in Denmark. Given his youth a council, presumably headed by Ulf, was responsible for day-to-day decisions, relying on distant leadership from the king himself. It might seem unusual to give such a young child positions of authority, even if they were only titular, but there were precedents for such a move from Ottonian Germany.

Whilst these stories of Godwin's military prowess are hard to find in earlier accounts, there is ample evidence that the earl became Cnut's most trusted deputy in England. He rose to the rank of *bajulus*, a new position but one that seemed to make him first amongst equals of all the ealdormen in the land. The *Vita Edwardi Regis*, a book written in praise of King Edward the Confessor, says that Godwin possessed a number of qualities that impressed Cnut; these were prudence, intelligence, strength, steadfastness, courage and eloquence.[34] All were virtues likely to appeal to the king.

Most of all, though, we can add loyalty. Godwin appears to have proved an unswerving lieutenant to Cnut though he would not prove to be quite so reliable with his ultimate successors. Certainly he seems to have accompanied Cnut on very few of his journeys abroad, suggesting that he was steering the helm of state in England whilst the king was away. This suggests that Cnut identified Godwin as someone that he could rely on, particularly around 1023 when Thorkell and Erik of Lade disappear from the stage. Although the exact sequence of events remains very unclear, some historians date Godwin's rise to become ealdorman of the whole of Wessex, and not just the eastern part of it, to around this date.[35] That said, although it cannot be proved beyond doubt, it has been persuasively argued from an analysis of Domesday Book that Godwin's real interests, certainly in terms of landholdings, remained very much in the east of the province.[36]

Gytha, Godwin's wife, was a remarkable enough woman in her own right. Her father Thurgils Sprakaleg was said to be descended from a bear. During her life, Gytha would be accused of being the focal point of a racket that involved the sending of pretty young slave girls back to Denmark. She was to bear at least nine children to Godwin. It is noticeable that some of their children were given very Danish names and others very English ones. The eldest son was called Sweyn. He always seems to have fitted in uncomfortably with the rest of the Godwin clan. He later claimed that his father was not Godwin at all but Cnut. His mother indignantly denied that this was so.[37]

The *Life of King Edward* [the Confessor] would speak of Godwin in the following terms, suggesting that he held great power:

> In the reign of this King Cnut Godwin flourished in the royal palace, having the first place among the highest nobles of the

kingdom and, as was just, what he wrote all decreed should be written, and what he erased, erased.[38]

Judging from the evidence of the surviving charters Godwin replaced Earl Erik as Cnut's first amongst equals. This in itself is not surprising. The 'greasy pole' of politics was as real in tenth-century England as it was for Disraeli nine centuries later. But most remarkably, a Scandinavian had been replaced in the king's good graces by an Anglo-Saxon. Erik continued to witness charters in 1023 after Godwin had moved to the top of the list. But he does not appear after that year and it is most likely as previously mentioned that this was the year of his death.

The fighting in Denmark was anyway brought to a satisfactory conclusion for the time being. Rather frustratingly, there is no record of any dramatic denouement to mark the culmination of this simmering feud between Cnut and Thorkell, no violent conclusion to this ongoing drama between king and Viking warlord. Thorkell just fades from view as far as the historical record is concerned.

Thorkell remains perhaps the greatest enigma of the time. He had plenty of that adventurism that characterised the Viking spirit. It seems that Cnut did not really know how best to deal with him. His exile to Denmark, if that indeed is what it was, was a rather strange move by Cnut. After all it removed Thorkell to a place where the king could far less easily keep an eye on him, making it potentially much easier for him to cause trouble. Cnut's need to go to Denmark to deal with him in person suggests that the plan was not a success.

One of the ways Cnut could try to secure the English throne was by patronage and some of the surviving charters from the times give us an insight into how he did this. So in England we find Cnut making a grant of land in Abbotsbury to one of his men named Ork. There was an abbey here which had fallen into ruin due to the exactions of Viking raiders. In later years Ork and his wife Tola, who were childless, restored the monastery, which was repopulated with Benedictine monks.[39]

There are in fact reasonably good records surviving that evidence the distribution of land in Dorset at the time, perhaps suggesting that Earl Godwin's interests lay more in the east of Wessex and that there was room in the west of the province to build a class of landowners below that of ealdorman that could be used to reward Scandinavian supporters of Cnut. One such was Agemund, granted land at Cheselbourne in 1019, whilst Ork was also given Portesham in the west of the county in 1024 and lands were given to a Scandinavian named Bovi at Horton. Over half a century later, the Domesday Book would note that each of the major urban boroughs of Dorset, that is Dorchester, Wareham, Shaftesbury and Bridport, at one time paid a tax to support the work of the *huscarles*, the king's enforcers, in the area.

Other records suggest that Ork was also granted land at Hilton in the county and that nearby Tolpuddle was in the possession of his wife. Although the original records that give this information in the cartulary of Abbotsbury are now lost, there is no real reason to doubt the authenticity of these accounts as the later copyists who noted them had no obvious ulterior motive for making such things up. These men are regularly found as witnesses to grants giving each of them lands in Cnut's reign but never outside of Dorset. It seems then as if they were a close-knit group looking after each other's interests, and vicariously those of Cnut also, but only in a very restricted geographical area. The use of the term *huscarl* in relation to them may suggest that they were even at one time part of his personal bodyguard. What better policy than to reward trusted and proven supporters of the king with land in potentially problematic parts of England?[40]

There is also evidence of Scandinavians being settled in the adjacent shire of Devon, potentially an even more problematic part of England for Cnut. The evocatively named 'Viking' who held land around Exeter must, we can reliably assume, relate to a man of Scandinavian origin; similarly, a man with the same name was active as a moneyer at Lydford at some time between 1029 and 1035 (and bear in mind that a man with this trade was no mere artisan but someone with considerable local importance).

The former of these men was certainly there for the long term as it is probable that he was still acting as a witness to documents in 1065 when Cnut had been dead for three decades. Domesday Book also records lands once granted to Ulf, Tovi, Siward and Ingvar in the shire, all names suggesting a Scandinavian origin. Again this suggests the possibility at least of deliberate colonisation by Cnut of potentially volatile areas with officials he thought he could rely on to defend his interests. Certainly the presence of Scandinavians in a region where not long before the Ealdorman Æthelweard had been removed would probably have been welcomed by the king.[41]

This division of land was a feature of the Viking years in England. In the past it had been a country of large estates owned by three classes: the king, the great nobles and the Church. Viking conquest saw the land being parcelled out to those who had fought with their armies. As such, something of a process that had been described as 'privatisation' of the land took place. Although this trend may have happened anyway, it was certainly strongly accelerated by the Viking conquests.[42]

Elsewhere in England, life went on. At around this time, on his return from Rome Æthelnoth was accompanied with a precious relic, the arm of St Augustine of Hippo, which he had purchased at Pavia for a hundred talents of silver and one of gold. He now presented this to Coventry Cathedral. At this time the archbishop began discussions on measures to right one of the Viking wrongs of recent years. The murder of Archbishop Ælfheah in 1012 was a stain that would be very hard to expunge from the record. Æthelnoth sought to do what he could to make amends and met the king publicly at St Paul's Minster in London accompanied by Beorhtwine, Bishop of Wells. Here they asked for, and received, permission to translate the martyred archbishop's remains to Canterbury.

On the day that this translation, as it was formally called, took place, the chronicler Osbern says that there was a strong Danish presence in the city to ensure that matters went off without incident. This might well have been an extremely prudent move; after all, the archbishop had been murdered by the Danes who were now running the country. The recent high levels of taxation would have done nothing to ingratiate Cnut to the Londoners, who had anyway been amongst the most loyal adherents to the cause of Æthelred II.

There were other reasons why the Londoners would be unhappy to see Ælfheah's remains moved. The presence of his relics in the city made it a centre of pilgrimage, which would have been an important source of revenue for London. In addition, there was a political element to this too. The archbishop was a thoroughly English martyr around whom opposition to the Danes might accrete. Moving his mortal remains elsewhere might burst a political bubble and calm down a potential source of opposition; on the other hand, the act of removing it might on the day lead to a violent outburst of anti-Danish sentiment, especially as the late King Æthelred II was also buried in St Paul's close to Ælfheah's last resting place. The people of London would not be happy to give his body up. It was a reason for great civic pride as well as, it may be assumed, a good source of income given the fact that many people came to pay their respects to the martyred archbishop.

It is most probable that Cnut ordered Ælfheah's remains to be removed as a way of defusing a potentially explosive situation. The archbishop had been killed by the very people whose king now also hailed himself as King of England. He had been slain in barbarous fashion after refusing to accede to Danish blackmail. No wonder that he was therefore a hero to some of the English people.

The translation ceremony, when it came, was extremely high-profile and as fulsome an apology for the killing of the late archbishop as it was possible to get. When the body of the slaughtered Ælfheah was exhumed it was said to be remarkably intact, 'free from every taint of corruption', a pre-requisite almost at the time for any holy man with supporters who wished to canonise him.[43] The king and Archbishop Æthelnoth, along with many other bishops and clerics, accompanied the disinterred remains of Ælfheah across the Thames to Southwark and from there to Rochester – in some accounts Cnut even steered the ship that made the short river journey to here. Then the king bade farewell to the party and Æthelnoth was then responsible for the onward journey. The stately procession made its way 'joyfully', according to the *Anglo-Saxon Chronicles*, on to Canterbury.

Here they were met by the Lady Emma and her son Harthacnut. There then followed a ceremony of great pomp and solemnity and with hymns of praise the sacred remains of Ælfheah were conveyed into the city. Here, on 11 June 1023, they were brought into the hallowed environs of Christ Church. For four days they lay in state, as we would now call it, awaiting reburial. This took place on 15 June in a ceremony led by the current archbishop, accompanied by Ælfsige, Bishop of Winchester and Beorhtwine of Wells. Ælfheah was put in a tomb just to the north of the altar, just about as special a spot for a burial as was possible. It was also, very helpfully from a public relations viewpoint, a way of Cnut making subtle recompense to Canterbury for the damage inflicted on it by Viking raids not so many years before.

Such treatment of a holy man like Ælfheah was far from unique in those days. The late King Æthelred had after all done something similar with his assassinated brother Edward. Back then it was possible for a saint to be unofficially recognised by popular demand to a far greater extent than is feasible in more modern times where a papal checklist must be complied with before formal canonisation takes place.

Not until 1078 would Ælfheah formally be recognised as a saint by Pope Gregory VII but his martyrdom certainly touched a nerve. Ælfheah was one of only two men to remain on Canterbury's calendar of saints after the Norman Conquest (Augustine was the other) when the Norman Archbishop Lanfranc struck most other Anglo-Saxon saints off it. Ælfheah was after all the first Archbishop of Canterbury to be killed whilst in office. It was probably quite easy to project his death as an act of martyrdom in defence of his faith even though he was actually killed by a drunken mob who were more incensed at his lack of cooperation in raising a ransom than for his religious intransigence.

Ælfheah would enjoy a remarkable renaissance in the late twelfth century. In 1174 the Choir of Canterbury Cathedral was destroyed in a fierce fire. When it was rebuilt some stunning stained-glass windows were included. They showed various episodes from the life of Ælfheah and they remain there still. There was a certain resonance in including these magnificent memorials in the building; just four years before the fire another martyred archbishop by the name of Thomas Becket had bled out his life in the cathedral. To reinforce the appositeness of this remembrance of Ælfheah, Becket's very last sermon had included a reference to the Anglo-Saxon martyr; Becket clearly knew what was coming.

Certainly Cnut, and other kings of his time, hoped to obtain reputational benefits from their support for events of this kind when a holy man's remains were moved to a new and high-profile resting place.

This was yet another astute move on the part of Cnut. He was effectively creating a shrine to a man murdered by his own people and if he was, as we would now say, undertaking a 'hearts and minds' campaign it is difficult to think of a more statesmanlike move, however much it upset the Londoners. But it was not only his English subjects who would have been touched by this move. So would the papacy. It is perhaps not too difficult to imagine that such a move might even have been suggested to Æthelnoth when he had met with Pope Benedict in Rome.

It was anyway a smart initiative on the part of a king who was still only a few years into the role. The following year, 1024, the international scene was changed with the death of Duke Richard II of Normandy. The death of this prominent lord created potential instability, a situation that was not eased with the rapid demise of his son just a year later. There is frustratingly little detail of Cnut's activities in England during this year, with only one known charter of lands in Dorset to the Scandinavian by the name of Ork.[44]

By 1025, Cnut had further problems back in Scandinavia to contend with. It is not difficult to imagine the situation: Cnut was effectively an absentee king at the time, never a particularly secure situation in those days. It seems quite plausible that his pro-English stance may even have alienated a number of his subjects back in Scandinavia. In any event, Cnut was forced to go back to Scandinavia and face up to a Swedish raiding army, though some accounts such as those of Snorri Sturluson suggest that the protector of Denmark in the king's absence, Ulf Sprakaleggson, was so frustrated at Cnut's long-term absenteeism that he wanted his son Harthacnut to take his place. This account suggests that Harthacnut, then a child of about eight years old, was proclaimed King of Denmark by Ulf at Viborg. Given the fact that he was so young, it was not hard to work out who wanted to be the power behind the throne. Ulf was showing dangerous delusions of grandeur.

These events signify that holding England and Scandinavia together was likely to prove problematic for any king. Separated as they were by the unpredictable waters of the North Sea, it would prove a great challenge for any ruler of both countries to keep this extended kingdom united. On his return to the Baltic, Cnut faced the raiding army in Skåne. Swedish army and naval forces, including men led by Ulf and Eglaf, faced up to Cnut and his men.

The outcome of the battle, if the *Anglo-Saxon Chronicles* are to be believed, was not all that Cnut desired: 'and there many men perished on King Cnut's side, both of Danish men and of English; the Swedes had possession of the place of slaughter'.[45]

It is not entirely clear who was at the head of the army opposing Cnut; the precise identity of Ulf and Eglaf is uncertain but the Ulf who was Cnut's brother-in-law had a brother called Eilifr who had previously been given land in western Mercia after the fall of Eadric Streona, so it was probably these men. The *Anglo-Saxon Chronicles* did not think it necessary to explain more about who they were so presumably they were well known to an English audience. It seems likely that Ulf and Eilifr were indeed former lieutenants of Cnut. Most seriously, forces led by King Anund Jacob of Sweden and Olaf of Norway were also moving to attack Cnut.

It was a natural thing for them to do. Cnut's power was evidently growing in both England and Denmark and the acquisitive intentions of Danish kings towards northern Scandinavia in the past and Cnut's long-term absences from Denmark perhaps encouraged them to make a pre-emptive strike in alliance with dissatisfied men from Skåne. Certainly several accounts suggest that the region of Skåne was badly mauled by a Swedish land army during the campaign.

The precise location of the battle is not clear. It has been plausibly suggested that the confrontation, which became known as the Battle of the Holy River (or Helgeå), may have taken place near Kristianstad in southern Sweden, which is opposite the easternmost part of Denmark and only a short sea crossing away. Another site suggested is close to modern Stockholm.[46] It appears to have been a sea-battle or one fought off an island close to the sea, though there may also have been a land fight as well. Significantly, although there are no definitive answers to the difficult question of who won the battle, not one source claims an overwhelming victory for Cnut.

King Olaf was there in his great ship the *Bison*, adorned with the golden figurehead of such a beast. According to Snorri Sturluson, Olaf – who fancied himself to be an engineer – laid a trap for Cnut's army by building a huge dam. He arrayed his forces on land, in clear sight of his foe. When his opponent led his men ashore to prepare for battle, the dam was burst open. Many of the ships moored by the shore were damaged and large numbers of men were drowned. Some men managed to get on their ships and cut the ropes, allowing them to float off with the floodtide; Cnut was one man who escaped in such a manner.

Olaf's fleet was standing offshore and attacked Cnut's ship but it was too powerfully defended to be taken. The situation was gradually brought under control. Seeing that a decisive victory was not likely, Olaf and Anund disengaged their fleet from the battle. As they made their way to safety, it appears that the Swedish portion of the force had lost the will to fight. This, anyway, is what happened according to the sagas and in the absence of much else in the way of evidence, we are forced to accept or reject it as we see fit.

In the end, this was not a devastating defeat for Cnut even if he had not decisively bested his enemies. There are suggestions that the Norwegian fleet was trapped in the Baltic and that many of the men on board their ships had to make a demanding trek across the country to reach their homes. This was a journey of 400 miles, made in the depths of winter. It must have been long, an exhausting march and a number must have perished in the attempt. The suffering undergone by the Norwegian warriors as a result would have done nothing to endear their king, Olaf – who had allowed the fleet to be trapped – to them. This may have helped to undermine his position in the longer run. The king had reached the high-water mark of his earthly career.

Cnut's excursions into Sweden and his claim to be king of part of the country rather than all of it differ from his claims to Norway, where he claimed to be ruler of the whole country even at a time when it was practically being ruled by someone else. Although Danish claims to rule Norway had only been made in recent generations, there does not appear to be a similar claim to govern all of Sweden. It has been plausibly suggested that those Swedes whom Cnut wished to rule were men who had previously served in his armies and therefore this was not a claim that applied to the country as a whole.[47]

Cnut soon after returned to Denmark and it was here, late in September, that a fatal drama was played out. Ulf's position in the recent campaign is ambiguous to say the least. Whatever the circumstances, he had returned with Cnut but clearly could not be trusted. Ulf invited Cnut to a feast, where he was entertained extravagantly. However, he was, according to some accounts, 'aggressive, vigorous and brave; but he was also tactless and careless in speech, and possessed a temper that was not easily controlled'.[48] Perhaps harsh words were exchanged; at any rate a chess game followed in which a bitter row ensued, the king evidently being a man who did not like losing. The two men parted on difficult terms.

The next morning the earl was in church in Roskilde. Men had been despatched by the king to get rid of him. The first man who entered the church demurred at committing such an act on holy ground. But one of Cnut's guards, Ivar White, had no such qualms. He carried out his orders and Ulf was no more. If true, this story suggests that, whatever exterior face the king might present, internally he was still a ruthless and even violent man; Ulf had after all been killed not in a fit of pique but when Cnut had had a chance to sleep on his decision. Ulf's wife, Estrith (Cnut's sister), was reassured after this act by generous gifts of lands from her brother. She was not, however, that reassured, for her son Sweyn seems to have been sent to Sweden for safety's sake until after Cnut's death.

This staining of sacred ground with blood was clearly not a very Christian act on Cnut's part. Cnut paid substantial compensation to his sister Estrith. With this, she built a new stone cathedral to replace the wooden stave church that Harald Bluetooth had had constructed there. Estrith would eventually be buried there along with her son, the future Danish king Sweyn Estrithsson, and there they remain to this day. Wall pictures of both of them still decorate Roskilde Cathedral along with another of Harald Bluetooth. More remarkably, the human remains of Estrith and her son Sweyn have been more recently discovered and casts of their skulls can still be seen. Sweyn has even had his face reconstructed so that we can see what he looked like. Unfortunately, the remains of Harald Bluetooth on the other hand have disappeared without trace.

These troubles with Ulf evidenced how difficult it was even for a strong king like Cnut to hold on to an extended kingdom and to trust men even if he knew them well. His need to juggle his resources to maintain control across a wide area was not surprising. After all, England and Scandinavia were both warrior societies with strong and hard-to-control warlords on the lookout to foster their own interests even at the expense of a king. With the wilds of Norway presenting a marked contrast to Denmark and with England separated from the remainder of Cnut's kingdoms by the unpredictable North Sea, it was a challenge for Cnut to retain control everywhere and in practice this extended empire was a barely viable proposition in the longer term, though Cnut was energetic in his efforts to preserve it.

These were trying times for the king. The result of the Battle of Holy River is another salutary reminder that Cnut was not a great warrior who was unbeatable in the field. Any long-term accomplishments he might make were not, it seems, due to strategic or tactical brilliance but were rather a result of human qualities like resilience and determination and the wisdom of his statecraft.

That statecraft was again evident in the way that Cnut continued to build relationships with Rome. In 1026 Archbishop Ælfric, who had succeeded to the Archbishopric of York on the death of Wulfstan in 1023, journeyed to the Pope from whom he received the pallium, the woollen cloak that was once reserved for the Pope but had by now been conferred by him on his leading churchmen as a symbol that they had been given papal authority to act on his behalf.

The granting of the pallium by the Pope was an important symbolic act. Ostensibly the Pope was responsible for making all senior ecclesiastical appointments. This however was difficult for practical reasons when the country was as far away from Rome as England was. Therefore, such senior appointments were often made by the king locally. The ceremony in which the Pope handed over the pallium was an important if retrospective sign that the Pope was content to support the appointment that had been made.

One impact of England on Denmark involved the currency. Coinage in Denmark was a relatively new phenomenon whereas in England it was part of a long-established and well-organised model. The coinage in Denmark was redesigned on the English model though some Danish variants were introduced into the design, such as with the use of snakes or dragons on the obverse of the coins. A number of mints were set up, such as that at Lund, again emulating the approach in England.

This was not perhaps the most striking reverse influence though. This came in the form of the development of the Church in Denmark, where Anglo-Saxon influence was 'more than traceable, it was massive'.[49] The very newness of the Danish Church made it ripe for some imitation from the English model. Early influences on the Danish Church had come from Germany but this policy had been reversed by Sweyn Forkbeard, who instead based his approach on the use of English bishops or Norwegian bishops who had been consecrated in England.

Cnut continued to develop his father's policy. He also installed English bishops in Denmark, including at Roskilde. This rather annoyed the German bishops, who felt that they had been uprooted from Denmark, as indeed in practice they had. The Archbishop of Hamburg-Bremen appealed to the German emperor, Conrad II, for support in the ongoing debate. This led to a rather un-Christian act when Gerbrand, Bishop of Roskilde, was seized on his way back to Denmark after being consecrated by Æthelnoth, the Archbishop of Canterbury. Gerbrand was held captive by the Archbishop of Hamburg-Bremen and forced to confirm his allegiance to the German Church and, as noted earlier, Cnut was pressured into changing his policy.

These unseemly events were creating an unacceptable situation. It was deeply embarrassing for the Church, of course, and that alone meant that it should be sorted out. But this was not all. It suited Cnut's purposes to be on good terms with Emperor Conrad and this was going to be difficult to maintain in current circumstances when there were tensions between the Danish and German churches. Cnut needed the Emperor's support, or at least neutrality, given continuing problems in northern Scandinavia. Something was needed to break the impasse and Cnut thought long and hard about how to bring this about. The scene was now set for perhaps the most memorable event in Cnut's entire reign.

7

Emperor of the North: The Years of Greatness (1027–1034)

Scandinavia was a difficult region for Cnut to rule. Whatever cultural similarities there might be, Denmark, Norway and Sweden were also different in key respects, not least in the determination of some of the people in the latter regions to fight off Danish attempts at domination. One thing that many from all three regions had in common, though, was their ferocity in battle. Little wonder that Adam of Bremen would write in terms of awe, 'behold the exceedingly fierce race of the Danes, of the Norwegians or of the Swedes' or of 'that piratical people' or that 'land of horrors'.[1]

The indecisive results of the Battle of Holy River apparently gave Cnut much food for thought. For a Viking king, even a very Christianised one, martial success was what gave him credibility and enabled him to maintain his grip on power. The fact that he had not yet made good on his claim to Norway would have rankled and it is likely that he was only biding his time before he could return to what he no doubt regarded as unfinished business. 'Florence' of Worcester mentions that in 1027 discontented subjects of Olaf in Norway were getting restive and were in return being generously supplied with gold and silver by Cnut.[2] If he could not conquer the country yet by force of arms, he could try and create the conditions for conquest by other means.

Cnut's decision to travel to Rome soon after perhaps gives some indication of the outcome of the Battle of Holy River. His decision to make his way there hints at unfinished business, of the need to develop more support in order to finish what he had started.

This argues against a decisive victory for Cnut at Holy River. But on the other hand, he felt strong enough to leave Scandinavia unattended whilst he went south, which he would surely not have done if he had suffered a decisive defeat.

It is also tempting to speculate that there might have been an element of atonement in all this. If he had indeed been responsible for the killing of Ulf in a church, it was not something that the papacy would look kindly upon, as King Robert the Bruce of Scotland would find out three centuries later. Certainly, the later sagas suggest that Cnut travelled to Rome as a pilgrim carrying the scrip and staff, the traditional insignia of such a traveller. This was perhaps quite conventional and expected; certainly he also went heavily laden with silver, gold and other riches. But perhaps there was also an element of conscience troubling the king, and taking on a penitential stance would be no bad thing from a political perspective.

The scene was set for the high point of Cnut's political career. 1027 was the year in which Cnut's rise to greatness was symbolically affirmed when he decided that he would at last travel in person to Rome rather than merely let his archbishops and bishops journey there. In March, Cnut attended the crowning of the Holy Roman Emperor Conrad II in the Eternal City, a mark of acceptance indeed. His welcome there was the ultimate sign of approval for the Viking king whose pagan antecedents now seemed a long way in the past.

Cnut's journey took him through Flanders, Francia and Italy. He was generous in his charitable acts as he travelled. The *Encomium* chronicler gives one example as a representative of the rest and his tale is the more convincing, perhaps, as he said he witnessed it himself. Cnut visited the monasteries of Nôtre Dame and St Bertin in the town of St Omer in the north of Francia. Here he acted humbly, praying for the intercession of the saints, with tears of piety rolling down his cheeks. He made generous offerings in all corners of the monasteries but saved the greatest for the high altar. Neither, it was said, was he niggardly towards the poor people he met in the area. These were classic acts of a pious Christian monarch.[3] He also made strenuous efforts to reduce the levels of taxation or tolls charged on travellers on the roads through Francia on the way to Rome. Generous contributions made by him were said to have reduced the levels charged by half.[4]

The conversations between Cnut and Pope John XIX in Rome seemed to go well. The king managed to negotiate some significant tax exemptions for the English Church; it would be very ironic if this was because of the great financial hardships suffered by the country in recent decades as he had played a notable part in causing them in the first place. He took a vow at the tomb of the 'apostles' in Rome that he would amend his life, an act which might be treated with cynicism from a modern perspective but which was in fact far from unique amongst men who were contemplating their life in the next world and believed that such actions in this one could help make for a more comfortable time in it.

The coronation of Conrad II and his wife Gisela took place on 26 March 1027, in the Church of the Holy Apostles in Rome. Not only was Cnut present, so too was Rudolf III of Burgundy, along with many leading churchmen including the archbishops of Cologne, Mainz, Magdeburg, Ravenna and Milan. The Emperor held land not just in Germany but also in Italy and he took the homage of several crucial nobles from the peninsula during his time there.

The highlight of the ceremony was when the Imperial Crown of the Holy Roman Empire was placed on Conrad's head. It was a magnificent work of art, bejewelled with magnificent gemstones which shone translucently when held up to the rays of the sun. It was an object that shouted out loud that the man who wore it was possessed of wealth and power that few if any men could hope to emulate. It certainly seemed to inspire Cnut for it was said that soon after he returned to England he had himself a crown made that was modelled on it.

These were important times for Cnut. It was to the mutual advantage of both him and Conrad to remain on good terms. Denmark had been rather too close to the German border for comfort during the reign of Harald Bluetooth and it was to Cnut's benefit that he could keep a friendly Emperor in Germany at arm's length. At the same time Conrad's extended territories to the south and east meant that he was more than happy to have a friendly Denmark to the north, a desire that was compounded because Conrad was involved in warfare in Poland and also had rebellion inside Germany to contend with. Cnut's concentration on affairs in England and Scandinavia meant that Conrad could rest assured that he would not have to worry about any interventions from the direction of Denmark, so the arrangement suited both men well.

The Emperor was also under regular threat from the direction of Poland, territories where the Danes had often found allies in their adventures and indeed where Cnut probably had family connections. Poland then did not cover the same territories as the modern country and its hold on coastal lands in particular was weak. But it was an important source of supplies for many, including the Danes, providing horses, cattle, game, fish, timber and hemp. This alliance with Cnut gave breathing space to Conrad II. Cnut had his unfinished business in the north to attend to, and he could now give it more attention. Conrad also had no distractions to worry about from that direction and indeed in 1029–30 he was on the offensive against his enemies in Poland.

Cnut returned to England in a roundabout way, going to Denmark first of all on his way back from Rome, perhaps evidence of a renewed confidence after the discussions he had been involved in but also again of unfinished business in Scandinavia. He sent back a long letter before his return, from 'Cnut, king of all England, and of Denmark, Norway, and part of Sweden, to Æthelnoth, metropolitan, and Ælfric, archbishop of York, and to all the bishops and prelates, and to the whole nation of the English, both the nobles and the commons'.

He explained his journey to Rome as one that was made in a search for forgiveness of his sins and for the welfare of his dominions and his subjects. He made particular reference to his visit to the tomb of St Peter. He laid emphasis on the fact that he had met not only the Pope but also the Holy Roman Emperor Conrad II. The Emperor had greeted him with honour, making lavish gifts to him. Cnut also asked for greater security for his people who were making pilgrimages to Rome (Burgundy, it seems, was a particular trouble spot for them). As a mark of these new friendships Conrad also at some stage ceded the border region of Schleswig to Denmark.

Cnut also mentioned that he had complained to Pope John about the excessive financial demands being made on the English Church, in particular when his archbishops were forced, by custom, to make the journey to Rome to receive the pallium; an insight into the fact that such events were far from being merely symbolic in nature. The Pope in return agreed not to do so in the future.

Cnut's letter went on in terms that were both almost confessional in nature and also firmly instructive to his officials:

> Be it known therefore to all of you, that I have humbly vowed to the Almighty God himself henceforward to amend my life in all respects, and to rule the kingdoms and the people subject to me with justice and clemency, giving equitable judgements in all matters; and if, through the intemperance of youth or negligence, I have hitherto exceeded the bounds of justice in any of my acts, I intend by God's aid to make an entire change for the better. I therefore adjure and command my counsellors to whom I have entrusted the affairs of my kingdom, that henceforth they neither commit themselves, nor suffer to prevail, any sort of injustice throughout my dominions, either from fear of me, or from favour to any powerful person.
>
> I also command all sheriffs and magistrates throughout my whole kingdom, as they tender my regard and their own safety, that they use no unjust violence to any man, rich or poor, but that all, high and low, rich or poor, should enjoy alike impartial law; from which they are never to deviate, either on account of royal favour, respect of person in the great, or for the sake of amassing money wrongfully, for I have no need to accumulate wealth by iniquitous exactions.

He moved towards a conclusion by saying that his planned diversion to Denmark was to restore peace there with those nations and peoples in the region who sought to have him removed from power. Pointedly, he said that his reason for going to Denmark first was to deal with 'those nations and peoples who wished, if it had been possible for them, to deprive us of both kingdom and life'.

Cnut's immediate priority at this time was Scandinavia. Ulf was dead and needed to be replaced. Eilifr also disappears without trace, so he had either suffered the same fate or managed to escape into exile. Interestingly, around this time the coin designs in Denmark changed and became more Scandinavian in appearance rather than largely emulating English styles, as if Cnut were emphasising that he had not forgotten where his roots lay. But England was not ignored either. Cnut demanded that the authorities there were to take care to ensure that all tithes and taxes due were to be collected as rigorously as ever; anyone in default 'will incur fines to the king, according to the law, which will be strictly enforced without mercy'.[5]

The sting in the tail of this letter, showing that the king was determined that all monies due were to be collected as thoroughly as always (though much of the money was to go to the Church), suggests that we should be careful not to read too much into it as concerns a complete transformation of Cnut. At the heart of this remarkable letter, and indeed of this whole visit to Rome, was politics and kingship.

The discussions in Rome were so positive first and foremost because they served the interests of all parties. The Holy Roman Emperor, for example, got what was effectively a quasi-alliance with a powerful neighbour to the north who could have caused great trouble to the lands to the south if he wished. The papacy, at this time in its history trying to secure its position more firmly, also benefitted from relations with this powerful man and was able to ensure that in return for easing up on the price charged for awarding the pallium to English bishops, other tithes would flow to it.

Cnut got not only some practical financial concessions, always welcome of course, but also something perhaps even more important to a proud monarch – legitimacy. Complaints of inequitable treatment against the English nation suggested, inter alia, that it could be exploited. Not anymore. Cnut was rubbing shoulders with the most powerful men in Europe and essentially being treated as something close to an equal. Quite a turnabout for a 'Viking' king.

Even the injunctions against his own officials to steer clear of corruption were both practical and political. Practical because the actions of corrupt officials stole wealth not just from the people but also often from the king. Political because anti-corruption messages in any age are popular with those who are being exploited, though even in the modern world we know only too well that it is one thing to preach anti-corruption, quite another to implement effective policies to deal with the issue.

It is interesting, though, to reflect further on whether Cnut himself was changed by the experience of his visit to Rome. In that world, as in ours, actions – even if small – speak louder than words and it is significant that Cnut's first act on returning later to England was to grant the rights that arose from the area on either side of Sandwich

Harbour to Christ Church, Canterbury. This was indeed a move imbued with symbolism, for previous Viking raiders had frequently used the port as their entry point to England. It was now no longer required for this purpose and had instead been gifted to the Church that the Vikings had so often plundered in the recent past.

All of this was extremely positive 'spin' for Cnut but in most cases such concessions are only made by giving up something in return. Cnut was a strong ruler but he was not quite a European superpower, whatever his propagandists might say. He had not yet even confirmed himself as king of all of Scandinavia. He was in no position to demand concessions from Emperor or Pope without giving something back. What that something was was shown when the bishopric of Roskilde subsequently came free. The new bishop, Avoco, was consecrated at Roskilde by Libentius, Archbishop of Hamburg-Bremen. In terms of the Church in Denmark, the Germans were back.

This did not bring an end to the dispute concerning the position of the Scandinavian Church in the longer-term and its domination by Germans, especially those from Hamburg-Bremen. Discussions with the Papacy concerning an independent Scandinavian archdiocese were ongoing several decades later and were still fiercely resisted by Hamburg-Bremen, who resented any resultant loss of influence. But in the short term the decision had gone to the German archbishop and it was sufficient to buy Cnut the time that he wanted. It is also an important indicator as to Cnut's thinking. He certainly wished to be thought of as a supporter of the English Church but he was fully prepared to sacrifice her interests if politics demanded it.

If England was by now a picture of stability compared to the decades of turmoil that preceded Cnut's reign, Scandinavia was in contrast still a volcanic melting-pot. The region was still struggling for its identity and powerful warlords continually strove for dominance over their rivals. The year 1027 appears to have been a watershed for Cnut, who resolved after the tough fighting which had culminated in the Battle of Holy River that he needed to assert his authority to a greater degree in the region.

In his long letter back to England he had called himself 'King of England, Denmark, Norway and part of Sweden'. These were grand claims but they were as yet a long way from total reality. The limited claim to part of Sweden rather than all of it made some sense at the time as this was still a fragmented region with many petty kingdoms further to the north.

As far as Norway is concerned, the situation was fairly clear cut. Although Adam of Bremen, like all chroniclers, is not always completely reliable, his assessment of this period strikes a chord: 'between Cnut and Olaf, the king of the Norwegians, there was continual war, and it did not cease all the days of their lives, the Danes struggling for dominion, the Norwegians in truth fighting for freedom'.[6]

Whilst it would be too simplistic to see this as a battle for national identity rather than a struggle for supremacy between two powerful warlords, one can see easily enough how Danish domination might irritate many Norwegians and equally how keen many Danish warriors might be to subdue the country (though for reasons of personal gain rather than national pride). But in any event it was clear that the conflict between Olaf and Cnut was by no means at an end.

Cnut attempted to drive a wedge between Olaf and the Norwegian aristocracy by the offer of something that attracted the latter group very much: money, or to be more accurate gold and silver. But many of these important subjects of the Norwegian crown had already, crucially, fallen out with King Olaf Haraldsson. This aristocratic group had shown signs of considerable independence in their outlook and resented attempts on the part of the Norwegian king to appoint royal officials who would limit their freedom of action. All these frictions inside Norway gave Cnut some very natural opportunities which he was keen to exploit.

He was careful to take appropriate preparations before setting foot in Norway. Snorri Sturluson noted that the envoys he despatched 'came north and brought much wealth with them. They fared widely during the winter, paying out the money that Cnut had promised for support in the autumn before; but they also gave money to others and thus bought their friendship for Cnut.' No doubt a good part of the funds came from his treasure trove in England and the people of that land played a significant financial part in the planned conquest of Norway. Occasional finds of hoards of contemporary English coins suggest as much.[7]

In 1028, Cnut added to his already sizeable domains when he went with fifty ships from England over to Norway and brought an end to the problems there, at least for the time being. He stopped en route to pick up reinforcements at the Limfjord in Denmark and then journeyed up the west coast of Norway towards Trondheim with what was reportedly an enormous fleet. He was apparently accompanied by earls Godwin and Hákon from England. Once ashore, he drove King Olaf from the land, who in the words of Snorri Sturluson had 'few folk and little dragons [i.e. ships], and took the country for himself. Whilst the *Anglo-Saxon Chronicles* are short on detail, a poet named Sigvatr was in the service of Olaf of Norway at the time and confirmed that Hákon, son of Earl Erik of Lade, was allied to Cnut. Another poet, with the grand name of Thorasin Praise-Tongue, told how Cnut sailed from Denmark with a fleet and landed unopposed at Trondheim, with Cnut's 'dragon' 'gleaming with steel and gold'. There was, it seems, no fight, suggesting just how deep the divisions between Olaf and many of his more influential subjects actually were.

Norway was a rugged region with a mountainous spine hemming in the barely farmable land in many places into very small corners. The sea acted as a natural barrier on the other side, giving the farmers there very little opportunity to expand. The main reliance in farming terms was on herds. The farmers relied on their cattle and their sheep for food, for milk and for clothing. Fruit was a very rare luxury indeed and Adam of Bremen credits this fact for the renowned ferocity of Norwegians as fighters.

There had been a long history of territorial disputes between the Norwegians and the Danes, who had sought to dominate Norway from time to time. Relationships between Norwegians and Swedes were typically more straightforward. Adam ascribes poverty as being the main driving force behind the piratical activities of Vikings from Norway. By Adam's time they had, despite unpromising beginnings, become good Christians in his opinion. They seemed to him to be content with their lot despite the avarice of some priests who attempted to fleece their flock by charging ridiculous amounts for services such as funerals.

But even in his time, half a century after Cnut's death, the far north of Norway remained another country, a land at the end of the world. This was a region considered to be peopled by magicians who had incredible insight and knowledge. They were even said to have sufficient powers to call sea monsters to the shoreline. The men lived in the woods and the women, it was said, grew beards. It was a land where a traveller – presumably a relatively rare creature – was more likely to meet a buffalo, an auroch, an elk or a bear than a fellow human being.

All this was another land and of little concern to Cnut, whose greater interest was in the south of the country and in the central region (around Trondheim in particular). Trondheim was about five days' sail from Denmark; to give this some context, it was said only to be one day's sail from here to Orkney. It could also be reached on foot from Skåne but this journey was slower and considered to be more dangerous because of the wild country in between. This was rough country, in virtual darkness in the north all day long during the winter and perishing cold. No wonder these were tough warriors given the life they had to face.

At Trondheim, at the very heart of Norway, at a point where in the summer months the daylight never truly disappears for long, the town had become an important trading place and at the time one of the major settlements in Norway, gripping tenaciously to the shoreline of the fjord on which it stood. Resistance to Cnut's invasion attempts was patchy and Olaf was forced to flee given an absence of any meaningful support. Hákon, coming over from his lands in west Mercia, was installed as Cnut's man in Norway now that the way was clear for him to do so.[8] Generous grants of land to Norwegians who had supported Cnut were also confirmed, having previously been made in England before Cnut had even launched his invasions. Even the bleak north was taken into account with generous grants to two men, the intriguingly named Thor the Dog and Harek of Tjotta, who amongst other things were allowed a monopoly of trade with the Finns.

It was appropriate that Hákon was allied with Cnut during these decisive events. This was a return to the old days when his father had fought alongside Sweyn Forkbeard at the Battle of Svold a quarter of a century before, when Olaf Tryggvason had been bested and Norway had fallen into the hands of the Danish crown for a time. This was logical; Cnut and Hákon's families were traditional allies; equally, Olaf's family was a traditional opponent of both. Olaf Haraldsson was forced to flee, first to Sweden, then to Novgorod. But for both Hákon and Cnut any sense of elation felt at this turn of events was short-lived; winning the battle proved to be far easier than winning the war. Cnut returned to England shortly after, stopping off in the Oslo Fjord, where he was proclaimed King of Norway. His triumph, though seemingly complete, was in reality anything but.

Cnut's subsequent plans seem to have been based on an acceptance that he could not rule such as extended empire alone. Hákon was given strong powers in Norway and Harthacnut was confirmed as ruler of Denmark, though as he was still a child a guardian would need to practically govern in his name until he was of age. Snorri Sturluson suggests that this task was allotted to Harald, the son of none other than Thorkell the Tall, suggesting just how complex and hard to interpret relationships with that late, great warrior had actually been.

Returning to England the year after his conquest of Norway, Cnut was forced to hurry back when the deposed Olaf returned in an attempt to recover his kingdom after Hákon had been drowned in an accident at sea. Some accounts suggest that he had been recalled to England and was to be replaced in Norway but that his ship foundered off Orkney.

The deprived Norwegian king sought to win back his lost crown but the outcome of this campaign was altogether more decisive than the last one. Olaf had been an unpopular king with many of his people and his return was opposed. Two armies faced up to each other; that of the Christian Olaf was inspired, according to Snorri Sturluson, by a skáld's rendition of the *Bjarkamál*, the Norse equivalent of *Beowulf*. It did little good. Not only did Olaf lose the battle that followed at Stiklestad near Trondheim Fjord, this time he also lost his life, a loss that did much to strengthen Cnut's position on the throne of Norway. It did Olaf little good in this world that he would later be canonised as an ideal of the Christian ruler, though it did secure for him a hallowed place in the hearts of later generations, especially in Norway. But he was every bit a warrior too, famed for his mighty axe named *Hel*, after the Viking goddess of death.

Adam of Bremen tells us that Olaf had ruled as a Christian king, rooting out the 'magicians' in the land in his efforts to obliterate pagan practices. Norway, Adam suggests, was rife with such depravities: 'although all barbarism overflows with their number, the Norwegian land in particular was full of these monsters. For soothsayers and augurs and sorcerers and enchanters and other satellites of Antichrist live where by their deceptions and wonders they may hold unhappy souls up for mockery by the demons.'⁹ It is a description that only lacks cave trolls to make it Tolkienesque.

Olaf later came to be seen as a saintly king. The Church in Norway was on the rise later in the century and needed a royal saint to help cement its position. The late King Olaf, an aggressive supporter of Christianity in every sense of the word, seemed the perfect candidate and he was duly canonised. With the inevitable supernatural overtones that frequently gild the saga tales of the time, Olaf's body was later disinterred. It was found to be miraculously intact and the nails and hair of the dead king had carried on growing as if he were still alive. It was suggested that this was not at all miraculous but rather resulted from the preservative qualities of the sandy soil, an argument that was soon disproved. When some of the king's hair was cut off and thrown into the fire to test whether a miracle was indeed involved or not, it refused to burn. And so the sanctity of the slain Olaf was proved and in death he proved a unifying figure for the Norwegian people, exactly the opposite of what he had been in life.

By the thirteenth century Olaf was regarded as the model of a just Christian ruler, helped in particular by the writings of Snorri Sturluson, from whose account the story of the miraculous disinterment derives. It is interesting and perhaps predictable that Adam of Bremen, who was much more contemporary, also suggests that opposition to Olaf stemmed from the fact that he had apprehended the wives of some of his nobles for sorcery, another allusion to possible pagan practices stubbornly hanging on in Norway.¹⁰ Eventually Olaf's tomb in Trondheim would become famed as a place of miracles, leading to his ultimate recognition as a saint. He became a focal point for Norwegians, who saw him as a protector of their traditions, which was ironic given his strident attempts to impose Christianity on the country where he had once been ejected by his own people.

That Scandinavia generally was a region that was still in transition from old pagan beliefs to Christianity is also suggested by other episodes related by Adam of Bremen. He wrote of events in Sweden at around the time that Cnut defeated Olaf. In his account he said that an English missionary named Wolfred went to Sweden on a mission to convert men to his faith. Here, 'he proceeded to anathematize a popular idol named Thor' which he did, rather unwisely, by walking up to it and shattering it into pieces with a battle axe. The outraged Swedes who witnessed this act of what they would have regarded as sacrilege promptly cut him to pieces.[11] Parts of Sweden certainly hung on to their old belief systems until long after other parts of Scandinavia adopted Christianity and Uppsala in particular remained a centre of more traditional practices for some time into the future. It was memorably said by one historian that 'in Sweden the darkness of heathendom still hung heavy and low'.[12]

Uppsala had become a byword for its allegiance to the old religion. Here there was a temple decorated with gold with the statue of Thor enthroned at its centre. Either side of him sat Odin (Wotan in Anglo-Saxon) and Frey. The red-headed Thor, who governed the rains, the thunder and the lightning and the crops, drove around the sky in a goat-pulled cart. Odin was the god of war, the Norse equivalent of Mars. Frey on the other hand brought peace and leisure, symbolised by the enormous phallus that he was adorned with.

The priests at the temple made offerings to the gods, to Thor in times of famine, to Odin when war threatened. Frey was the recipient of offerings when marriages were celebrated. There was also a great feast held there once every nine years. The heads of different animals were offered up to the gods at such times. The offerings would be made daily, one of each type of creature every day for nine days, a grand total of seventy-two altogether across the feast as a whole. The bodies of the sacrificed were then put up in sacred groves by the temple; horses and dogs hung there along with, most disturbingly, humans. Some of them were apparently drowned in a sacred fountain that was close to the temple whilst there was also a tree nearby that bloomed in both summer and winter.

Once the sacrificial victims had been slaughtered, their blood was sprinkled everywhere, over the walls of the temple and on the congregation of the people. This was the world that bordered on to the territories of the most Christian King Cnut, a strange and terrible land indeed where human sacrifice was still practised. No wonder Viking warfare was savage.

Sweden remained fragmented long after Denmark and Norway moved towards centralised states. The vast forests of the country helped keep it naturally partitioned. There were certainly important trading centres in the Viking era there, like Birko. But a powerful centralising king did not emerge at this time. Sweden tended to look east, where the expeditions of the Rus brought vast wealth back to the area. But few men returned with pretensions as sea-kings but rather preferred to build powerbases far from home. However, a large merchant class did emerge which was very careful to ensure that a dominant king did not trample down their rights. It is probably no coincidence that for a long time the monarch of Sweden was elected rather than being a hereditary position. The long attachment to paganism as opposed to Christianity may also be explained by the absence of a strong centralised monarchy.

Paganism therefore continued to hold stubbornly on in some parts of Scandinavia. It is of note that even in England, a nominally Christian country for centuries, there were still instances of much older beliefs surviving. A tenth-century charter describes how a widow had taken such a dislike to an acquaintance that she had taken to making a wax doll of them and driving nails into it to cause them suffering. Her estate was duly forfeited to the Crown and she was drowned by London Bridge.[13]

Olaf's teenage half-brother, Harald Sigurdsson (though he is much better known by his nickname of Harald Hardrada – 'the ruthless'), was also present at the battle fought by the fjord near Trondheim. Though struck down, he survived and became King of Norway in 1047. His links with England were far from over, though he would take a long, roundabout route to get there, which included the Mediterranean, Sicily, Constantinople, Asia Minor, Russia and the Holy Land.

He led a great Viking army that invaded England in 1066 in the aftermath of the death of Edward the Confessor. King Harold II of England rushed north to meet this host and decimated it at the Battle of Stamford Bridge. Amongst the thousands of dead was Harald Hardrada, having achieved the 7 feet of English ground that he was promised by Harold as his prize. It was said that he died early in the battle, having been struck in the throat by an arrow. He had refused to wear armour, being in a state of *berserkergang* or blood-lust driven ecstasy.

Stamford Bridge, that later battle, is often seen as the end of the Viking Age. It was also in its own way very nearly the end of Anglo-Saxon England as, at the end of the battle, Harold II heard that the Normans had landed far to the south and rushed to meet them and his date with destiny at Hastings. But perhaps this earlier battle, at Stiklestad, marked the onset of the Viking Twilight, when Viking fought Viking in a decisive encounter here on the banks of a Norwegian fjord and when the King of Norway fell, leaving a clear field for his bitter rival.

The elimination of Olaf Haraldsson seemed to have secured the country for Cnut, who was now at the peak of his powers. Olaf had taken his young son Magnus to the court of his brother-in-law Jaroslav in Novgorod. Novgorod was far from Norway and it seemed that this was the end of the dynasty's involvement in Norwegian affairs but such was not in fact the case.

In 1030 Sweyn, Cnut's son by his first wife Ælfgifu, was sent to Norway to rule along with his mother, who acted as his regent whilst he was still too young to rule; something had to be done to fill the vacuum left by Hákon's death. It would not be a happy time for the Norwegians and it was suggested that she acted in a peremptory and oppressive way, so much so that this period in the country's history was long remembered for its harshness.[14]

Yet it is unlikely that Cnut's wife and young son would have unilaterally embarked on imposing such a harsh regime without Cnut's say-so. He was a stern overlord in England and there is no reason to assume that he would not act in the same way in Norway. Indeed, laws that stipulated that the testimony of a Dane should heavily outweigh that of a Norwegian seem guaranteed to breed resentment.

It was very difficult to make such punitive laws stick in the country; Cnut was not present and his main focus was elsewhere, so this period of harsh government in Norway does appear to be a miscalculation on his part which proved to be counter-productive as his government of the country did not last for very long. These contrasted with successful policies, more based on appeasement, that he had used well elsewhere. This is so surprising that some historians even query whether this interpretation of Cnut's harsh rule is correct.[15] Yet he would not be the first, nor the last, person in history to fall into the fatal trap woven by hubris if he had in fact overstepped the mark. In any event, before too long Cnut appears to have lost the support of the same powerful factions that had helped give him Norway in the first place.

There are some suggestions that it was not taxation that was the problem but harsh climactic conditions in Norway. Food was so scarce that the population was forced to exist on cattle feed and tree bark during these days. Men, in that superstitious age, contrasted these terrible times with the much gentler conditions of Olaf's reign and wondered quite what they had done by driving him out. If this seems unlikely to us, we are perhaps looking at the eleventh century with twenty-first-century eyes. In the 1080s, a letter was sent from Pope Gregory VII to Denmark, in which he said that he had heard that priests and a group of women were being blamed for crop failures in the country and were being persecuted.[16] In other words, looking around for scapegoats to blame in the event of crop failure and famine was not unknown in those days.

Norway was part of an imperialist venture for Cnut. He gained nothing from it and, even if he had held on to it, the payback he would have received financially would have been meagre compared to the investment in it. These included bribes he had paid, fleets and armies he had equipped, and the men he rewarded for their efforts. But former Danish kings had claimed to rule Norway and it was an understandable human wish for him to emulate and match them (especially, we might speculate, as one of them had been his illustrious father). But no Danish king had really made their claims realities and none had ever actually conquered the country. Probably Cnut was inspired to go one better than them.

Something certainly seems to have changed with his journey to Rome. Even the skálds, the court poets and praise-givers, picked up on it and, as they were highly skilled in saying what their royal listeners wanted to hear, they were a good gauge. One of them, called Sigvatr, spoke of Cnut as a ruler who was 'dear to the emperor and close to the Pope', glorying in his status as a pilgrim.[17] It was all very different from his pagan predecessors, who had been lauded for their glory in battle. These were certainly changed days and Cnut was a long way from an archetypal Viking king.

Several skálds are known to have visited Cnut's court in England during his reign. As well as Sigvatr, there were other men famous at the time such as Ottar the Black and Thorarin Praise-Tongue. Their job was to praise the king and keep him and his entourage entertained in the dark nights spent in the long halls, dimly lit but full of conviviality and comradeship (at least on the surface). The court poets were highly prized and often had a particular attachment to a specific king or other great man and their services were jealously guarded by their patrons. Sigvatr, for example, had King Olaf as his patron when he visited Cnut and could not be lured from him. Several short works were composed lauding Cnut's prowess by these men but their brevity and infrequency suggest a short acquaintance with him, as if they were visitors passing through his court, rather than a longer relationship.

Cnut also had to retain some focus on England even given all these north European activities. He is ironically often best remembered now for an event that might never have happened at all, the famous incident when he tried to halt the incoming tide. This is first mentioned by Henry of Huntingdon in the twelfth century. Henry told how the king ordered his chair to be placed on the sea-shore when the tide was coming in. He said to the tide that 'you are subject to me, as the land on which I am sitting is mine, and no one has resisted my overlordship with impunity. I command you, therefore, not to rise on to my land, nor to presume to wet the clothes or limbs of your master'.

The sea of course took no notice of such commands and drenched Cnut's feet and shins. This caused him to remark to his courtiers that 'the power of kings is empty and worthless, and there is no king worthy of the name save Him by whose will heaven, earth and sea obey eternal laws'. After this event, Cnut no longer wore a crown but placed it on a Crucifix. Read like this, Cnut's action in trying to turn back the sea was not to demonstrate his power but rather to demonstrate its limits to hyperbolic and sycophantic courtiers.[18] The exact location of this event, if it ever happened, is a mystery though Southampton is one place where later legend suggests it took place and nowadays there is a Canute Road in the city. Thorney Island (Chichester Harbour) has also been linked with it.

Another place associated with this legendary event is Bosham in Sussex, a pretty small town by the sea that had much greater significance in Anglo-Saxon times. There is another legend – no more than this on current evidence – that a young daughter of Cnut drowned in the millstream here and was buried in Holy Trinity Church in Bosham. Speculation about this was encouraged by the discovery of the stone coffin of a young child which suggested architectural links with the right general period during some work done in the church in the nineteenth century.

Shortly after returning from Rome, probably in 1027 (there are mentions in the *Anglo-Saxon Chronicles* of a journey to Rome in 1031 so either one date has been quoted in error or there were two visits), Cnut made his way north to Scotland where King Malcolm II, seeing what a redoubtable enemy he might be, submitted to him, probably at Fife, and became his man, though if the *Anglo-Saxon Chronicles* are to be believed it was not an arrangement that he held to for very long. Along with Malcolm, two other kings in Scotland called Mælbeth and Iehmarc also paid homage according to Henry of Huntingdon.[19] Iehmarc (or Echmarcach mac Ragnaill) was of Gaelic-Norse descent and later ruled part of Ireland around Dublin, the Isle of Man and some of the Western Isles and Galloway. Mælbeth was properly known as Mac Bethad mac Findlaith, the anglicised version of which will be instantly familiar to many: Macbeth.

Echmarcach man Ragnaill would later become king in Dublin after the death of the redoubtable Viking leader there called Sihtric Silkbeard in 1036. Sihtric, head of those mainly Norwegian Vikings who had established a strong foothold in Ireland, appears to have witnessed several charters at some time on behalf of Cnut and certainly seems to have modelled his currency on that of Cnut.[20]

Malcolm had been king since 1005 and was known as Máel Coluim Forranach, 'The Destroyer'. However, although regarded as High King of Scotland, he was not the sole king in the country. There were also kings in Galloway in the south-west and in the Western Isles. There was also a strong Anglo-Saxon interest in the south-east. In return Malcolm showed a strong interest in English affairs along the border and in 1018 he had installed his grandson Duncan (later Duncan I of Scotland) as king in Carlisle after winning a battle against the Angles of Northumbria at Carham in the same year. Eadwulf Cudel – Uhtred's brother who ruled in Bernicia, described by a chronicler as 'a very sluggish and timid man'[21] – had been badly beaten in that conflict and had been forced to cede lands held in south Lothian back to the Scots.

Mention of these confrontations is a useful reminder that Anglo-Scottish affairs were often difficult long after the Romans decided to build Hadrian's Wall and long before the era of William Wallace and Robert the Bruce. There had been an attack on Durham in 1006 in which the Scots had been repulsed, suffering great losses in the process. It was said that the walls of Durham (then a new town in many ways; the first cathedral there had only been started in 995) were decorated with many Scottish heads placed on pikes after the attack, their hair meticulously combed by the women of the city who were rewarded with prizes of cattle in return for their labours. Clearly the English did not just have Viking raiders to worry about.

The other two named men with Malcolm including Macbeth were probably under-kings who were his men. The reasons for the meeting are unclear but there are several possible explanations and perhaps there was more than one motive involved. The most obvious was to protect England's northern borders, especially as Malcolm had violently seized Lothian some ten years before. Moray (northern Aberdeenshire) was also in a state of upheaval which would allow Macbeth eventually to become mormaer (or lord) there, his lands possibly stretching as far north as Caithness and Sutherland. And even more to the north there was a Norse kingdom in Orkney, where the ruling regime was friendly towards Cnut's rivals in Norway.

The meeting with Malcolm and the other kings, an exercise in geo-politics, resulted in a promise of peace and friendship being made to Cnut. However, this was perhaps less than was desired; for example there was no promise to provide practical aid in times of war. In the event this was very much a one-off meeting and Cnut paid little attention to Scottish affairs afterwards, being far too occupied elsewhere to worry about it. But it was another action that could be interpreted as being inspired by imperialist tendencies and it emulated those of former English kings, notably the much-remembered Edgar who had also laid claim to the allegiance of British rulers outside of England.

As Cnut's reign continued in England there was an ongoing transfer of power away from Scandinavian lords to Anglo-Saxon ones, though not completely so. By 1030 the two most prominent secular lords were both English, Earl Godwin in Wessex and Earl Leofric in Mercia. However, Earl Siward of Northumbria makes a single appearance on a charter of 1033. He was of Scandinavian descent and became more prominent in the later reigns of Harthacnut and Edward the Confessor. He would in the 1050s be involved in a successful war against Macbeth, an involvement that would be alluded to in Shakespeare's masterpiece half a millennium later. This is not without indirect significance;

Siward's emergence in the 1030s at about the time that King Malcolm made his limited submission to Cnut suggests that the latter had appointed him as earl at about this time and had in the process resolved ongoing difficulties with the descendants of Uhtred in the north of Northumbria by replacing them altogether.

Siward's provenance is of note. He was said to have a Danish father and he was not noted in English affairs before becoming Earl of Northumbria in around 1033; rather more intriguingly, his great-grandfather was said to have been the offspring of a union between a noblewoman and a white bear. This suggests that Cnut was appointing his own man from outside of England, without consulting existing vested interests in the region; such a man was more likely to be loyal to him. Siward's main interest was in the southern part of Northumbria around York but when an opening appeared in the northern part of Northumbria, around Bamburgh, in 1041 Siward was quick to take advantage of the opportunity. His nickname was *Digera*, which in Old Norse means 'the Strong', and he seems to have lived up to it on this occasion. His position in Northumbria was no doubt helped by a judicious marriage to the late Earl Uhtred's granddaughter, Ælflaed.

We can read into this greater interest in the affairs of both Scotland and Northumbria that something had happened to Cnut to encourage him to take proactive measures to increase his involvement or at least his influence there. Perhaps this was partly as a counter to the powerful earls of Orkney who were allied to Cnut's opponents at the time. Certainly in Scotland Macbeth would prove to be a persistent opponent of them. But it is hard to avoid the speculation that he was also inspired by his closer connections to the Emperor to become more imperial himself. Allied to his aggressive actions in Norway, certainly Cnut appeared to be in expansionist mood.

He was supported by a loyal coterie of powerful earls in England. The emergence of Godwin, Leofric and Siward was about the advancement of men who all shared something in common. All of them were to an extent what we might now call nouveau riche. Only Leofric came from a long-established noble family in the upper echelons of the ruling hierarchy and even then not from the very highest levels.[22] It was as if Cnut was trying to replace the old school with one of his own.

This was a wise strategy on Cnut's part. The advancement of all of these men was due to the patronage of the king and therefore they owed more than just loyalty to him. Their position depended to a large extent on his ongoing support. It would therefore be a rash move on their part to do anything that might jeopardise that support, meaning that their own survival was to some degree dependent on that of the king.

Evidence that Cnut was seeking to pay off a few metaphorical debts to the Almighty can be found in 1032 when the Church of St Edmund, 'king and martyr', was dedicated at Bury St Edmunds. Given the part of the Vikings in causing the death of the king in 869 and the alleged disrespect paid to him by Sweyn Forkbeard, a psychologist might see in this act a monarch who is trying to right a few wrongs. It was said to be 'a church with princely magnificence' and the abbot who was responsible for it was also granted large estates.[23]

There were also probably very practical reasons behind this too. Edmund was a martyr to the English people in the same way that Archbishop Ælfheah had been. Both men were slaughtered by Danish raiders in cold blood, both standing defiant against what was seen as a heathen threat (even if by Ælfheah's time a number of the Vikings had ostensibly adopted Christianity). It was significant perhaps that the new Church of St Edmund was dedicated not on an anniversary directly connected to the saint but on the same date that the Battle of Ashingdon had been fought in 1016.

The building of a new church here and that at Ashingdon as well as the translation of Ælfheah's relics to Canterbury a decade before may be seen as an attempt at reconciliation and restitution. This can also be read in his patronage of Cerne Abbey in Dorset, a holy site that had quite probably been pillaged by Viking raiders just a few decades before. We do not know if these efforts were sincere and piously motivated or were rather just good politics. In any event, it was a statesmanlike move once more on Cnut's part.

Honouring the dead, especially those of the fallen enemy, was not the norm for the times. The later chronicler Orderic Vitalis notes that piles of bones were scattered around the battlefields of Stamford Bridge and Hastings decades after the event. The leaving of the bones of the enemy slain for carrion to help themselves to was a symbol both of contempt and of absolute victory for it was required that the lords of those who fell in battle should arrange for decent burial for them and not to do so was a mark of deep dishonour. To be left for the 'beasts of battle' to devour – the great black ravens and the wolves of the forest – was shameful. The Vikings certainly knew of this and at one time had carried a banner with a black raven – the 'Landwaster' – which they carried into battle, warning their enemies what to expect after they had fallen.

Other men of Scandinavian descent followed Cnut's lead in providing for the Church. In 1030, Tovi the Proud is recorded as financing the building of a church at Waltham. It was said that Tovi had found a figure of the Crucified Christ on his estates. Such donations show how the 'new' religion was becoming more firmly established amongst the northern warrior caste by this stage. Tovi and Osgot Clapa had appeared as witnesses to charters in the mid-1020s, showing that a new class of Anglo-Scandinavian 'minister' was appearing at Cnut's court by this time.

There are still some occasional unexpected reminders of these amazing years in England when the world of the Vikings, men who had not too long before been pagans, came into contact with that of Christendom and managed to find a way of coexisting. The museum in the undercroft of York Minster has several such mementoes. In this remarkable space, built on the very stones of the Roman basilica where Constantine, the Roman ruler who first adopted Christianity as the state religion, may well have been first acclaimed Emperor, there are several relics of the late Viking period. There are gravestones where traditional Viking pattern designs are interlaced with a Christian crucifix probably dating back to tenth-century Jorvik (York). But even more incredible perhaps is the Horn of Ulf, exactly contemporary with the reign of Cnut (dating to around 1030).

This is a large drinking horn, probably carved from the tusk of an elephant, which came initially from Italy, most likely from Amalfi or the surrounding region. It is said that Ulf presented it to the Minster as a token of the surrender of some of his lands and possessions to the Church. In the legend which has grown up around the Horn, Ulf is supposed to have laid it, filled with wine, on the altar of the Minster as a symbol of the transfer of his lands. It has exquisite carvings on it including a figure of a unicorn, a lion killing a deer and a gryphon (a mystical fusion of lion and eagle), which may well have been inscribed by Islamic craftsmen. This is of course a legend (though the land grants were confirmed in the reign of Edward the Confessor), and not a historically proven set of facts, but it does sum up rather well the fusion of cultures of the time: not just Anglo-Saxon and Scandinavian but that of paganism and Christianity. The links with Italy and Islamic craftsmen serve too as an eloquent reminder of just how global the Europe of the time was.

Certainly Cnut was a man who seemed as if he wished to go out of his way to demonstrate great respect for the Church. He was magnificently liberal with his donations at Winchester according to William of Malmesbury, making gifts to both the Old and the New Minsters. Amongst his contributions to the latter was a stunning gold cross which later found its way to Hyde Abbey, which was built when the New Minster was demolished in the early twelfth century.[24] The quantity of precious gems he gave astonished those who witnessed the bequests he made, though the chronicler suggests that this was at the instigation of his wife Emma, who wished to distract him from martial ventures.[25] But the description of this magnificent cross certainly gives the impression that this was in every sense a treasure, composed as it was of 500 lbs of silver, thirty marks of gold, three diadems and three footrests of pure Arabian gold. The abbey continued to hold a fascination for Emma even after Cnut's death as she was noted as gifting a relic, the head of St Valentine, to it in 1041.[26]

There is a remarkable piece of evidence to back up the story concerning the cross. A contemporary and well-known illustration of the event can be seen as the frontispiece to the *Liber Vitae* – The Book of Life – of Winchester, a volume that according to biblical precedent is due to be opened on Judgement Day. The compilation of an earthly Book of Life was one way that an individual could help ensure their passage into Heaven.[27] Having one's picture included, as Cnut and Emma did in this particular volume, was presumably of great help in this respect.

Cnut is shown clutching a cross, though intriguingly the one shown lacks any sign of precious jewels so maybe it is not the one which he presented. Above him, an angel places a crown on his head, probably an allusion to the heavenly crown that he can expect to wear when he receives rewards in paradise granted as a result of being a good Christian king in his lifetime. Emma kneels opposite him on the other side of the altar on which the cross is placed, with her regal Anglo-Saxon name Ælfgifu next to her. At the head of the page Christ hovers in glory above the cross, bestowing His own divine favour on Cnut and Emma as a result of their beneficence.

What can we read into this contemporary portrait of Cnut? No doubt it is a stylised picture, drawn by an artist who wished to present the king in a favourable light. But that is useful enough, for it tells us how Cnut himself wished to be seen. We see a confident man, clutching the cross boldly with his right hand whilst his left grasps his sword. A Christian king in one respect, a mighty warrior in another – certainly a good enough summary of how Cnut wanted to project himself.

He looks middle-aged, a tidy beard and a full head of hair suggesting nevertheless that he still possesses vitality; this perhaps is misleading as Cnut had only four years left to live when this picture was drawn. Whilst Emma looks slightly sideways at the cross, as if afraid to peer at it full-on, his pose is one of boldness, staring directly and unapologetically at the Christian symbol. This is a man who wishes himself to be seen as someone who will tackle a problem head on, who will not prevaricate but will confront whatever challenge may face him head-to-head; a man, in other words, not to be resisted.[28]

This is also an image which is imbued with imperial undertones. It is stylistically different to any other Anglo-Saxon art of the time. Instead it closely resembles Continental models of the period, particularly those of the German Ottonian court. Specific allusions were made to Roman emperors in the image. It is very easy to see the imperial pretensions in all of this and again hard to avoid the conclusion that Cnut's journey to Rome and his insight into Conrad's court had been a life-changing experience. Even coin changes on Scandinavian currency in the late 1020s show glimpses of contemporary German imperial inspiration and differ significantly from the English models that had previously been the basis of Cnut's currency in the region. This was a complete break with any previous precedents, for although German currency had circulated in Denmark before it had never been used as a model on which to base local coins.[29]

In later times, Cnut would be credited for the magnificence of his court. Of course, the usual caveats about saga writers who lived several hundred years later apply, but when Snorri Sturluson says that visiting Scandinavians found 'greater magnificence than in any other place, both as to the number in daily attendance and as to the furnishing and equipments of the palaces that he owned and occupied',[30] he should not be dismissed out of hand. Such grandeur would fit with the image that a king with imperialist pretensions would want to project and was also possible given the financial resources available to him.

Cnut would have been glad for the opportunity in 1032 to appoint his own man to the bishopric of Winchester. In that year Ælfwine became bishop. Before his appointment he had been one of Cnut's priests and was therefore a well-known quantity to the king. From the following year, he normally appeared as the third witness on Cnut's charters following the two archbishops. In a very hierarchical society such symbols mattered much. He certainly seems to have been close to the king, in his inner circle indeed, and a man that Cnut would be keen to promote as a loyal supporter.

Before his appointment as Bishop of Winchester, Ælfwine had played a key role in persuading Cnut to allow the relics of St Mildred to be translated to St Augustine's Abbey in Canterbury (according to some accounts the king would have been persuaded rather easily as he gave thanks to the saint for saving him from shipwreck whilst on the way back from Rome).[31] The body of Mildred was translated to Canterbury on 18 May 1030 though the abbey in Thanet from which it was moved was by then in a position of steep decline and had no nuns and only a few clerks. With a painful sense of irony, it appeared that the church there had never got over a Viking raid on it in 980.[32]

Ælfwine would remain close to Cnut for the rest of his reign and would long outlive him, becoming a key adviser also to Edward the Confessor. He was also close to Emma of Normandy, allegedly too close if some possibly scurrilous rumours are to be believed. There were other acts of religious donations that marked Cnut's reign such as the gifting of a magnificent reliquary containing the remains of a fourth-century Spanish saint, Vincent, or the translation of the remains of St Wystan at Evesham Abbey. These were ways for the king to demonstrate his piety, ingratiating himself with his subjects and his God at the same time.

These 'translations' of saintly relics were a common feature of the time. It meant moving the remains of saints from their original, normally humble, resting places to somewhere more grand. This usually followed a series of miracles connected to the saint, so much so that their former place of burial was no longer considered worthy of them.

Cnut was adept at using Church appointments in which he played a vital part as a way of securing and advancing his interests. When vacancies came up, men who were known to him and in his favour would be put in place wherever possible. Winchester was clearly a special place to him; such can be inferred from his decision to be buried there and so the appointment of Ælfwine to the bishopric can be seen as suggesting a strong connection between king and cleric. It was also an important place, one of the great cities of England and in those days navigable from the sea by means of the River Itchen, which was open to shipping which it is not now. Its importance to England at the time cannot be overstated.

Another man who must be regarded as being in Cnut's inner circle was Dudoc, appointed as Bishop of Wells in 1033. Before this he had been given lands in Somerset and Gloucester, a further sign that he was in favour. Dudoc was not of English stock and came from the Continent, from Lotharingia. This was the region in which Cologne was placed, a city that had become a very significant ecclesiastical and imperial centre. It is possible that Dudoc had come back to England with Cnut when he returned from his imperial tour in 1027, when he is known to have been in the vicinity of Cologne. He too would comfortably outlive Cnut, living well into the reign of Edward the Confessor and dying in 1060.

Perhaps the most remarkable appointment, though, was not at one of the major religious sites of the time but at the new church built at Ashingdon and dedicated back in 1020 to commemorate the battle that was fought there and those who died in it. Cnut had a young priest in his entourage by the name of Stigand and he was made a chaplain at Ashingdon. The name is Norse but that of his brother Æthelmaer is English. He therefore seems to have come from a family that somehow bridged two cultures to a certain extent.

Stigand is shadowy during Cnut's reign, only appearing as an occasional witness to a diploma; indeed, so little is heard of him in the early part of the reign that some historians consider that the suggestion that he was appointed as the cleric responsible for the minster at Ashingdon is incorrect.[33] In later life, though, he would become an adviser to Emma of Normandy and was made Bishop of Winchester in 1047. He played a part in the power-politics of pre-Conquest England and achieved the ultimate prize of Archbishop of Canterbury in 1052, though in controversial circumstances. He, however, hung on to the bishopric of Winchester at the same time, which might suggest someone of a rather mercenary disposition, though such actions were by no means unique.

On the death of Edward the Confessor in 1066, Stigand led the funeral service. Some accounts also claim that he crowned Harold Godwinson as his successor (he is certainly shown doing so in the Bayeux Tapestry). He managed to survive the Norman invasion for a short time and William the Conqueror retained his services for a while. But then in 1070, his usefulness done, he was deposed by the king. He was subsequently imprisoned and died in captivity in 1072, being buried in the Old Minster in Winchester, close by Cnut.

Another example of Cnut's ability to mix politics with Church appointments may be found in the appointment of Ælfweard as Bishop of London in 1035. London was a prime ecclesiastical prize, ranking only behind Canterbury, York and Winchester in terms of the hierarchy of the English Church. It was said that Ælfweard was a relative of Cnut's and certainly the installation of someone from the king's party in London would have been very welcome as the city was always a headache for him. Ælfweard was previously Abbot of Evesham but he did not give up this position on his appointment to London, even though Church law required him to. Here again is a good example of turning a blind eye to the niceties of canon law.

This was a welcome opportunity for Cnut to put his mark on the Church in London. The uncomfortable nature of his relations with the clerical establishment there was well evidenced by his removal of the remains of the late Archbishop Ælfheah from there to Canterbury in 1023. In addition, he made generous gifts to Westminster Abbey, then relatively unimportant, which was outside the city of London. A tradition grew up that he gifted several relics to the abbey, some of them relating to St Ciriacus, another, more significantly, of the martyr king and saint Edmund. There were also relics connected to St George.

Most significantly of all, though, was the possible donation of a relic related to no less a person than Ælfheah himself. If true this was a remarkable move. It meant that when the saint's body was exhumed, Cnut had taken the opportunity to help himself to a relic, allegedly his finger (it was suggested that he also gave a relic of Ælfheah to the Old Minster at Winchester at some stage). That was striking enough but to donate it to a religious house in the London region but not to St Paul's, which had been a site of pilgrimage for the slain archbishop, seemed to forcefully make a point against that august church and the bishop whose religious home it was. The expropriation of lands belonging to the bishopric at Southminster would only accentuate the point.[34] In this respect it is also probably more than coincidence that in 1023 the Abbot of Westminster died and was replaced by a man named Wulfnoth; there are some suggestions that he was sponsored by Cnut, no doubt as a way of building up his influence in London.[35]

There are a number of surviving records of Cnut's gifts to various churches though we cannot be sure at this remove that the list is complete and fully representative. But it appears that he was later a particular beneficiary of Durham and of St Cuthbert especially, again maybe a sensible political move to try and ingratiate himself with the local population in an area of England that to a significant extent remained outside the mainstream of the country. That this appears to have happened only later on in his reign is also significant, particularly given other steps he took to strengthen his influence in Northumbria at around this time.

That said, his 'gifts' to Durham were also possibly to an extent selective. Rather than grant new lands to the cathedral, he quite possibly put pressure on some of the leading secular men in the region to return lands that had previously been transferred from the Church to them. This was a way of both ingratiating himself with the Church and also putting an independent-minded local aristocracy back in their place. The cost to Cnut, apart from walking barefoot for five miles in an act of pilgrimage, might not personally have been that great.

His visit to Durham comes across as a particularly astute move. The church there was only a few decades old, having been founded in 995, and housed the sacred relics of St Cuthbert, perhaps the most hallowed of all English saints at the time and even allegedly the inspirer of Alfred the Great's fightback from Athelney when he appeared to the king in a dream. Cuthbert had died in 687 and was then buried on Lindisfarne, where he had been bishop for a while. Of course, the Viking raids had made this a location of very doubtful security and eventually the sacred remains of the saint had been moved elsewhere in an attempt to protect them.

The body of the saint then underwent a rather peripatetic existence. It was housed for a short time at Ripon and for a longer period at Chester-le-Street. But even here it did not appear to be safe. It ended up at last on top of a steep hill above the River Wear, now perhaps most famous for its beauty but then more attractive for its impressive defensive qualities for which it had been noted by Uhtred of Bamburgh. Cnut's homage to this most influential of English saints, one who was closely connected to the Anglo-Saxon royal family, was likely to endear him to his subjects, especially those in the remote and difficult to control area in the faraway lands of Northumbria. Again, as with St Edmund and others, the fact that he was so respectful to a holy man who had suffered indirectly at the hands of the Vikings (even if he had by then been dead for several centuries) could also be interpreted as an exercise in bridge-building.

Cnut's attachment to religious establishments was, however, selective. At other times Cnut experienced difficulties with particular churches such as those of Ramsey Abbey or Ely (though later in his reign those with the first-named abbey seem to have improved). It is perhaps noteworthy that these were two East Anglian abbeys, where maybe there was more local opposition to Cnut's reign. This, after all, was an area where the troublesome Earl Thorkell had held sway for a while and a number of East Anglian men had died in battle against the Danes: indeed, Ashingdon itself was on the southern fringes of the area and many prominent East Anglians – including a number of churchmen – had died there. Cnut therefore seems to have chosen to have built strong links with churches, or churchmen, who served his purpose.

It was no blank-cheque arrangement in play here and some prominent foundations, such as Worcester Cathedral, seem to have received nothing at all from him although nearby Evesham Abbey, which appears to have been headed by a relative of Cnut, did rather well.[36] Indeed, there are very few suggestions of Cnut making gifts to foundations in west Mercia at all other than to Evesham. This may be, some have suggested, because the region had become almost a separate province in its own right during recent times, especially when under the control of the much-despised Eadric Streona. Even King Æthelred had made few recorded gifts there.

Cnut had been more active in terms of making gifts in Wessex. Even there, though, he was selective. He had been overwhelmingly munificent to Winchester and also to Abingdon and it may be no coincidence that these had also received lavish gifts from Æthelred. He also made recorded donations to other foundations in the region, such as to Sherborne. However, his involvement in Church affairs in the area was almost timid in comparison with what it was elsewhere. There are suggestions that Cnut intervened in attempts to place his own candidates into vacant sees at both Sherborne and Wells early on in his reign but with limited success. Cnut did not, it seems, at that stage have the confidence to push the point. It was only in later years that he was forceful in such matters in Wessex, perhaps now having become much more certain of his position. The region had probably been on the verge of revolt early on in his reign when ealdorman Æthelmaer was expelled but that was now long in the past.

As the years advanced, there was evidence of another ghost to put to rest. One of Cnut's most astute moves was his decision to appoint Æthelnoth as Archbishop of Canterbury. It is perhaps significant given Æthelnoth's beginnings that in 1032 Cnut granted financial privileges to the abbey at Glastonbury, though there is no evidence of gifts from the king at any other part of his reign, showing again that his involvement in Church affairs in this region was selective.[37] He even at some stage journeyed there to pay his respects at the tomb of Edmund Ironside. He left an ornate cloak decorated with peacock feathers at the tomb. This was an item with several symbolic dimensions to it. It was associated with Byzantine emperors, laying out a link with one of the foremost world powers of the day, and it was also a Christian symbol associated with resurrection (some of the catacombs of ancient Rome have paintings of peacocks on the walls).

Cnut confirmed all the privileges granted to the church at Glastonbury by his regal Saxon forebears in Wessex as well as more recent predecessors as King of England such as Alfred, Æthelstan and Edgar. He also made gifts to Wilton, where St Edith, the sister of Æthelred II, had served and where according to some accounts Emma had had that king buried. In paying homage to these former rulers who had reinforced the importance of Glastonbury Abbey and also the king with whom he had fought a bitter war, it was as if Cnut was taking great care to look to his legacy and how history, or more likely in those times the Almighty, would judge him in the future.

The connection with St Edith was a curious one. There is a moral tale told by William of Malmesbury that Cnut did not at first approve of her and suggested that she had not merited the veneration she had received as a saint. He ordered her shrine to be opened and when this was done she rose up and struck him. If we are to believe this tale, the king was of course dumbstruck and did penance for his sin at once. The miraculous 'resurrection' of St Edith did the trick.

The gift to Glastonbury was perhaps occasioned by the rather convenient death of Edmund just a few weeks after agreeing to split England with Cnut, an event now some years in the past. No involvement of the latter in Edmund's demise has ever been proved but it was an event that was very helpful to him. It would be surprising if no tongues had wagged at the time, especially given Cnut's probable involvement in the death of Earl Uhtred of Northumbria. By making such gestures now he was perhaps hoping to make his peace with the English people and also the spirit of the late king and the God whom Cnut would have expected to answer to for his actions some day.

This strange reunion must have engendered some odd feelings in Cnut. Here he was in the presence of his former great adversary, paying him great honour. Glastonbury, with its great abbey, was a sacred place. The age-old tor stood like a sentinel behind the monastic establishment. The tower which stands there today is a much more recent construction but even in Cnut's day there was a monastery at the top of the lonely hill. In later medieval times the place would be inextricably mixed with stories of Arthur and Joseph of Arimathea but by the eleventh century it was an important place in its own right.

Modern historians tend to see Cnut's relationship with the Church as being almost entirely a politically inspired expedient. Support for the Church certainly had its political uses. His Viking ancestors had brought chaos to the English Church but here was Cnut building it up and defending it. It even contrasted favourably with the actions of some Anglo-Saxon kings such as the luckless Æthelred, who had been regarded as being an enemy of the Church when he took action to regain Crown property which had been handed over during the great monastic reform movement in the mid-tenth century, though he had subsequently mended his ways.[38]

We cannot know whether or not Cnut was genuinely pious, though there is no good reason to think that he was not. But many of his interactions with the Church were at least politically beneficial so they served a double purpose even if he was deeply religious as a man. In a country where many of his Anglo-Saxon subjects may still have thought of him as a usurper and of possibly being implicated in the all too convenient death of Edmund Ironside, his actions can also be seen as a determined and well thought-out attempt to foster support and evolve a sense of legitimacy for himself and his dynasty. Yet that does not mean that he was not also, by the standards of the time, a genuinely devout Christian ruler. He was of course a man as well as a king. It would not be unusual if he were to genuinely fear for his own immortal soul as many other men of the time did, even those (or perhaps especially those) who could also be ruthless and merciless in their actions. If his penitence and piety served more than one purpose, then so much the better for that.

There is widespread evidence of the scale of Cnut's generosity, whether it be to the church of Winchester, those of Peterborough or Cologne or the splendid gifts to Duke William of Aquitaine (a land that had, like England, suffered much from Viking raids in former times and where perhaps some bridges also needed to be rebuilt).[39] We should believe that these accounts are true as they are often penned by the recipients. No doubt this helped secure his reputation in the history of the Church. However much his motivations may be questioned, even if ultimately we cannot prove that he was not a genuinely religious man, he may well have been such. Many of his gestures and penitential actions were very public and can be read as part of a show on his part. But at the same time they were what was expected of a king at the time and he played the part, if this is what it was, very well.

When all is said and done he was a man with a shady past with even shadier antecedents. Even in his lifetime, Vikings that his dynasty claimed to lead were hacking the life out of an archbishop in a very public act of violence, hardly the actions of a Christianised people. Seen from this perspective, the munificent gifts can be viewed as manipulative gifts dressed as spiritual donations with which to strengthen his own position, ones that furthermore were often financed by other people such as his subjects or the very Church he was claiming to espouse. Perhaps as an eleventh-century king, Cnut was genuinely motivated by what was to happen to him in the life to come, but we would be guilty of naivety to assume that he had no concern for his life on Earth at the same time.

A good illustration of this can be identified in the gift of a shrine that he and Emma made to Abingdon. It was an expensive piece of work and Cnut wanted people to know it. The inscription on the shrine stated that 'King Cnut and Queen Ælfgifu [Emma] commanded this shrine to be wrought with 230 mancuses of refined gold and two pounds of silver'.[40] Clearly everyone who saw this – or those who could read the inscription anyway – would be impressed with their regal power and generosity. If they might also pray for their immortal souls too, then so much the better.

There were signs by this stage that there was ongoing concern about the possible intervention of Normandy in English affairs. Emma's sons from her marriage to Æthelred were now grown to adulthood. William of Jumièges tells a story that in 1035 Cnut made an offer to divide the country of England with one of them, Edward, and there are other titbits which hint at him being regarded as the rightful King of England by the Norman court. Events soon after Cnut's death would suggest tensions too.

The references to Edward are not sufficiently detailed or consistent to be regarded as incontrovertible evidence, but they are nevertheless suggestive that there were problems in Cnut's mind as far as Normandy was concerned and William of Jumièges, the later Norman chronicler, suggested that a Norman invasion fleet set out but was defeated by the weather; this was probably in 1029 or 1030 as in the period after this the duchy was heavily involved in a civil war in Francia. Allied to the fact that Duke Robert of Normandy had been quick to divorce Cnut's sister Estrith – if indeed he had ever married her at all – and there is reason to believe that matters were far from well between England and Normandy at this stage, even though Robert was Emma's nephew.

Any tension between Cnut and Robert was brought to a permanent conclusion when the latter died on pilgrimage to Jerusalem some time before 1035, making his way east after a harsh famine had badly affected his duchy. Interestingly, there were also stories of famine in Norway at around this time, events that may have contributed to the resistance towards Sweyn and Ælfgifu in the country; this, along with other accounts of terrible deprivation in Europe at the time, suggests very hard times indeed for parts of the Continent.

Duke Robert left behind him a young son and heir, an eight-year old boy who had come from a relationship with the daughter of a tanner from Falaise whose name was Herleva. It is far from clear that there was ever a marriage involved but this did not prevent the boy from duly becoming duke. He would have many trials to survive before his position was secure but at the end of these he would be a mighty warlord. The young duke's name was William and three decades later England would have cause to regret that he had ever succeeded as duke at all.

Cnut too needed to think about succession. With his life drawing towards its concluding years, Cnut decided that Harthacnut should continue looking after Denmark. He sent troops with him to help secure the government of the country. It has the sound of a king who is getting old, in body if not in terms of years of life, who realises that he has not long left in this world and wishes to put his affairs in order whilst he still can. Sweyn, his son from his first marriage to Ælfgifu, was at one stage to have Norway. However, by 1034 it had been lost to Magnus, the son of Olaf Haraldsson, barely more than a child but showing signs of great promise. 'Florence' of Worcester could not stop himself from referring to rumours that Sweyn was not Cnut's son at all but that his father was really a priest of dubious morality.[41] The dispossessed Sweyn found sanctuary in Denmark where he is thought to have died in 1035.

It is significant that the proclamation of Magnus as king whilst still only ten years old took place when Cnut was still alive. The young boy was called back from Novgorod after a period of resistance against Ælfgifu and Sweyn led by prominent Norwegians such as Einar Tambarskjelve, who was married to the late Earl Hákon's sister, and Kalv Arnesson. Olaf Haraldsson, Magnus's late father, was canonised and Norway was now free of Danish rule. It would remain so for the next three centuries. In fact, the boot was now firmly on the other foot. When the crown of Denmark came free in 1042 with the end of Cnut's direct line it was Magnus of Norway who staked a claim to be the next king of the country. In Norway, Magnus ultimately proved himself a popular ruler, avoiding the excesses of his father so well that he was awarded the sobriquet 'the Good'.

Life was running out; Cnut was tired and aware that his end could not be postponed much longer. Even though he was not old, there are hints of some kind of illness bothering him, something that some of the sagas refer to, including a suggestion that he was suffering from what was termed 'jaundice'. Whatever the reason, Cnut was to die before his time. The words of the *Encomium* may be hagiographical but they are nonetheless a remarkable epitaph for a man who started life as the younger son of the fiercest Viking warrior of his age and ended it as a pillar of the Christian establishment:

> The Lady Emma, his queen, mourned together with the natives,
> poor and rich lamented together, the bishops and clerics wept

with the monks and nuns; but let the rejoicing in the kingdom of heaven be as great as was the mourning in the world! These wept for what they had lost, but let those rejoice over his soul, which they take to themselves. These buried his lifeless body, but let those lead his spirit aloft to be rejoiced over in everlasting rest. Mortals alone wept for his departure, but for his spirit let the heavenly citizens as well as mortals intercede. Let us earnestly pray God that his glory may increase from day to day; and since he has deserved this by his benevolence, let us pray every day: 'May the soul of Cnut rest in peace. Amen.'[42]

8

Cnut the Great:
A Life Assessed (1035)

It was on 12 November 1035 that Cnut's reign came to an early
end. He died at Shaftesbury, the Dorset hillside town with the
dominating view of the Blackmore Vale below, home to a great
abbey, founded by Alfred the Great. It was a place of long
historical associations with the royal family of Wessex. If it was
perhaps appropriate that a king who had been born Danish and
had essentially made himself feel at home in England should die in
such a thoroughly English town, it was equally so that his death
took place within a few yards of where the martyred king, Edward,
lay buried. Yet there is an irony in that supposed Englishness.
In England Cnut is rarely referred to as 'Great', that accolade
normally belonging to the wholly Saxon Alfred. In Denmark he is
rarely referred to without the epithet.

There is some evidence that Cnut knew that his end could not
be far off. He had visited the nearby abbey town of Sherborne in
earlier years when the church was in a sorry state and the roof
was leaking badly. He and Emma made generous contributions to
it then. Now he made another grant to the church in the form of
the manor of Corscombe in Dorset. In return for his donation to
the monks there, he asked that daily prayers be said for his soul.[1]
Although this was by no means an unusual convention, in such
circumstances it does not appear to be too rash a speculation that
Cnut was thinking about his own mortality and was taking steps
to protect his soul in the Hereafter. It is probable that he was not
even forty years old when he died.

Prayers for the soul were much needed now that the king was dead. A legend developed that his heart was cut out and buried in a small casket at Shaftesbury. A small glass container, 'the Shaftesbury bowl', was unearthed during an archaeological dig at the abbey: it was speculated that this could have contained Cnut's heart, though Edward the Martyr's lung was another possible candidate. The rest of Cnut's remains were taken to Winchester where they were buried in the Old Minster and eventually ended up in an ornate box, a mortuary chest that dates to the sixteenth century of which there are several examples in what is now the cathedral. Here he was part of a somewhat random collection, sharing a box with his wife Emma, Bishop Ælfwine and William II, the successor to William the Conqueror.

The king's bones would be desecrated by Parliamentarian soldiers during the Civil Wars of the seventeenth century. Therefore we cannot be sure that the remains that are now stored in the chest actually belong to him – in fact, as the box in which they supposedly repose is made up solely of arm and leg bones whilst another with allegedly only one Saxon king in it contains no less than five skulls, it certainly does not contain all of him.

The Roundhead soldiers responsible for this outrage allegedly used the thigh bones to break the medieval stained glass in the east window. Indeed, we cannot even be sure that any of the bones in the boxes in the first place were ever those of whom they were supposed to be. The Old Minster had been demolished when the present Norman cathedral was built and thereafter the bones could have been lost or mixed up as far back as the end of the eleventh century.

At the time of writing this book, attempts are being made to see if DNA matches can prove which bones belong to which monarch. As well as Cnut, the mortal remains of his wife Emma of Normandy, five earlier Saxon kings and three Saxon bishops are thought to be in the chest collection. Unfortunately when they were re-packaged after the Civil War came to an end, they were mixed up and there is no certainty which bones belong to which individual.[2] Matching Cnut's DNA may, however, be possible because recently the remains of Sweyn Estrithsson, his nephew who was buried in Roskilde, and also his sister Estrith, were examined intensively and could prove a potential match.

Some particular challenges have arisen as a result of these modern scientific interventions. The bones after all include those of consecrated English monarchs and bishops. Therefore they need to be treated with special respect and as a result a temporary laboratory has been set up in Winchester Cathedral in the Lady chapel there rather than allow them to be taken away from this sacred ground for testing. It would be fitting if the bones of Cnut, and indeed his wife Emma, were at last allowed to rest in peace at the end of these procedures, this time hopefully with greater confidence that they are actually in the right place.

It is apt that we cannot even be sure where exactly Cnut's bones are. There are limits to so much about the evidence we have for him and his times. When re-writing the story of Cnut, we have to make the most of the limited documentary evidence that we have. The *Encomium* for example does not say much about the reign of Cnut other than in a retrospective sense, almost in the style of an obituary. The writer noted that he was the Emperor of five kingdoms: England, Wales, Scotland, Denmark and Norway. This seems to be stretching a point. There is no evidence that he ever actually ruled Scotland other than in a limited nominal sense and none at all for his subduing the Welsh although there is some that suggests occasional raids from England into the Welsh hinterland from time to time. Even Norway could not be regarded as being securely Cnut's as by the time that he died he had lost his grip on it.

The writer of the *Encomium* also noted that Cnut was a great patron of the Church, 'a friend and intimate of churchmen, to such a degree that he seemed to bishops to be a brother bishop for his maintenance of perfect religion, to monks not a secular but a monk for the temperance of his life of most humble devotion'.[3] His generosity towards the Church made a great impression, as no doubt he intended that it should.

Cnut's status as a ruler of European reputation was confirmed posthumously when the year after his death his daughter Gundhild was married to Henry, son of the Holy Roman Emperor Conrad II. The groom would later become Emperor Henry III. He and Gundhild had been betrothed some years before when they were still children, which explains why there was no marriage during

Cnut's lifetime. This was a prestigious match and would only have been considered if the bride had been a suitably important prize for such an important husband.

This in itself is evidence of the standing to which Cnut had risen. Unfortunately, the match did not have a long-term impact on European affairs as Gundhild died just two years later. The Danish alliance was important to the Empire for political purposes as a way of ensuring that its northern borders were protected so that greater attention could be paid to more lucrative parts of her extended territories, which stretched far down into the Italian peninsula. It was also, of course, very useful to Cnut. If he had lived and wished to recover Norway, he would need a secure frontier to the south of Denmark.

Whilst relationships with the Holy Roman Empire are reasonably well documented, there is limited surviving material on Cnut's links with other European powers. However, there is the occasional hint of strong ties with some contemporary rulers. For example, the Aquitanian chronicler Adémar of Chabannes wrote of yearly embassies from Cnut to Duke William the Great of Aquitaine. The English king sent great treasures to Aquitaine and received even greater ones in return; there was talk of a beautiful codex adorned with golden letters as one such gift.[4] It was potentially very useful to have alliances in Francia outside of Normandy as a form of counterbalance to possible complications emanating from the duchy.

We know perhaps more of Cnut's relationship with the Church than of anything else, for the simple reason that more written records have survived. The Church was, by the standards of the day, a soundly administered bureaucracy, which meant that many transactions were relatively well documented. By Cnut's time it was a well-established power and for a Christian monarch it offered a few potential challenges but also a number of opportunities. It held considerable influence over secular affairs and therefore relationships with it needed to be properly nurtured, something that Cnut seemed very well aware of. In so doing, there would be mutual benefits for both parties.

One way this could be done was by the patronage of saints. The importance of the lives and examples of such holy men and women was a strong phenomenon by the early eleventh century. They were much valued for their sanctity and the inspiration of their lives and their presence on earth was marked by the display of relics, the spiritual homes of which, the churches in which they rested, had become centres of pilgrimage.

These centres of pilgrimage, and the iconic saints that they commemorated, played their part in building the power of the Church. Cnut's cultivation of certain favoured saints helped him to strengthen links with the clerisy. It is noteworthy that he made various donations and gestures of support to 'martyred' English kings and saints such as St Edmund and the comparatively recently slain St Edward. Such moves can be seen as gestures designed to emphasise his piety – and even, in the case of Edmund, a sense of restitution for the actions of his forbearers – whilst at the same time fostering closer links with the English kingdom that he claimed to rule.

The Church had become very rich as a result of societal changes that began in the tenth century and continued under Cnut. Domesday Book, half a century later, recorded Canterbury and Winchester as being the richest and second-richest religious establishments in the country and their wealth was immense. Monastic establishments were also wealthy and during Cnut's reign that at Bury St Edmunds was a particular beneficiary of royal and noble largesse. In 1020 a new stone church here had been built on his orders, soon followed by further donations from him and Emma, including a grant from the latter of 4,000 eels yearly from Lakenheath. Yet even so there was evidence that Christianity had a stronger grip in the south of England that it did in the north. A legal document, the Law of Northumbrian Priests, which was probably compiled during Cnut's reign, forbade heathen practices, witchcraft and idol worship, suggesting that there was a need to make such prohibitions.[5]

It is an important reminder that Cnut's dynasty was still in relative terms new to Christianity. In a time when the support of the king was critical to the wellbeing of the Church, and where she could in return provide strong political and practical support to the monarch, Cnut and the Church needed each other. But the Church was more strongly established in England than she was as yet in

Denmark and so the shape of the English religious establishment was not much changed by the Danish conquest. Instead she probably helped to shape the king and through him Denmark, though in this respect it was not just English but also German and other clerics that played a role.

Cnut, who was baptised as Lambert when he became a Christian, was outwardly very pious but nevertheless continued to value things from his pagan Viking past. This particular 'Christian name' was associated with the Piast dynasty who ruled in Poland for a time and was probably given him by his mother when he was young, emphasising his probable Slavic origins.[6] There was also, though, a duality to all this: at the same time he was also a patron of the skaldic poets with their pagan heritage who made the lives of those who were dead live once more. That said, even English monarchs had not completely forgotten their roots. It was possibly during the reign of Æthelred II that the surviving version of the Anglo-Saxon epic *Beowulf* was written down, an intriguing work with undoubted pagan origins but noticeably Christianised and therefore sanitised for a more contemporary audience.[7]

Cnut was certainly capable of acts of public humility which helped reinforce the veneer of piety that attached to him. When he visited the tomb of St Cuthbert in one of his rare excursions to Northumbria, he allegedly walked the last five miles barefoot. This is by no means an unbelievable tale. In 1051 Sweyn Godwinson, son of Earl Godwin of Wessex, went on pilgrimage to Jerusalem as a mark of repentance for his sins. Sweyn had been involved in the murder of Bjorn, brother of Sweyn Estrithsson, King of Denmark, and nephew of Cnut (and therefore his own blood-relative). One account of his death on his return homewards tells of him dying of exposure in the mountains of Asia Minor, where he was walking barefoot in the winter as a sign of penitence.

Contemporary or near-contemporary Church writings emphasise Cnut's humility, a reminder to those who succeeded him to act in the same way. By adopting such a pose Cnut was acting out the paradigms expected of an earthly king by the Church, a role model to other rulers and as such a very useful tool for the religious establishment who needed such examples. We can assume that Cnut saw political as well as spiritual benefits arising as a result of acting in this fashion but so too no doubt did the Church.

Cnut may have been acting out a part when he made himself into a model Christian king, the complete antithesis of the pagan Viking warlords whose blood ran in his veins. But it was certainly a convincing performance if he was. Geoffrey of Cambrai was prior at Winchester half a century after his death and he wrote some verses on the king which, translated into English, read as follows:

> Cnut, sprung from the ancient blood of kings,
> Had greater power than countless kings,
> He girt his noble brow with a triple crown
> While he reigned over Danes, English and Norwegians.
> And he who had been a proud robber, bloodied against the foe,
> Held the office of king over those subject to him.
> Often leaving the joyous banquets of his own table,
> He became a companion of poor monks.
> Putting aside pomp, amid a needy crowd,
> A fellow slave, he served the slaves of God.
> The last light shone for him on the twelfth of November,
> And the last day becomes the first day for him[8]

If Cnut was playing such a role without genuine underlying beliefs, he certainly took in Geoffrey and many others like him, though his generosity towards Winchester would certainly have helped convince them of his sincerity. It was a consummate performance.

The country of England that Cnut bequeathed to his successors was a very different one than that which he had inherited. From what we can glean from the surviving records, this had been in the main a time characterised by peace compared to what had preceded him. What fighting marked Cnut's reign had generally been in Scandinavia, though there were several possible plots to replace him in England. But Cnut had felt confident enough in the security of England after the early years to leave it for some fairly long periods of time. There had certainly been evidence that England

and Scandinavia had come to terms with each other. The greatest of Anglo-Saxon nobles, Earl Godwin, had named his sons Sweyn, Harold, Tostig and Gyrth, all fine Scandinavian names, whilst the very Norse Tovi the Proud called his son Æthelstan. England was almost in danger of becoming cosmopolitan.

Yet it is necessary to avoid over-romanticising Cnut's view of England as some historians have tended to do in the past. There is a risk of assuming that because Cnut spent the largest proportion of his time as king in England, he felt a deeply held affection for the country. He may have done; we do not have conclusive evidence one way or the other. But more likely he spent much of his time in the country so that he could keep an eye on it. It was after all the source of much of his wealth, and that wealth was a way of building and keeping power. The most likely explanation of his presence in England is that Cnut's attachment to the country was a largely pragmatic one.

Neither did England show excessive warmth towards him. There was no royal biographer, no equivalent of Asser, the Bishop of Sherborne who write a famous biography of Alfred. The *Anglo-Saxon Chronicles* say little about Cnut. This is perhaps unsurprising; he was after all first and foremost a conqueror of the people whose history they are chronicling. More surprising perhaps is that he made relatively little impression on the saga-writers, rating much less attention than Harald Hardrada, who followed shortly after him.

But Cnut failed in one thing. He left behind a messy, tangled line of succession. This has even led some historians to claim that Cnut's death was sudden and unexpected. However, this is not necessarily the case. Cnut's generous donations in later life, whilst not at odds with events earlier in his reign, could suggest a man who knew that his health is failing and that his end might be not too far off. And Harthacnut's position in Denmark was under threat at the time Cnut died so it is very possible that he could not have left for England even if he wanted to. This would leave Denmark wide open to attack from Norway.

Nevertheless, Harthacnut's continuing absence from England at a critical time after Cnut passed away, however sound his reasons, was to have drastic consequences for his position there. It is most likely that he was declared King of Denmark in Cnut's lifetime as a way of establishing his legitimacy whilst his father was still alive. Such moves were by no means unusual in those times and were practised elsewhere on occasion, for example by the Capetian dynasty in Francia. It helped now to protect Harthacnut's position in Denmark but was less effective in doing so in England.

After Cnut's death, Emma took up residence in Winchester. It had taken Cnut nearly two decades to build a strong empire; it was a matter of weeks before it started to unravel. The throne of England was claimed by Harold Harefoot, who stated that he was the son of Cnut and the Lady Ælfgifu of Northampton, though the *Anglo-Saxon Chronicles* insisted that this was untrue. He pounced on many of the riches of the late king, seizing them from Emma who was powerless to stop him. This not only deprived her of her wealth, it also effectively took away her power.

A legend grew up that the two children born to Ælfgifu of Northampton from her 'marriage' to Cnut were both fathered by other men, Sweyn to a cobbler and Harald to a priest. It is a story that may well have owed much to Emma, anxious to blacken the character of her ostensible rival and also debar her children from any claim to the throne of England or anywhere else. She seems to have been a woman who would not let much get in the way of her ambition. But Ælfgifu was still alive and was soon in prime position to extract a fierce revenge for her effective disinheritance. The scene was set for a dark period in English history and a series of plots and counter-plots of Machiavellian proportions.

Emma's life had taken a sudden and terrifying turn for the worse and it was not about to get better. She was effectively under house arrest in Cnut's palace at Winchester. Harthacnut appeared to be in no hurry to come back from Denmark and England was divided in his absence. The south of the country broadly stood behind Harthacnut, the north for Harald, though this is probably a gross over-simplification. Emma's arch-rival Ælfgifu of Northampton was now in the ascendancy. The state of chaos was evidenced by the actions of the moneyers; some minted coins with Harald's head displayed, some with Harthacnut's, and some even kept their options open by minting coins for both. Others, perhaps wiser than the rest, carried on producing ones with the reassuring figure of Cnut displayed as if hankering after a miraculous resurrection.[9]

Then another complication was added to this already incendiary mix. Emma's sons from her marriage to Æthelred, Edward and Alfred, now decided to stake their claim, further muddying the waters. They abandoned the security and comfortable anonymity of Normandy and returned to England. Whether this was at the active suggestion of Emma is not clear. She may have given up on Harthacnut and cynically attempted to exploit her other sons for her own benefit; it would seem rash to put it past her. There was talk of a letter encouraging them to return to England. It began plaintively 'Emma, Queen in name only'. Others suggested that this was a forgery artfully created by Harold Harefoot, although as the accusation comes from Emma's apologist in the *Encomium*, this claim should be treated with caution.

But return the two absentee sons did. Edward made his way to Southampton with forty ships. It was a sizeable force and conveniently close to Winchester and his mother whilst also ideal for a quick getaway if the attempt failed. Alfred, however, ended up in Kent after sailing across from Flanders. This ultimately had fatal personal consequences. Why he journeyed through Kent is unclear. It is unlikely that he was making his own bid for the throne as dividing forces amongst the natural supporters of Æthelred's sons would not be a sensible strategy. Rather, the *Anglo-Saxon Chronicles* suggest that he was on his way to link up with his mother in Hampshire.

At Guildford he met with Earl Godwin, who greeted him in friendly fashion. But when his guard was dropped the earl's men fell on him and his escort, which was a large one. They were seized and bound. Many of Alfred's men were slaughtered in cold blood. Archaeological digging in the area in the 1920s found the remains of several hundred men from the right period of history who bore all the characteristics of being executed. Thrown into prison first of all, Alfred was then taken to Ely where he was blinded, probably by warriors loyal to Harold Harefoot rather than Godwin's men. In this appalling state he was found by the monks at Ely, with whom he died soon after.

According to the *Anglo-Saxon Chronicles*, no worse act had taken place since the Danes came;[10] a significant statement indeed when one considers that Godwin, one of the prime causes of this, was of English and not Danish stock (though he had clearly thrown in his lot with the Scandinavian dynasty). Regardless of the politics of removing a rival to the throne, it was a despicable act. There were suggestions that Godwin and Emma had been managing to maintain a working relationship of sorts up until this point. That moment had now passed.

Godwin seems to have at first sided with Emma whilst she stood out for the rights of Harthacnut. Her recall of her two sons by Æthelred, if we assume that it was at her instigation that they returned, suggests that Harthacnut's claim was felt to be increasingly unlikely to be sustained. Godwin was presumably no friend of the old regime in Æthelred's line, as his father Wulfnoth had been at odds with him. Now that Edward and Alfred had returned, he had clearly decided to change sides. Perhaps egged on by his Scandinavian wife and certainly not wishing to see a return to the chaos of the pre-Cnut years, Godwin decided that now was the time to do a sharp about-turn. Like many men of the time, self-interest seemed to be the prime motivator.

These shocking events were seized upon by those chroniclers that opposed the usurpation of Harold Harefoot. The writer of the *Encomium Emmae Reginae* partly blamed Harthacnut for this turn of events. In his view, his 'absence gave an unjust invader a chance to enter the bounds of his empire, and this man, having secured the kingdom, killed the king's brother under circumstances of most disgraceful treachery'.[11]

Much as Emma may have wished otherwise, she could not overturn the accession of Harold without Harthacnut and she was driven from England soon after 'without any mercy to face the English winter'[12] before making her way to exile on the Continent, though to Flanders rather than Normandy. England submitted to Harold because, it was said, Harthacnut had spent too long in Denmark. Edward managed to escape from England and across the Channel to safety. His part in the drama was far from over.

Godwin acquiesced to the taking of the English throne by Harold and indeed if we accept these accounts, he actively aided it. Maybe this was just a pragmatic acceptance of realpolitik but it made him look untrustworthy. His unsavoury involvement in the blinding and subsequent death of Alfred left a stain on his character that was hard to wash off. This is despite the fact that these last terrible events took place in Ely, far from Godwin's heartlands, which suggests that Harold may have been responsible for them. Whoever was to blame for the final act of this black drama, Godwin had played a key role in the events leading up to it.

There is an interesting reference made by 'Florence' of Worcester that England was, at an earlier stage, to once more be divided with Harold getting the north and Harthacnut the south. The decision as to who got what was apparently to be made by the drawing of lots.[13] It is an allusion to a country that was still not quite at peace with itself, whose people did not yet think of themselves as one homogeneous whole, not yet completely what we might call a nation. This also suggests that despite Cnut's great achievements, even such an outstanding ruler as him could not mould England into one unified land given the various racial and political factions that then existed. Now, after his death his own family were at war with each other. It was a vendetta that would have done Shakespeare in his pomp proud, where one wife fought against the interests of another and brothers took up arms leading opposing factions. It was in short a familial mess.

Even the Anglo-Saxons in Cnut's England were divided. Earl Leofric of Mercia supported Harold whilst Godwin had initially supported Harthacnut but then changed sides. Godwin was showing himself to be a Machiavellian operator in the mould of Eadric Streona. Emma, in exile now, was forced to be patient but not for too long, for on 17 March 1040 Harold died, leaving the way open for Harthacnut to return to England and take up the crown or, in the slightly less balanced words of the writer of the *Encomium*, 'divine vengeance followed, smote the impious one, and restored the kingdom to him to whom it belonged'.[14]

This was, it seemed, a further miracle, another divine intervention to bring England to her senses. Harthacnut was already waiting across the Channel with a fleet when the young Harold died, supposedly of natural causes. But the timing was as fortuitous as was the demise of Edmund Ironside several decades earlier so there is circumstantially fuelled suspicion of foul play (though no firm evidence for it). Emma returned to England and with her came her son from her first marriage to Æthelred, Edward. Godwin managed to dextrously change sides again. Harthacnut, however, also did not enjoy the fruits of kingship for very long, for on 8 June 1042 he too expired.

It was said that Harthacnut was excessively fond of the good life; a later source remarked of him that he was renowned for the generosity he exhibited in the feasting hall. But he was a chip off the old pre-Cnut Viking block, a man who saw England as a source of wealth to be thoroughly exploited without giving something back in return. His fierce retribution in Worcestershire after several of his heavy-handed officials had been killed trying to grab yet more money from the local populace became a dark stain on his character. It was as if the worst days of Sweyn Forkbeard had returned. It seems unlikely that many would have mourned his passing after an excessively heavy drinking session at the marriage of Tovi the Proud, a retainer to Cnut, at Lambeth on the Thames. Tovi was celebrating his union with the daughter of Osgot Clapa, another man who was close to the late, great king. It was like a final swansong for the old regime. Harthacnut's sudden death was like an allegory for the fall of Cnut's England.

In the aftermath of Harthacnut's unexpected demise, the repercussions of Cnut's unfinished business in Scandinavia were exposed. A few years previously Harthacnut had entered into an agreement with Magnus of Norway, the main ingredient of which was that whichever man died first, the other would succeed to all his lands. This meant, in theory at least, all of Norway, Denmark and England. Magnus was resisted in Denmark by Sweyn Estrithsson but on Harthacnut's death he succeeded in taking the throne there. This agreement with Harthacnut gave Magnus and his successor Harald Hardrada a claim that was an ongoing threat to stability across Cnut's old empire. There would be several further Viking raids on England before 1066, though not on the same scale or of the same frequency as those previously seen.

After the sudden death of Magnus in 1047, his uncle Harald Hardrada took Norway but Sweyn Estrithsson reasserted his claim to Denmark, leading to more years of fighting there. This lasted until 1064 and finally Sweyn managed to seize power and proved himself to be a very capable King of Denmark. In the interim, there were yet more Viking raids; this time Denmark, not England, was the target. This confirmed the inherent weakness of any 'Empire of the North'. Scandinavia itself was not united and if there were internal tensions still to sort out there, how then could England be firmly assimilated in the Empire? Cnut worked around this issue during his reign by focussing on England as his core priority but this was at the expense of the other territories he claimed to rule, especially Norway. Even Cnut the Great left an empire that was already starting to fragment and we must therefore conclude that in the circumstances that pertained at that time it was impracticable.

These problems with Scandinavia suggest that the extended nature of this Empire of the North made it unsustainable given the situation that pertained in the opening decades of the eleventh century. The formidable Sweyn Forkbeard had struggled to retain Norway even before he was set on the conquest of England and Cnut had been forced to leave England on several occasions in attempts to keep control of Scandinavia. Even he failed in Norway. If such great personalities as Sweyn and Cnut could not maintain control across these extended territories, there was no chance that lesser men would.

Yet it is also important to emphasise that Cnut's reign was an important part of an ongoing process of development in Scandinavia that had been taking place for decades, even centuries. The extraordinary success of Scandinavian adventurers, whether raiders or traders, had brought great wealth into the region. This can be seen in developments as varied as the evolution of jewellery, the appearance of more sophisticated furniture in the region and the evidence of imported luxuries such as wine and glassware. Cnut's contribution to the continuing growth of Denmark and its evolution into a nation state that became an integral part of western Europe was extremely significant, even if it did build on the successes of others such as his father Sweyn Forkbeard and his grandfather Harald Bluetooth.

He also left in England a powerful class of Anglo-Scandinavian rulers and Danish influence continued in England for some time after he was gone. Earl Godwin, the most powerful man in the country after the king for several decades, was married to a Dane and his brood of children continued to have links with Scandinavia. Other men of Danish descent continued to play a key role in the affairs of England, both nationally and locally. Earl Siward continued to hold sway in Northumbria and the names of men like Osgot Clapa and Tovi the Proud continue to be mentioned with regard to English affairs. So too, more locally, do men like Ork in Dorset. And it worked the other way around too. Much later in the century, men with the distinctly English names of Ælfnoth and Ælfweard appear to have been minting coins for Danish kings in Denmark.[15] More worryingly for King Edward the Confessor and his successor Harold, Scandinavians continued to lay claim to the throne of England.

After Harthacnut's premature demise, the throne of England went to Edward and thereby reverted to a Saxon line of kingship. Edward ruled on until 1066, becoming renowned for his sanctity (though this may well be the invention of a royal hagiographer) and therefore known as King Edward the Confessor. He would be an idealised model for many later medieval kings of England and was forever associated with the building of a great abbey at Westminster (though a more modest monastic house existed there previous to this). Yet here he betrayed the fact that he was no Saxon traditionalist, for the minster was the first church in the Norman Romanesque style to be built in England. He had become, in other words, to some extent a Norman (Norman warriors were present in Herefordshire in the 1050s) and this was to lead to many complications when he died in 1066.

Edward was crowned on Easter Day 1043 at Winchester, to date the last time that an English monarch was so honoured there or anywhere else outside Westminster. The day was significant, associated as it was with resurrection and new beginnings. So too was the place, for here were buried the mortal remains of Cnut, Edward's stepfather, and Harthacnut, his half-brother. In its own way it was a claim to legitimacy on Edward's part as, given Magnus of Norway's claims, it was not at all legally or morally clear that the throne was his to take.

It was far from guaranteed that Edward would be chosen as king. He was not, after all, of Cnut's bloodline and there were many powerful men in the country now whose ancestors were Danish rather than English. Harthacnut, who was only about twenty-three when he died, left no heirs but Sweyn Estrithsson was seen by some as his natural successor. Again, though, Sweyn was far away in Denmark just as Harthacnut had been when Cnut died. Anyway, that awkward treaty made between Harthacnut and Magnus would now, theoretically, kick in. And Sweyn would have enough to concern him in protecting his position in Denmark without worrying about England.

Edward had returned to England in the latter part of Harthacnut's reign. Quite why he did so we cannot be sure, though it is possible that the calculating wiles of Emma were behind the decision. Perhaps she feared that the start of Harthacnut's reign had been ill-starred and the return of someone from the Anglo-Saxon bloodline, a true descendant of Cerdic, would buy some public favour. After showing little interest in her son for many years, she now apparently needed him again. Maybe Harthacnut was ill and in the absence of an heir in the form of a son, an alternative was needed; we should assume that Emma had no wish to be caught out by another disputed succession. Certainly it may have seemed preferable to many that an Anglo-Saxon should become king rather than a Norwegian like Magnus.

There was one man who was kingmaker in the succession to Harthacnut. Nearly a decade after Cnut's death, the strong triumvirate that gave his regime solidity was still at the high table: Godwin in Wessex, Leofric in Mercia and Siward in Northumbria. But of these the most powerful was Godwin. Edward was naturally suspicious of him; after all he was the man who was significantly responsible for the blinding and savage death of his brother Alfred. But he must have been persuaded somehow that the great earl, the power behind the throne in Cnut's time, could be trusted. Perhaps, when all was said and done, Edward had little choice; without Godwin's support, he probably had little chance of becoming king.

The murder of Alfred would nevertheless loom large over Godwin. He had had to make an enormous peace offering to

Harthacnut when he had come over to England, though whether Harthacnut's anger was real must be in doubt (he and Alfred were only half-brothers and there is little evidence that they spent any time together). Godwin presented Harthacnut with a magnificent ship along with eighty warriors, fully equipped and sumptuously weaponed with axes adorned with gold and silver bindings, and shields with golden studs. The men wore gold rings weighing sixteen ounces on each arm. Godwin managed to ingratiate himself with Harthacnut. Now he had to repeat the trick with Edward. That must have been difficult – but not too difficult. Both men needed each other. In the end expediency triumphed above any thoughts of morality, as it normally does.

But England it seems had had enough of the Danish bloodline. Her people turned to the Anglo-Saxon dynasty again. The experiment with Danish kings in England had come to an end. In some ways it demonstrates the essential fragility and impermanence of Cnut's achievements. Yet in others it accentuates the magnitude of his success that he alone was able to do what his successors had not: keep a grip on both Denmark and England for fifteen years and at the same time become a man of substance on the European stage. It reinforces the fact that his reign was one of immense and, in its own way, unrivalled personal achievement.

Yet this is only half the story. Some of Cnut's main Danish supporters carried on for a time with little change to their roles or the lands that they held. According to one prominent modern historian of the period, the witness lists to the royal charters issued in the early years of Edward's reign show 'massive continuity' from the reign of Cnut.[16] Even Anglo-Saxons had been changed by Danish influence. Earl Godwin for example had married into the Danish royal family and his sons, including the man who became King Harold II of England and died at Hastings, were therefore half-Danish. Even some of the troops fighting and dying in that fateful battle at his side were of Danish descent. The Bayeux Tapestry shows many warriors on the 'English' side who were equipped with axes that look distinctively Danish. Nationalities and racial origins had become blurred.

However, as time went on there were strong suggestions that Edward bristled at the Anglo-Danishness of his father-in-law's dynasty. Gradually, prominent Danes were removed from power. Cnut's niece Gundhild and her children were exiled from England in 1044. Osgot Clapa was deprived of his East Anglian estates in 1046; he returned on a raid a few years later but was forced back to the Continent after achieving not a great deal.

By 1049 there are no Scandinavian names witnessing charters.[17] Only in remote Northumbria, far removed from the centre of power in the south of England, did Earl Siward retain power. Edward refused to support Sweyn in Denmark against the attacks of Magnus from Norway, despite encouragement from men like Godwin to do so. It was a dangerous game. Once Denmark fell, England might be next. The problem resolved itself when Magnus died before his time in 1047.

The remarkable Emma died in England on 7 March 1052. She was buried in Winchester close to her second husband Cnut and their son Harthacnut. It is probably significant that Edward allowed his mother to be buried next to her second husband rather than with her first, and his natural father, in St Paul's. During the latter years of her life, she briefly retreated from the public eye, losing most of her remaining treasures in the process. She recovered some of her former position at court but she was effectively finished in the political arena. Edward had seemingly become suspicious of his mother, who had after all managed to switch from being the consort of Æthelred to that of Cnut with remarkable dexterity. In the process she had largely abandoned her sons from her first marriage for years.

It was only months after Edward's accession before he turned on her. Relations had been so difficult between the two that it was even said that Emma would have preferred Magnus of Norway to be king rather than Edward.[18] It was yet another example of the complex relationships that marred the family lives of two departed kings and rivals, Æthelred and Cnut, and continued to do so even long after they took leave of the world stage.

Even Godwin though was not immortal. The year after Emma's death, he died. He too was buried in the Old Minster at Winchester, close to his great royal benefactor Cnut in an increasingly crowded mausoleum. Relationships with the English king were difficult, despite Edward's marriage to Godwin's daughter, Edith.

So bad did matters become that for a time Godwin was forced into exile though he returned soon after with a large army at his back and matters were hastily, if superficially, patched up. Given this, Godwin's death not long after probably came as a relief to the king.

Edward's marriage failed to produce an heir. In the absence of one, attempts were made to reintegrate the children of Edmund Ironside, who had been in exile in Hungary. They had not seen England since they were babes in arms, some three decades before. The only surviving son, Edward, had done well at the Hungarian court and had made an excellent marriage to Agatha, a relation of the Holy Roman Emperor. He came back to England in 1057, only to die shortly after his return. He was buried in St Paul's close to King Æthelred, his grandfather. He left a son, no more than five years old, called Edgar and two daughters, Margaret and Christina.

Siward of Northumbria died in 1055 and Leofric of Mercia in 1058, the last of the great earls appointed by Cnut outliving him by almost a quarter of a century. Siward was also an outwardly religious man. Siward founded a church in York in which he was buried. However, he could not forget his Scandinavian roots – it was dedicated to St Olaf, in life one of Cnut's most consistent opponents. Godwin had effectively been replaced by his son Harold and other members of his house, such as his brother Tostig, ensured that King Edward 'the Confessor' struggled to remove himself from their shadow. Of prominent Danes in England there was barely a trace by this time, though far to the north the shadow of the Norwegian Harald Hardrada loomed like a distant cloud threatening a tempest. Ultimately, his death at Stamford Bridge in 1066 would give Anglo-Saxon England perhaps its greatest victory in 600 years. Just a few weeks later it would suffer its worst and terminal defeat at Hastings. Such are the vagaries of history.

Given the subsequent demise of the ruling Danish dynasty in England, how should we assess Cnut's life? It is perhaps worth, referring to the words of a man who did not really approve of how he took the throne but nevertheless could not ignore his qualities.

William of Malmesbury said of him that 'though he obtained the sovereignty unjustly, yet he conducted himself with great affability and firmness'.[19] It must be admitted though that the mention of firmness strikes a more resonant note than does affability, especially as the word from which it stems, *mansuetudo*, in modern terms means 'gentleness'.[20]

Although details of the short reigns of both Harold and Harthacnut are scanty, what remains does not inspire hopes that they were ever likely to make a favourable impression. The legacy of Cnut was therefore limited in the longer term, or at least in England this was the case. It was much greater in Denmark, though, when also taking into account the reign of his father Sweyn Forkbeard and his grandfather Harald Bluetooth.

There was no permanent establishment of a ruling Danish dynasty in England and in all probability England made a greater mark on Cnut rather than vice-versa. The design of the Danish Church and currency along English lines suggests as much. No doubt the greater wealth of England also proved an immense boon to Cnut in his enterprises across the length and breadth of his empire but for the people of England the benefits of Cnut's reign were more limited in the long term.

But there is little doubt that there were shorter-term benefits. During his lifetime Cnut brought stability to England, albeit at a hefty price to taxpayers in the country. The Danegeld of Æthelred's reign continued but in a different guise, now in the form of legal taxation – *heregeld* or 'army tax' – rather than what was effectively 'protection money'. But although taxes were heavy, at least the persistent violence stopped. There were several attempted coups against Cnut's rule but they were not accompanied by large-scale warfare. We must assume that the people of England were extremely grateful for this.

The stability of the country during his reign shows that Cnut's policy of creating a new aristocracy in England with men like Godwin, Leofric and Siward advancing at the expense of the old regime worked whilst he still lived. Therefore, in his lifetime it was a successful tactic. After his death, however, the stability soon evaporated and infighting quickly broke out. Therefore it can be argued that success was only possible when there was a strong central authority in place (such as Cnut) in order to make the policy work.

It is also the case that during these years the secret of success in many parts of Europe and not just England or Denmark was successful expansionism. This gave rulers the chance to dispense their patronage, reward their supporters and therefore keep them under control. This policy had worked in Ottonian Germany, it had worked in Carolingian Francia, it had worked in tenth-century England with its all-conquering monarchs and it had also worked for Cnut. It would continue to work, spectacularly well, for Duke William of Normandy, though at a huge cost to the country that he conquered.

The problem was that when the expansionism stopped it was difficult to find an alternative way of rewarding ambitious supporters without depriving others and therefore creating internal dissent. This may be seen as a fatal weakness of Æthelred's England. Successful patronage was at the heart of successful kingship at the time and Cnut's energetic expansionism enabled him to reward men well, be they secular or ecclesiastic. Æthelred on the other hand was in no position to do the same.

With regard to the government of England, Cnut's policy was innovative. Whilst he sought to gain the maximum personal advantage from his kingship (which can hardly be said to be unique in the annals of history) his attempts to make himself more acceptable to his English subjects were a marked contrast to the ruthless suppression of the conquered by an alien power evidenced by William the Conqueror half a century later. On the other hand the latter conquered England far more effectively on a permanent basis by squeezing the life out of Anglo-Saxon society, particularly at the ruling levels in the country.

In England at least, Cnut carefully cultivated as many trappings as he could of what was expected of an English king, which would no doubt increase his legitimacy with his subjects there. So we find him as a patron of some places closely associated with former monarchs: Shaftesbury and King Edward 'the Martyr', Glastonbury and the great Edgar (as well as Edmund Ironside), Wilton and St Edith and Winchester, closely associated with Alfred, where Cnut was buried in what was effectively an Anglo-Saxon royal mausoleum.

Cnut was careful to link his reign with that of King Edgar in particular. The homilist Ælfric of Cerne wrote of Edgar that he was a 'noble and resolute king [who] exalted the praise of God everywhere among his people, the strongest of all kings over the English nation'.[21] This was a man that Cnut would like to be compared to. At the same time he cultivated links with important English clerics who were also associated with the previous ruling Anglo-Saxon dynasty. In many ways this was a very successful policy despite his Scandinavian roots. He noticeably referred back to the reign of Edgar almost as a role model for his own, most significantly in the adoption of his laws.

Cnut's approach to England might be regarded as an interesting experiment which worked well whilst he lived but did not long survive him. The same could not be said in Scandinavia, where his tactics were more traditional. By imposing his sons Sweyn in Norway and Harthacnut in Denmark he hoped to maintain stability in those lands. It worked in Denmark to a large extent but only at the expense of Harthacnut effectively giving up his claim to England. It did not work in Norway at all, mainly because the tough fighters in that distant and demanding country had no wish to be ruled by a Dane.

In fairness to Cnut and his legacy, it must be said that the demise of Harold and Harthacnut, both in their twenties, was premature even by the context of those much more dangerous times when life expectancy was much shorter than it now is. Even Cnut's death at around the age (probably) of forty was still fairly young. This can be regarded as little more than bad luck, though contemporaries might be more likely to attribute it to the Hand of God. But the problems experienced between Harold and Harthacnut when Cnut died did not inspire confidence that things would have been better had they lived longer.

In assessing Cnut as a king it is important to remember that he was also a human being, with strengths and weaknesses, virtues and blind spots, skills and deficiencies. Calling a man 'Great' does not make him superhuman. As a wise Norse poet suggested, 'no man is so good as to be free from all evil; nor so bad as to be worth nothing'.[22] It is also important to remember that even though Cnut died young his reign covered twenty years, not an age certainly but enough time to evolve into the role. As time passed, so did Cnut change and adapt.

So when we first see Cnut as a young man his start was unimpressive, as he was ejected from England in a short space of time. Yet given his youth and probable inexperience, we should not be surprised at this. That he was caught off-guard is perhaps forgivable but also suggests something else: that Cnut was not a military prodigy. Indeed, his career suggests a warrior who was stoic and determined but not necessarily a brilliant military tactician. We do not know enough of the detail to be sure of this, but judged by results alone, apart from the triumph of Assandun there were no decisive victories (and even Assandun might have been Pyrrhic in nature).

However, although it was important for a king of those times to be brave and inspiring in battle, Cnut was not the only English monarch to know defeat as well as victory. That other monarch with the moniker 'Great', Alfred, also suffered several heavy reverses. But both men showed themselves to be more than capable of coming back from these and fighting through to success and this was a crucial quality as rulers from this and other times, such as Robert the Bruce of Scotland, demonstrate well.

It is also important to note that, crucial though military prowess was, it was not the only requirement of a good king. Political acumen was also vital and Cnut had it in abundance. So we see that even in England Cnut adopted contrasting policies in different parts of the country. In western Wessex it was subtly installing his own men into positions that were locally important; in western Mercia and London it was a much more direct approach. Northumbria was largely left to its own devices until later on in his reign.

So too with his Scandinavian possessions. In much of Denmark it was a light touch that seems to have been the norm. However, in Skåne the opposite was the case, suggesting a thorough suppression of the previous aristocratic dynasty. He did not really demonstrate fully his long-term approach to Norway simply because it was not his for long enough. But his initial tactics of effectively buying the support of the aristocracy there were so successful that the country fell to him virtually without a fight, so here we see Cnut cleverly using his not insignificant wealth to buy support.

His visit to Rome in 1027 seems to have changed his view of kingship. After his return we see much stronger imperialist tendencies. He no doubt had the confidence to act on these after his discussions with Conrad II and if he was inspired by first-hand sight of the trappings of empire, he was not the first or the last person to be so moved. On his return the imperial crown was copied, the Danish currency changed to a more Germanic style, Norway was invaded and the nominal subservience of Scottish kings was gained. Northumbria too became more integrated with the rest of England. This is compelling collective evidence of a man whose view of kingship had fundamentally changed to one that was altogether on a grander scale.

Cnut should not be thought of as a thoroughly modern king. A more balanced assessment than that is needed. One modern commentator said of Cnut that 'we can see a broad conception of his role emerging in Cnut's mind and acts; but monarchy still depended on fear as well as on loyalty and good government, and the Viking in Cnut never disappeared'.[23] This is as good an assessment as any. He may have gone out of his way to be a Christian king but those who crossed his path in a negative fashion tended not to last for very long. That he felt comfortable with new approaches to kingship appears clear enough but that he also was shaped by the old Norse traditions and upbringing he had is similarly apparent. That is unsurprising, for few people are not formed in part by the environment in which they develop. And the Viking North was certainly an environment unlike any other.

Cnut evolved the concept of Viking-era kingship in some important ways even if he was not completely innovative. His use of the Church as an ally for the secular state in Denmark was impressive but it built on trends started before him by Harald Bluetooth and possibly even continued by Sweyn Forkbeard, though the acerbic commentary on his reign by the waspish Adam of Bremen makes it hard to be sure. But Cnut certainly took it to a new level. At the same time he seems to have respected many Viking conventions in Denmark especially and continued to make use of the skálds, the

Viking equivalent of bards, who extolled his virtues though this time as a Christian king and a friend of emperors. Even the poets were changing.

So Cnut passed from human view and into the realms of history. The Battle of Hastings in 1066 turned England on its head, but it was not the end of Danish involvement in the country. After William of Normandy became King of England, attempted Danish invasions were launched. There was one in 1069 and another in 1075 which achieved little of long-term note but did succeed in raiding York Minster. The last was in 1083, with Danish forces linking up with others from Norway and Flanders and King William forced to rush back from campaigning in France to deal with the threat. But these events never materialised into anything of real substance. The attempt in 1083 was a rather disappointing non-event, a real damp squib, when compared to the aggressive efforts of earlier times and it marked the effective end of Scandinavian raids on England. The Viking age had announced itself explosively in the country nearly three centuries before but had gone out with a whimper.

England had changed forever. After Hastings, Edmund Ironside's grandson Edgar was elected king in place of the slain King Harold. In fact, as an aetheling he had far more claim to the throne than the Godwinsson who had died at Hastings did. But it was a position that would not hold. William was far too strong, though Edgar did escape to live a long life. His sister Margaret, however, would play a part in the future history of England. She married Malcolm III of Scotland and their daughter Matilda married King Henry I – but that is another story. Soon after 1066 Anglo-Saxon England breathed its last, several decades after the ruling Danish dynasty in England expired. The world, and England especially, would never be the same again. Despite this, the Anglo-Saxon epoch was missed. Margaret, for example, showed her roots clearly enough with the names given to her four eldest sons: Edward, Edmund, Æthelred and, Edgar.

In its own way the Anglo-Saxon dynasty lived on. The bloodline of Cerdic may have died out in the male side (it is easy to think this happened when William triumphed at Hastings but Harold Godwinsson was not of the bloodline either) but through the female it survived, albeit in a somewhat diluted form. It continues to flow in the veins of the reigning British monarch, though watered down by the emergence of new dynasties, such as the Tudors, Stuarts and Hanoverians, at which point the line of descent became quite distant and indirect. It is appropriate that what links there are to the line of Cerdic and Woden stem from the granddaughter of Edmund Ironside, a brave and determined English hero who led a gallant but futile defence against the stoic and ultimately triumphant Viking king, Cnut the Great.

Bibliography

Primary Sources

Alexander, Michael, *Beowulf – A Verse Translation*, Penguin, Harmondsworth, 1973

Alexander, Michael, *The Earliest English Poems*, Penguin, Harmondsworth, 1970

Campbell, Alistair (ed.), *Encomium Emmae Reginae*, Royal Historical Society, Cambridge University Press, Cambridge, 1998

Doubleday, H. Arthur and Page, William (ed.), *A History of the County of Hampshire, Volume 2*, Victoria County History, London, 1903

Forester, Thomas (trans.), *The Chronicle of Florence of Worcester with the two Continuations*, Henry G. Bohn, London, 1854

Giles, J. A. (trans.), *William of Malmesbury's Chronicle of the Kings of England*, Henry G. Bohn, London, 1847

Greenway, Diana (trans.), *Henry of Huntingdon – The History of the English People 1000–1154*, Oxford University Press, Oxford, 2009

Lunde, Paul and Stone, Caroline, *Ibn Fadlān and the Land of Darkness*, Penguin Classics, London etc., 2012

Page, William (ed.), *A History of the County of Kent, Volume 2*, Victoria County History, London, 1926

Storm, Gustav and Hearn, Ethel Harriett, *Snorri Sturluson – The Sagas of Olaf Tryggvason and of Harald the Tyrant*, Valde Books, 2009

Swanton, Michael (trans. and ed.), *The Anglo-Saxon Chronicles*, Phoenix Press, London, 2000

Tschan, Francis J. (trans.), *Adam of Bremen – History of the Archbishops of Hamburg-Bremen*, Columbia University Press, New York, 2002

Wright, A. P. M. and Lewis, C. P., *A History of the County of Cambridge and the Isle of Ely: Volume 9, Chesterton, Northstowe, and Papworth Hundreds*, Victoria County History, London, 1989

Secondary Sources

Barker, Katherine, Hinton, David A., and Hunt, Alan (ed.), *St Wulfsige and Sherborne*, Oxbow Books, Oxford, 2005

Barlow, Frank, *Edward the Confessor*, Yale University Press, 1997

Barlow, Frank, *The Godwins*, Routledge, Abingdon and New York, 2013

Bolton, Timothy, *The Empire of Cnut the Great – Conquest and the Consolidation of Power in Northern Europe in the Early Eleventh Century*, Brill, Leiden and Boston, 2009

Brøndsted, Johannes, *The Vikings*, Penguin, Harmondsworth, 1971

Brook, Nicholas with Thacker, Alan, *St Ælfheah (St Alphege) from Deerhurst to Martyrdom (1012): Some Millennial Reflections on Religious Ideals*, Deerhurst Lecture, 2012

Brooke, Christopher, *The Saxon and Norman Kings*, William Collins & Co., Glasgow, 1975

Carroll, Jayne, Harrison, Stephen H., Williams, Gareth, *The Vikings in Britain and Ireland*, The British Museum, London, 2014

Chandler, John, *A Higher Reality – The History of Shaftesbury's Royal Nunnery*, Hobnob Press, East Knoyle, 2003

Coker, John, *Coker's Survey of Dorsetshire, 1732*, reprinted Dorset Publishing Company, Sherborne, 1980

Cullingford, Cecil N., *A History of Dorset*, Phillimore & Co., Chichester, 1999

Davis, Terence, *Wareham, Gateway to Purbeck*, Dorset Publishing Company, Wincanton

Finberg, H. P. R., *The Formation of England*, Paladin, St Albans, 1974

Fletcher, Richard, *Bloodfeud – Murder and Revenge in Anglo-Saxon England*, Penguin Press, London etc., 2002

Hall, Richard, *Exploring the World of the Vikings*, Thames & Hudson, London, 2007

Harrison, Mark, *Anglo-Saxon Thegn AD 449–1066*, Osprey, Oxford, 2009

Heath, Ian, *The Vikings*, Osprey, Oxford, 2008

Higgitt, John, *Odda, Orm and Others: Patrons and Inscriptions in Later Anglo-Saxon England*, Deerhurst Lecture, 1999

Higham, N. J., *The Death of Anglo-Saxon England*, Sutton Publishing Limited, Stroud, 1997

Hill, Paul, *The Anglo-Saxons at War 800–1066*, Pen & Sword, Barnsley, 2014

Hilliam, David, *Winchester Curiosities*, Sutton Publishing Limited, Stroud, 2008

Hinton, David, *Discover Dorset – Saxons & Vikings*, The Dovecote Press, Wimborne, 1998

Jones. Gwyn, *A History of the Vikings*, Book Club Associates, London, 1973

Larson, Laurence Marcellus, *Canute the Great*, G.P Putnam's Sons, New York and London, 1912

Lawson, M. K., *Cnut – The Danes in England in the early Eleventh Century*, Longman, London and New York, 1993

Loe, Louise, Boyle, Angela, Webb, Helen and Score, David, *'Given to the Ground' – A Viking Age Mass Grave on Ridgeway Hill, Weymouth*, Dorset Natural History and Archaeological Society Monograph Series No. 22, 2014

Norton, Elizabeth, *Elfrida – The First Crowned Queen of England*, Amberley, Stroud, 2014

O'Brien, Harriet, *Queen Emma and the Vikings*, Bloomsbury, London etc. 2006

Pollington, Stephen, *The Warrior's Way – England in the Viking Age*, Blandford Press, London, 1989

Rahtz, Philip and Watts, Lorna, *Glastonbury – Myth & Archaeology*, The History Press, Stroud, 2009

Richard, Julian D., *Viking Age England*, Batsford, London, 1994

Rumble, Alexander (ed.), *The Reign of Cnut – King of England, Denmark and Norway*, Leicester University Press, London and New York, 1999

Sheppard, Alice, *Families of the King – Writing Identity in the Anglo-Saxon Chronicles*, University of Toronto Press, 2004

Wahlgren, Erik, *The Vikings and America*, Thames & Hudson, London, 2000

Williams, Ann, *Æthelred the Unready – The Ill-Counselled King*, Hambledon and London, London and New York, 2003

Wilson, David, *The Vikings and their Origins – Scandinavia in the First Millennium*, Thames and Hudson, London, 1970

Audio

Harl, Kenneth H. (Professor, Tulane University), *The Vikings, The Great Courses*, a series of thirty-six lectures

Notes

Prelude

1. A united country that we would recognise as England did not yet exist; instead there were smaller kingdoms such as Wessex, Mercia and Northumbria.

2. The Portland reference is from the *Annals of St Neots*; see Note 5 in *Anglo-Saxon Chronicles*, 54.

3. *Beowulf*, 58.

4. *Anglo-Saxon Chronicles*, 54.

5. Richards, 10

6. Carroll, Harrison and Williams, 6–7.

7. Finberg, 157

8. Brøndsted, 22

9. Jones, 1.

10. In Barlow, *Edward*, 3

11. *Corpus Poeticum Boreale*, in Larson, 184.

12. Jones, 202.

13. From *Voluspá* in Larson, 189

14. Earlier ambitious Anglo-Saxon kings had called themselves 'Bretwalda', the exact meaning of which is unclear but should be thought of as something akin to an overall ruler. Ironically, the *Anglo-Saxon Chronicles* list eight such kings at the end of the ninth century but do not include Offa of Mercia, probably the most powerful king before Alfred the Great. Neither man in practice ruled Northumbria.

15. Norton, 125.

16. Ibid., 115–116.

17. See entry for the year 978, *Anglo-Saxon Chronicles*, 122.

18. Richards, 13.

19. *William of Malmesbury*, 162

20. The surviving versions of the *Anglo-Saxon Chronicles*, of which there are nine, include variants from scribes at Winchester, Abingdon (two versions), Worcester, Peterborough and Canterbury. These different variants are by no means identical and there is indeed considerable variation between them so it is important to note when referring to them which particular version is being used.

21. *Anglo-Saxon Chronicles*, 123.

22. Larson, 294.

23. Gaimar's *History of the English* places the murder in Wiltshire; Norton, 145. The accounts of William of Malmesbury and Henry of Huntingdon provide most of the detail described.

24. In an interesting twist, when Shaftesbury Abbey was sold into private hands in the twentieth century what should happen to Edward's remains became a matter of extended dispute only settled by a legal ruling. Eventually it was decided that they should be interred in a setting near Brookwood Cemetery, which eventually took place in 1984. The Russian Orthodox Church in which the remains now lie is the Saint Edward the Martyr Orthodox Church. The king's feast day in the Orthodox Church's calendar is 18 March.

25. Norton, 50.

26. Chandler, 31.

27. In the highly hierarchical Anglo-Saxon world an ealdorman was in the top rank, followed by a thegn, then a ceorl and finally slaves. Many of the warriors in the local fyrd are likely to have been either thegns or senior ceorls. See Harrison, 10.

28. *William of Malmesbury*, 165. It has been pointed out that this might not be an act of repentance for the murder of Edward at all but that these were more general acts of humility often adopted by older men and women as a way of improving their spiritual health prior to their death: see Norton, 193.

29. Norton, 153.

30. From the Peterborough version of the chronicles in *Anglo-Saxon Chronicles*, 123.

31. *Anglo-Saxon Chronicles*, 122.

32. *Florence*, 126. Dunstan had not enjoyed good relations with Æthelred right from the start. He baptised the king when he was a baby and was horrified when, during the ceremony, 'he defiled the sacrament by a natural evacuation' and predicted a troubled life for the infant as a result – see *William of Malmesbury*, 166. He had also been opposed to the wedding of King Edgar and Elfrida, considering it to be adulterous. See Norton, 61. Dunstan seems very much to have been a 'fire and brimstone' kind of cleric who did not hold back when offended.

33. For an alternative suggestion that this was not at all a rash act but a way of bringing the Vikings to battle, see Pollington, Chapter 3.

34. Quotes from the translation of *The Battle of Maldon* by Douglas B. Killings, see www.english.ox.ac.uk/oecoursepack/maldon_resources.

35. Pollington, 66.

36. Ibid., 67.

37. Hall, 7.

1 England

1. Lawson, 15.

2. It is symptomatic of the problems of interpreting chroniclers of this time that many historians think that the work of 'Florence' of Worcester was written by a contemporary of his, John, who in the past has only been given credit for small inputs to the work. Some historians indeed now invariably refer to John

of Worcester in their work. I will avoid doing so hereafter but the potential confusion should be noted.

3. See, for example, Peter Sawyer in Rumble, 16.

4. In Lawson, 1.

5. Pollington, 91.

6. *Encomium*, 9.

7. *Olaf*, 51.

8. Timothy Reuter in the Introduction to *Adam of Bremen*, xvii.

9. The modern wireless technology Bluetooth is named after him. He is still a very well-known figure in Denmark.

10. *Encomium*, 9.

11. *Adam of Bremen*, 72.

12. Absalom was the favourite son of King David of Israel but rebelled against him. See the Book of II Samuel in the Old Testament.

13. See Bolton, 170.

14. *Olaf*, 51–52.

15. *Encomium*, 9.

16. Lawson, 7.

17. *Olaf*, 81.

18. *Adam of Bremen*, 80.

19. *Olaf*, 72.

20. See NASA research paper *Asteroids, Comets, Meteors*, 1991, 385. This can be found at http://articles.adsabs.harvard.edu/cgi-bin/nph-iarticle_query?bibcode=1992acm..proc..385M&db_key=AST&page_ind=2&plate_select=NO&data_type=GIF&type=SCREEN_GIF&classic=YES.

21. Lawson, 23.

22. Ibid., 81.

23. Higham, 33.

24. *Olaf*, 49.

25. Lawson, 16.

26. *Olaf*, 77.

27. *Olaf*, 98.

28. Harl, Lecture 20.

29. The World Factbook lists Norway as having the seventh longest coastline in the world, and has the United Kingdom at twelfth and Denmark at sixteenth.

30. Norton, 194.

31. *Anglo-Saxon Chronicles*, 133.

32. Williams, 16. The evidence from the coin hoard is from Hinton, 68. A significant part of the hoard can be seen at Gold Hill Museum in Shaftesbury.

33. *Anglo-Saxon Chronicles*, 133.

34. Norton, 193–194.

35. *Encomium*, 5.

36. *Henry of Huntingdon*, 6, who also mentions that Archbishop Dunstan on his deathbed in 988 foresaw such events.

37. O'Brien, 14.

38. The use of several names for wives was not uncommon: there were other examples of Norman women taking both Frankish and Scandinavian names – see Jones, 229 and Hilliam, 72.

39. Norton, 171.

40. Higham, 40.

41. The nickname was ironic as the name Æthelred means 'noble counsel'. 'Æthelred Unræd' therefore means 'noble counsel no counsel'. Norton, 168. The regular use of 'Æthel' at the start of a number of Anglo-Saxon names – technically known as the 'prototheme' – means 'noble' and was commonly applied as part of the name for many, male or female, higher up the social scale.

42. Charter of Æthelred to St Frideswide's Minster of 1004, quoted in footnote 9, *Anglo-Saxon Chronicles* 135.

43. Henry of Huntingdon, 7.

44. Williams.

45. *William of Malmesbury*, 185.

46. See BBC website, www.bbc.co.uk/news/uk-england-oxfordshire-17595823.

47. Higham & Ryman, 348; see also Loe et al., xxii.

48. Loe et al., 211. See also David Keys at http://www.smithsonianmag.com/history/a-viking-mystery-59648019.

2 Sweyn Forkbeard

1. Henry of Huntingdon, 7.

2. *Anglo-Saxon Chronicles*, 135.

3. Ibid.

4. Heath, 11.

5. There is some confusion in the *Anglo-Saxon Chronicles*, which also mentions Hertford but for practical reasons Thetford would appear a more likely target.

6. *Anglo-Saxon Chronicles*, 135.

7. Harrison, 9.

8. D. M. Metcalf quoted in Williams, 68.

9. In Barker, Hinton and Hunt, 73.

10. William of Malmesbury, 185.

11. See Larson, 32.

12. Peter Sawyer in Rumble, 17.

13. See Carroll, Harrison and Williams, 60.

14. Henry of Huntingdon, 8.

15. Also called Cuckhamsley Knob or alternatively Scutchamer or Scotsman's Knob, an old prehistoric barrow now located in Oxfordshire and a prominent point on the Ridgeway.

16. Williams, 72.

17. O'Brien, 46.

18. http://news.bbc.co.uk/2/hi/uk_news/4561624.stm.

19. Lavelle, 117.

20. Williams, 74.

21. See Lawson, 58–59.

22. Barker, Hinton and Hunt, 66.

23. See Hill, 43.

24. Lawson, 59.

25. When Estrith married Ulf is unclear, with some arguing that this marriage did not take place until long after the events described occurred.

26. *Henry of Huntingdon*, 8–9. Incidentally, the depiction of Vikings with horned helmets is now largely considered to be a much later, probably nineteenth-century, invention. However there are illustrations of pre-Viking age Scandinavian gods shown wearing such helmets; Heath, 52.

27. *Anglo-Saxon Chronicles*, 138.

28. Lawson, 37.

29. See Williams, 106.

30. *Anglo-Saxon Chronicles*, 141.

31. Barker, Hinton and Hunt, 113.

32. Bolton, 44.

33. *Henry of Huntingdon*, 11.

34. *Florence*, 121. *William of Malmesbury*, 184, blamed Thorkell, who will appear frequently in the story in later times, as being the 'chief cause' of the Archbishop's murder. This seems doubtful given his change of sides not long after.

35. *William of Malmesbury*, 168.

36. Sheppard, 108.

37. See Williams, 109.

38. O'Brien, 75.

39. Modern historians tend to support a birthdate of around 995. See for example Barlow, *The Godwins*, 31.

40. *Encomium*, 13.

41. *Florence*, 122.

42. See Williams, 121.

43. *Florence*, 122.

44. Alexander, *Earliest English Poems*, 12. He is writing of Anglo-Saxon poets but it would apply equally as well to their Norse counterparts.

45. *William of Malmesbury*, 171.

46. *Florence*, 124.

3 Cnut of Denmark

1. *Florence*, 123.

2. See Bolton 10, footnote 4, which summarises the evidence for the non-election of Sweyn.

3. Barlow, *Edward*, 54.

4. *Anglo-Saxon Chronicles*, 145.

5. Barker, Hinton and Hunt, 1.

6. O'Brien, 86. Chance discoveries in the 1920s of Viking axes and grappling hooks in the Thames mud appear to add substance to the tale.

7. A good description of London at the time can be found in O'Brien, 98.

8. Higham, 34.

9. *William of Malmesbury*, 191. See also *Henry of Huntingdon*, 13 – Ironside 'because he possessed tremendous strength and remarkable endurance in warfare'.

10. Higham, 73.

11. *Florence*, 124.

12. Sheppard, 108.

13. See, for example, *Encomium*, 15.

14. Bolton, 156.
15. In Lawson, 90.
16. Adam of Bremen, 49.
17. *Encomium*, 17.
18. Ibid., 19.
19. See *Anglo-Saxon Chronicles*, footnote 2, 146, quoting Stenton, *Anglo-Saxon England*.
20. Higham, 61.
21. *William of Malmesbury*, 191.
22. *Encomium*, 19.
23. Larson, 67.
24. *Adam of Bremen*, 91.
25. *Florence*, 112.
26. Higham & Ryman, 346.
27. Davis, 14. A 'hide' was originally measured by the value and resources an area of land could produce, though by the time of the Domesday Book in practice it was more related to the size of the land but even that could vary from one part of the country to another.
28. Ibid., 15.
29. This was an upgrading of the penalty from the previous one of 'merely' losing a hand for such crimes. The strengthening of the penalty took place during the reign of Æthelred; see Lavelle, 81.
30. Lavelle, 78. Similarly, the mint at Chichester may have been moved to the hillfort of Cissbury near Worthing.
31. Cullingford, 36. However, it should be noted that the primary or archaeological evidence for this is not strong. See Hinton, 68, who says that raids in Dorset during this late Viking period 'have not left a physical record in burnt churches and abandoned villages'. The author is a recognised expert archaeologist specialising in the period in Dorset so is a highly credible commentator.
32. Coker, 86.
33. Examples from Brøndsted, 38–39.

4 Ironsides

1. Jones, 229.
2. *Florence*, 125.
3. See Bolton, 40.
4. See Higham, 41–46.
5. Pollington, 85.
6. Wilson, 73–74. The term 'Riding' comes from an Old Norse word that means 'a third part'. They were sub-divided into smaller parts called wapentakes, another word of similar ethnic origin.
7. Williams, 133.
8. At the time, the irony would have been lost on the English as George would not become their national saint until later medieval times.
9. *Anglo-Saxon Chronicles*, 148.
10. *William of Malmesbury*, 165.
11. Norton, 39. This was in the year 956.

12. *William of Malmesbury*, 169.

13. *Adam of Bremen*, 91.

14. See *Snorri Sturluson – Olaf*, 49.

15. Higham and Ryan, 341.

16. *William of Malmesbury*, 169.

17. *Florence*, 127.

18. *Anglo-Saxon Chronicles*, 148 and 149.

19. In Williams, 17.

20. Norton, 152–154.

21. O'Brien, 91.

22. The *Anglo-Saxon Chronicles* say on the Rogation Days, between 7 and 9 May that year; *Anglo-Saxon Chronicles*, 148.

23. In Larson, 87.

24. *Encomium*, 23. The dates and events here are at odds with those in the *Anglo-Saxon Chronicles*, which do not mention the surrender of the city to Cnut. The dating in the *Chronicles*, which state clearly that Æthelred died on St George's Day, assert that his demise occurred before the siege of London began, whilst the *Encomium* suggests that it was after it began.

25. Penselwood itself lies right on the border of Dorset with Somerset and in fact is itself in the latter county. Gillingham was a royal manor at the time.

26. It should be said that there are other claimants to be the spot where this crucial earlier battle was fought. But Penselwood is in the right general location for the battle for the seventh-century Saxon victory allowed them to move on to the line of the River Parrett in Somerset. And Penselwood is recorded as Penna in the Domesday Book.

27. For example, Larson, 88.

28. Such as when an army sent to put down a revolt led by the nephew of Alfred the Great, Æthelwald, occupied the hillfort of Badbury Rings near Wimborne in Dorset on their way to try to defeat him.

29. See, for example, the charter to Sherborne Abbey in 998, in Barker, Hinton and Hunt, 12. Later in the eleventh century, the Danish defences of Roskilde used beacons as an early warning system extensively.

30. Hill, 54–55.

31. Hill, 54. He makes mention of *herepaths* in Dorset which could have been used for the fyrd to march along. One ran through the old hillfort of Nettlecombe Tout, known in more recent times as the site of a beacon and probably used as such much further back in time too. The name probably derives from *tot* or *tute* which is an Anglo-Saxon word linked to a beacon site.

32. Pollington, 74.

33. Hill, 148 and 153.

34. Ibid., 83.

35. *Florence*, 129.

36. *Encomium*, 23.

37. The latter version from *Florence*, 130.

38. Peter Sawyer in Rumble, 17.

39. *Encomium*, 25.

40. *Anglo-Saxon Chronicles*, 150.

41. Ibid. Again there is a difference between the timing of Eadric's latest defection, which the *Chronicles* suggest took place in 1016, and that in the *Encomium* which implies that this was in the previous year.

42. It has been suggested that the battle may have taken place at either Ashingdon in south-east Essex or at Ashdon in the north-east of the county. See Lawson, 20, and Williams, 146–147, who argues strongly for the latter.

43. Heath, 50.

44. *Henry of Huntingdon*, 14.

45. Ibid., 15.

46. *Encomium*, 27.

47. Lawson, 20.

48. *Henry of Huntingdon*, 15.

49. Lawson, 79.

50. *Florence*, 131.

51. Rahtz and Watts, 114.

52. *William of Malmesbury*, 195.

53. *Adam of Bremen*, 92.

54. *Henry of Huntingdon*, 16. It should be said that most accounts place Eadric's execution some time after the death of Edmund.

55. Larson, 102.

56. *Encomium*, 31.

5 King of England

1. Florence, 132.

2. Barlow, Edward, 138–139.

3. Further information in O'Brien, 60–61.

4. Larson, 137.

5. Richards, 54.

6. Bolton, 61 and note 66.

7. Higham, 98.

8. Higham, 5.

9. Lawson, 83.

10. A very straightforward and lucid explanation of charters and writs can be found in Barlow, *Edward*, 146–147.

11. See table in Hill, 50.

12. See Higham, 100.

13. See Bolton, 62–63.

14. Bolton, 63.

15. Bolton, 75–76.

16. Fletcher, 24.

17. *William of Malmesbury*, 197. Other accounts suggest that the killing of Eadric took place earlier in the year.

18. *Encomium*, 33.

19. Bolton, 69.

20. The theory concerning the plot is presented in Higham, 82–88.

21. Adam of Bremen, 107.

22. See, for example, Norton, 45. Similar doubts resulting from a union along these lines were attached to the legitimacy of the great tenth-century English king Æthelstan as well as to Edmund Ironside.

23. Lawson, 132.

24. *Encomium*, 33. Similar dismissive comments about her were made by *William of Malmesbury*, 191, who patronisingly said that Edmund Ironside 'was not born of Emma, but of some other woman whom fame has left in obscurity'.

25. Higham, 80.

26. See Fletcher, 101.

27. See Sheppard, 114–115.

28. Keynes in Rumble, 45.

29. Lawson, 89.

30. Barlow (*The Godwins*) is a strong supporter of the theory of Godwin's royal descent – see the Godwin family tree on page 21.

31. Finberg, 153.

32. Bolton, 17.

33. Ibid., 35.

34. Ibid., 42.

35. There is a very useful summary of the charters by Simon Keynes in Rumble, 48–54.

6 King of Denmark

1. Lawson, 9–10.

2. *Adam of Bremen*, 187.

3. Although Copenhagen later replaced Roskilde as the capital of Denmark, the latter remains the royal mausoleum of the current ruling Danish royal dynasty.

4. See *Ibn Fadlān*, 45–55.

5. Bolton, 169.

6. Bolton, 199.

7. Bolton, 171.

8. Bolton, 221–222, 232.

9. Richards, 26.

10. *Adam of Bremen*, 51.

11. *Adam of Bremen*, 198.

12. Niels Lund in Rumble, 31.

13. The arguments concerning the role of the Church in Denmark at this time are well explored by Niels Lund in Rumble, 32–35.

14. It was contemporary practice to have the Archbishop of York also as Bishop of Worcester in the last part of the tenth and the first part of the eleventh centuries.

15. Quoted in Williams, 135.

16. See Higham, 104.

17. See Bolton, 80.

18. Bolton, 86.

19. Larson, 166.

20. Lawson, 60–61.
21. O'Brien, 125.
22. Lawson, 61–63.
23. Larson, 341.
24. O'Brien, xvii.
25. Wright and Lewis, 307.
26. Bolton, 213.
27. *Henry of Huntingdon*, 16. Henry is in fact conflating events from a number of different years in this statement which is in effect a summary of many such.
28. See Simon Keynes in Rumble, 67–70.
29. *William of Malmesbury*, 204.
30. *Adam of Bremen*, 93.
31. Larson, 158.
32. Bolton, 218.
33. *Henry of Huntingdon*, 16.
34. Barlow, 38.
35. See Bolton, 47.
36. See Bolton, 49–50.
37. See Barlow, *The Godwins*, 33, who is not completely dismissive of the rumours though accepting that they cannot be proved.
38. Quoted in Rumble, 85.
39. Coker, 30. See also Thomas Hutchins, *The History and Antiquities of the County of Dorset*, London 1774.
40. Bolton, 51–53.
41. Bolton, 58.
42. Richards, 31.
43. *William of Malmesbury*, 168.
44. Lawson, 99.
45. *Anglo-Saxon Chronicles*, 157.
46. Lawson, 99.
47. Peter Sawyer in Rumble, 19.
48. Larson, 221.
49. Lund in Rumble, 39.

7 Emperor of the North

1. *Adam of Bremen*, 222–223.
2. Quoted in Lawson, 100.
3. *Encomium*, 37.
4. *Henry of Huntingdon*, 17.
5. The letter is quoted in full in *Florence*, pps 137–139.
6. *Adam of Bremen*, 94.
7. In Larson, 235.
8. Discussed in Lawson, 100–101.
9. *Adam of Bremen*, 94.
10. Ibid., 96.
11. Ibid., 97–98.
12. Larson, 180.

13. O'Brien, 32.

14. Norton, 159.

15. See Bolton, 275–283.

16. Ibid., 287.

17. Ibid., 295.

18. *Henry of Huntingdon*, 17–18. Another chronicler, Gaimar, places these events on the Thames at Westminster rather than on the sea-shore.

19. Ibid., 17.

20. Lawson, 106.

21. In Larson, 140.

22. All three men would try to improve their position through advantageous marriages. Leofric would do so by marrying Godgifu – not to be confused with the daughter of King Æthelred of the same name. Godgifu, which means 'Gift of God', would be far better known to later generations as 'Lady Godiva'.

23. William of Malmesbury, 198.

24. Hilliam, 107.

25. *William of Malmesbury*, 198.

26. Doubleday and Page, 116–122.

27. O'Brien, 151.

28. The manuscript has been digitised by the British Library and may be viewed online at http://www.bl.uk/manuscripts/Viewer.aspx?ref=stowe_ms_944_f006r.

29. Bolton, 297–300.

30. Larson, 262.

31. O'Brien, 211.

32. Page, 151.

33. See Bolton, 94.

34. Higham & Ryman, 363.

35. See Bolton, 87–89.

36. Lawson, 154.

37. *William of Malmesbury*, 203, and Lawson, 156. Bolton suggests that this journey probably took place much earlier on in his reign, some time around 1020: see 95.

38. Norton, 168–170.

39. Further details in Lawson, 159.

40. See Higgitt, 11. A *mancus* was a gold coin.

41. *Florence*, 140.

42. *Encomium*, 39.

8 Cnut the Great

1. Lawson, 65–66.

2. See http://www.hampshire-history.com/secrets-of-winchesters-mortuary-chests/ and Lawson 65–66.

3. *Encomium*, 37.

4. Lawson, 115.

5. Ibid., 120.

6. Bolton, 215.

7. Lawson, 131.

8. Quoted in Barlow, 30.

9. O'Brien, 170.

10. *Anglo-Saxon Chronicles*, 160.

11. *Encomium*, 7.

12. *Anglo-Saxon Chronicles*, 160.

13. *Florence*, 140.

14. *Encomium*, 7.

15. Bolton, 312.

16. Barlow, *Edward*, 75.

17. Ibid., 89.

18. See Barlow, *The Godwins*, 52.

19. *William of Malmesbury*, 196.

20. Williams, 9.

21. In Fletcher, 24.

22. From the *Hávamál* in Brøndsted, 251.

23. Brooke, 138.

Acknowledgements

I would like to thank all those who have helped in the development and finalisation of this book. Special thanks to Jonathan Reeve at Amberley who encouraged me in the idea of exploring the life and times of one of the more interesting but largely forgotten English kings and also indirectly introduced me to Denmark, a sometimes overlooked (in England at least) gem. As always it is a pleasure to work with Amberley, both Jonathan and his ever helpful colleagues.

I would also like to acknowledge those who have supported and travelled with me in my discovery of Cnut. We have shared many places near and far, including those on our doorstep, some for the first time, which have been inspirational. Particular thanks to my daughter and research assistant, Deyna Bartlett, who has done a great job helping me through the process.

Index

Aalborg, Denmark 192

Abbotsbury, England 187, 211, 212

Abingdon, England 251, 254

Absalom, son of king David 49

Adam of Bremen, chronicler 44, 45,
48, 49, 52, 120, 136, 159, 176,
189, 191, 192, 195, 196, 197, 208,
222, 229, 230, 232, 233, 281

Adam, biblical character 23

Adémar of Chabannes, chronicler
261

Ælfgar 42

Ælfgar Maew, lord of Tewkesbury and
Cranborne

Ælfgifu of Northampton, 'wife' of
Cnut 85, 106, 118, 121, 176, 177,
178, 202, 236, 255, 256, 266

Ælfgifu, daughter of Thored of
Northumbria 68

Ælfgifu, queen of England see Emma
of Normandy

Ælfgifu, wife of Uhtred of Bamburgh
100

Ælfheah, archbishop of Canterbury
(also abbot of Bath and bishop of
Winchester) 84, 96, 97, 98, 103,
105, 157, 165, 213, 214, 215, 242,
248, 249

Ælfhelm, ealdorman of Northumbria
68, 85, 92, 106, 121

Ælfhun, bishop of London 105

Ælflaed, wife of Siward earl of
Northumbria 241

Ælfmaer, abbot of St Augustine's,
Canterbury, later bishop of
Sherborne 95, 96

Ælfmar Darling, English 'turncoat'
149

Ælfric of Cerne and Eynsham,
homilist 69, 87, 112, 138, 279

Ælfric, archbishop of Canterbury 54

Ælfric, archbishop of York 220, 225

Ælfric, ealdorman of Hampshire 41,
42, 74, 156

Ælfric, king's high reeve 64

Ælfryth; see Elfrida

Ælfsige, abbot of Peterborough and
bishop of Winchester 105, 214

Ælfweard, bishop of London 248

Ælfweard, king's reeve 96

Ælfwig, bishop of London 111

Ælfwine, bishop of Winchester 246,
247, 259

Ælgar, English moneyer 127

Æthelings Valley, Wessex 63

Æthelmaer the Stout, ealdorman of
Wessex 80, 103, 116, 173, 207

Æthelmaer, brother of Stigand 247

Æthelnoth, archbishop of Canterbury
205, 206, 208, 213, 214, 216, 221,
225, 251

Æthelred I, king of England 174, 186

Æthelred II, king of England 18, 24, 25, 40, 42, 53, 56, 57, 64, 65, 68, 79, 81, 84, 87, 92, 94, 98, 99, 100, 113, 118, 121, 126, 128, 131, 132, 140, 156, 159, 161, 168, 177, 185, 186, 187, 200, 201, 215, 252, 263, 278
  and 'Danegeld' 39, 52, 95, 277
  and defence of England 90, 91, 93, 129
  and Eadric Streona 83
  and London 103, 114, 130, 172, 213
  and St Brices Day Massacre 72
  and Thorkell the Tall 122, 124
  attitude to church 36, 251, 253
  coinage of 50, 166
  coronation of 32
  death and burial of 134, 139, 165, 214, 276
  flight from England 104, 105, 107
  marriage to Emma 66, 67, 69, 74, 178, 254, 267, 270
  perceptions of as king 88, 106, 135, 136, 137, 181, 202
  relations with Edmund Ironside 123
  return to England 111, 112, 150, 180
  succession as king 26, 29, 31, 41, 138
Æthelric, bishop of Sherborne 80
Æthelstan Half-King, English nobleman 35, 69
Æthelstan, king of England 21, 25, 31, 131, 163, 186, 252
Æthelstan, son of Æthelred II 68, 92, 115, 185
Æthelstan, son of Tovi the Proud 265
Æthelstan, son-in-law of Æthelred II 94
Æthelweard, ealdorman of West Wessex 169, 174, 175, 207, 213
Æthelweard, king's reeve 63
Æthelweard, son of ealdorman Æthelmaer 173, 205, 206, 207

Æthelwold, Saint and Church reformer 88
Æthelwulf, King of the West Saxons 186
Agatha, wife of Edmund, son of Edmund Ironside 173
Agemund, Viking landowner in Dorset 212
Aidan, monk and Saint 14
Alani 197
Alcuin of York, English scholar 14, 30
Aldhelm, Saint 128
Alexander, Michael, modern scholar 104
Alfred the Great, king of England 11, 20, 21, 25, 31, 37, 40, 53, 69, 79, 83, 84, 102, 106, 114, 126, 138, 142, 155, 163, 182, 186, 188, 250, 252, 258, 265, 274, 278, 280
Alfred, son of Æthelred II 105, 161, 177, 267, 269, 273
Alfred's Tower 142
Amalfi, Italy 243
Amazons 196, 197
Anglo-Saxon Chronicles 13, 15, 23, 26, 30, 33, 56, 72, 73, 90, 93, 98, 104, 114, 116, 134, 142, 154, 159, 177, 214, 216, 217, 239, 266, 267, 268
  and Cnut 99, 265
  and Edmund Ironside 115, 139, 151
  and Æthelred II 135, 136
  background to 17, 28, 52, 108, 118, 162
  different versions of 27, 32, 63, 64, 82, 89, 94, 105, 137, 138, 180
  mention of comets in 53
Annales Cambriae 54
Ansgar, Saint 43
Anund Jacob, king of Sweden 217
Aquitaine 261
Århus, Denmark 120, 191, 193
Arthur, king of legend 159

Ashingdon, Battle of (1016) 154, 155, 157, 158, 159, 199, 242, 247, 248, 250
Aslac, charter witness 186
Assandun, Battle of see Ashingdon
Asser, bishop of Sherborne 265
Athelney, England 21, 155, 188
Augustine, Saint and theologian 88
Avoco, bishop of Roskilde 228
Aylesford, England 153

Baffin Island 61
Baldr the Beautiful, Viking god 43
Balkans 73
Baltic Sea 45, 50, 51, 119, 189, 190, 194, 196, 208, 216, 218
Bamburgh, England 41, 241
Bath, England 22, 103
Battle Abbey, England 200
Bayeux Tapestry 77, 144, 146, 248, 274
Beaduheard, king's reeve 13
Bedford, England 94
Bedfordshire, England 132, 167
Benedict VIII, Pope 216
Beorhtric, king of Wessex 13
Beorhtric, son of Ælfheah 174, 175
Beorhtwine, bishop of Wells 213, 214
Beothric, brother of Eadric Streona 91, 92
Beowulf 13, 43, 144, 263
Berkshire, England 83, 93, 95, 169, 239
Bernicia, England 26, 86, 133, 168
Bersi the Strong, Viking 58
Bison, ship 217
Bjarkamál, Norse saga 232
Bjor, Viking 180
Bjorn, son of Estrith 90, 263
Black Sea 76
Blackwater, River, England 34
Blair, Peter Hunter, historian 88
Bodmin Gospels 207
Boleslaw, king of Vindland 51, 58
Bosham, England 238

Bovi, Viking landowner in Dorset 212
Bradford-on-Avon, England 64
breidox 125
Brentford, England 151
Brian Boru, Irish king 20
Bridport, England 212
Brittany 115
Broad Clyst, England 64
Brownsea Island, England 128
Brunanburh, Battle of 22
Buckfast Abbey, England 207
Buckinghamshire, England 94, 132, 167
Burghal Hideage 127
Burgundy 225
Bury St Edmunds, England 107, 242, 262
Byrhtferth, monk 29
Byrhtnoth, ealdorman 33, 34, 35, 36, 39, 64, 143, 148

Caithness, Scotland 240
Cambridge, England 94
Cambridgeshire, England 94, 95
Canterbury, England 92, 95, 96, 99, 156, 165, 214, 215, 242, 246, 262
Carham, Northumbria 239
Carl, son of Thurbrand 134
Carlisle, England 239
Caspian Sea 76
Cenwalh, king of Wessex 83
Cerdic, king of Wessex 23, 107, 158, 173, 176, 185, 273, 282, 283
Cerne Abbey, England 56, 88, 128, 242
Charlemagne, emperor 19, 23, 120, 191
Charles the Simple, Frankish king 99
Charles VI, king of France 161
Chartres, Francia 207, 208
Chertsey Abbey, England 165
Cheselbourne, England 212
Chester, England 22, 130
Chester-le-Street, England 250
Chilterns, England 93

Christ Church, Canterbury, England
185, 187, 214, 228
Christchurch (Twynham), England
126
Christina, sister of Edgar the Ætheling
276
Cirencester, England 206, 207
Clovis, Merovingian king 43
Cluny 201
Cnut, king of England, Denmark and
Norway 12, 25, 27, 37, 38, 45,
46, 59, 61, 62, 72, 75, 76, 81, 110,
111, 121, 139, 152, 153, 163, 168,
170, 171, 176, 180, 181, 182,
188, 207, 220, 225, 226, 253, 256,
265, 266, 268, 269, 270, 271, 273,
274, 275, 276, 277, 278, 279, 281,
282, 283
and Ashingdon 154, 156
and battle of Holy River 217, 218,
223
and coinage 166, 194, 267
and Denmark 192, 193, 197, 198,
199, 208, 209, 255
and Eadric Streona 160, 175
and earl Godwin 210, 211
and Edmund Ironside 131, 157,
159, 173
and journey to Rome 222, 224,
227, 245, 281
and killing of Ulf 219
and London 140, 141, 149, 150,
151
and invasion of England 121, 126,
127, 128, 129
and Norway 167, 229, 231, 232,
233, 236, 237
and Scotland 239, 240, 241
and Skåne 195
and Sweden 196
and turning back the tide 238
and Uhtred of Northumbria 132.
133, 134
and Wessex 169, 187
becomes king of England 158, 161,
165, 174
burial 259, 260, 272

charters of his reign 185, 216
death 257
defeated and flees England 116,
117, 119, 130, 136
division and government of England
184, 186, 280
early life of 50, 52, 100
in attack on England with Sweyn
Forkbeard 99, 102
marriage to Ælfgifu of Northampton
106, 118
marriage to Emma of Normandy
177, 179, 183
offered crown at Southampton 137
relations with church 201, 202,
203, 205, 206, 214, 215, 221, 228,
242, 243, 244, 246, 247, 248, 249,
251, 252, 254, 261, 262, 263, 264
relationship with Thorkell the Tall
82, 124, 146, 200, 204
Cologne, archbishop of 224
Cologne, Germany 247, 253
Columba, bishop and Saint 20
Columbus, Christopher 77
Conrad II, Holy Roman Emperor
221, 223, 224, 245, 260, 281
Constantine, Roman emperor 44,
243
Constantinople 15, 76, 198, 235
Cookham, England 85
Corfe, England 28, 29
Cork, Ireland 54
Cornwall, England 33, 55, 56, 169,
207
Cornwell, Bernard; novelist 11
Corscombe, England 95, 258
Cosham, England 123
Courland 196
Coventry Cathedral, England 213
Cranborne, England 148, 186
Cricklade, England 126, 129, 166
Crouch estuary, England 154
Culloden, Battle of (1746) 145
Cumbria, England 26, 53, 57, 134
Cuthbert, bishop and Saint 14
Cwichelm, king of Wessex 83
Cwichelm's Barrow 83

Cyclopes 197

Danaskrogár 157
Danegeld 39, 40, 52, 64, 79, 80, 91,
  95, 97, 158, 179, 277
Danelaw, England 21, 25, 26, 41,
  101, 102, 117, 131, 139, 152, 170
Danevirke 47, 120
David, biblical king 49
De Obsessione Dunelmi 133
De Oratione Moysi 87
Dee, River, England 22
Deerhurst, England 157
Deira, England 26, 86, 133
Denmark 15, 43, 46, 47, 48, 49, 51,
  52, 58, 59, 71, 75, 76, 100, 106,
  109, 110, 119, 121, 123, 144, 163,
  164, 173, 178, 188, 189, 191, 192,
  195, 198, 199, 204, 205, 206, 210,
  211, 218, 220, 222, 225, 226, 231,
  234, 237, 256, 271, 274, 278
  church/Christianity in 44, 196,
  208, 221, 228, 263, 281
  Cnut as king of 38, 116, 167, 197,
  203, 217, 258, 260, 277, 280
  development of towns in 193, 194
  geography of 17, 45, 50, 60, 62
  Harthacnut in 209, 216, 232, 255,
  265, 266, 268, 270, 279
  relations with Germany/Holy
  Roman Empire 22, 120, 224, 245,
  261
Derby, England 102
Devon, England 33, 55, 56, 63, 64,
  68, 73, 103, 148, 169, 184, 186,
  212
Dewlish, England 186
Dissolution of the Monasteries 185
Dneiper, River 76
Domesday Book 133, 154, 184, 210,
  212, 262
Dorchester, England 14, 212
Dorset, England 56, 126, 128, 142,
  148, 169, 184, 186, 212, 216, 258,
  272
Drogo, count of the Vexin 177
Dublin, Ireland 20, 54, 76, 164, 239

Dudoc, bishop of Wells 247
Duncan I, king of Scotland 239
Dunstan, Archbishop of Canterbury
  and Saint 24, 32, 33, 206
Durham, England 239, 249, 250

Eadgyth, daughter of Æthelred II, king
  of England 86
Eadnoth, bishop of Dorchester 156
Eadric Streona, ealdorman of Mercia
  86, 91,97, 101, 104, 107, 122,
  127, 130, 166, 167, 171, 187, 207,
  217, 251, 269
  and killing of Ælfhelm 85, 92,
  106, 121
  and killing of Edmund Ironside
  159, 160
  becomes ealdorman of Mercia 84
  killed on orders of Cnut 174, 175,
  176, 183, 206, 207
  treachery of 93, 128, 129, 132,
  137, 147, 148, 149, 153, 155, 156
Eadulf, son of Uhtred of Bamburgh
  134
Eadwig ('Edwy') the Ætheling, brother
  of Edmund Ironside 174, 175,
  176, 206, 207
Eadwulf Cudel, brother of Uhtred of
  Bamburgh 168, 239
Ealdgyth, wife of Edmund Ironside
  122
Ealdred, son of Uhtred of Bamburgh
  134
East Anglia, England 41, 77, 93, 94,
  95, 100, 105, 106, 131, 156, 158,
  166, 167, 184, 206, 250, 275
East Riding, England 133
Echmarcach man Ragnail (Iehmarc)
  239
Edgar the Ætheling 276, 282
Edgar, king of England 22, 23, 24,
  25, 103, 158, 163, 166, 168, 174,
  180, 181, 240, 252, 278, 279
Edith, saint, sister of Æthelred II 74,
  138, 252, 278
Edith, wife of Edward the Confessor
  275

Edmund Ætheling, infant son of Edgar
and Elfrida 24, 25
Edmund Ironside, king of England
32,132, 141, 149, 151, 152, 153,
161, 162,174, 175, 176, 251, 253
abducts Ældgyth 122
at battle of Ashingdon 154, 155,
156, 158
at battle of Penselwood 146
at battle of Sherston 147, 148
becomes king of England 137, 138,
139
death 159, 160, 183, 187, 253,
270
descendants of 165, 173, 276, 282,
283
early life of 68, 115
fight against Cnut 130, 131, 134,
140
relationship with Æthelred II 123
Edmund, King and Saint 105, 144,
242, 249, 250, 262
Edmund, son of Edmund Ironside
173
Edward, King and Saint 24, 27, 28,
29, 30, 33, 109, 110, 127, 129,
138, 140, 215, 259, 262, 278
Edward, son of Æthelred II (later King
Edward the Confessor) 105, 132,
140, 161, 162, 210, 235, 240, 246,
247, 270, 275, 276
and earl Godwin 268, 274
becomes king of England 272, 273
in Normandy 177, 255
returns to England after death of
Cnut 267
returns to England as envoy of
Æthelred II 111
Edward, son of Edmund Ironside
173, 276
Eider, River 189
Eilifr, Viking warrior 90, 171, 217
Einar Tambarskjelve, Norwegian
opponent of Cnut 256
Elfrida, queen of England 24, 25, 27,
28, 29, 30, 31, 36, 56, 65, 67, 186
Elsworth, England 205

Ely, abbey, England 36, 156, 201,
250, 267, 268, 269
Emma of Normandy, queen of
England 66, 68, 73, 92, 121, 139,
140, 214, 246, 248, 256, 266, 267,
268, 269, 270, 273
burial 259, 260
death 275
flees to Normandy 105
marriage to Cnut 177, 178, 179,
183
marriage to Æthelred II 65, 67, 69,
114, 115, 123, 132
relations with church 202, 244,
245, 258, 262
Encomium Emmae Reginae 48, 50,
121, 141, 146, 147, 148, 153, 154,
160, 174, 177, 178, 179, 183, 223,
256, 260, 267, 268, 269
background to 66
Enham, England 87, 89
Erik Bloodaxe, Viking warrior 43,
57, 86
Erik Hákonarson, Earl of Lade 58,
59, 62, 134, 150, 166, 167, 168,
174, 185, 204, 206, 208, 210, 211,
230
Erik the Red, Viking 61
Erik the Victorious, king of Sweden
49, 54, 58
Essex, England 95, 167
Estland 196
Estonia 53
Estrith, sister of Cnut 51, 90, 171,
179, 199, 219, 255, 259
Evesham Abbey, England 175, 246,
251
Exe, River, England 63
Exeter, England 63, 64, 68, 73, 212

Falaise, Normandy 255
Felixstowe, England 152
Fife, Scotland 239
Finns 231
Five Boroughs, England 101, 102,
121
Flamborough Head, England 22

Flanders 54, 223, 267, 268, 282
Florence of Worcester, chronicler 41, 95, 96, 97, 142, 146, 147, 148, 158, 161, 222, 256, 269
Folkestone, England 33
Forest of Dean, England 158
Francia (France) 19, 40, 43, 75, 78, 150, 190, 223, 255, 266, 278, 282
Frey, Scandinavian god 16, 43, 234
Frisia; see Frisland
Frisian Sea 189
Frisland 49
Frome, River, England 126
Fulbert, bishop of Chartres 207, 208
Fyn (Funen) Denmark 191
fyrd 19, 142, 145, 152

Gainsborough, England 100, 101, 106, 109, 116, 117, 118, 133, 139
Galloway, Scotland 239
Geoffrey Gaimar, chronicler 160
Geoffrey of Cambrai, prior of Winchester 264
George VI, king of England 90
Gerbrand, bishop of Roskilde 208, 221
Germany 22, 47, 189, 224, 278
Gisela, wife of Conrad II 224
Glastonbury, England 158, 206, 251, 252, 278
Gloucestershire, England 157, 171, 247
Godfred, king of Denmark 120
Godgifu, wife of Drogo, count of the Vexin 177
Godwin Porthund, assassin 85
Godwin, bishop of Rochester 96, 99
Godwin, ealdorman of Lindsey 156
Godwin, English earl 92, 169, 173, 208, 240, 241, 263, 265, 270, 272, 275, 277
as charter witness 185
as Cnut's lieutenant in England 210, 211
and Edward the Confessor 273, 274, 276
death of 275

role in death of Alfred 267, 268, 269
with Cnut in Denmark 208, 209
with Cnut in Norway 230
Godwin, English moneyer 50
Gokstad ship 76
Gorm the Old, king of Denmark 46, 120, 178, 189
Goths 195
Gotland, Baltic island 196
Great Fire of London (1666) 135
Greece 196
Greenland 15, 60, 61
Greenwich, England 98, 140, 157
Gregory VII, Pope 215, 237
Griotgard the Quick, Viking 58
Gudrod, son of Erik Bloodaxe 57
Guildford, England 267
Gundhild, daughter of Cnut 260, 261
Gundhild, mother of Cnut 51
Gundhild, niece of Cnut 275
Gundhild, sister of Sweyn Forkbeard 70
Gunnar, mother of Emma of Normandy 65
Guthrum, Danish raider 53, 102
Gyrth, son of earl Godwin 265
Gytha, daughter of Sweyn Forkbeard 51, 62, 167
Gytha, wife of earl Godwin 209

Hadrian's Wall 22, 239
Hagia Sofia, Constantinople 15, 199
Hákon, charter witness 186
Hákon, son of Erik of Lade 166, 167, 175, 230, 231, 232, 256
Halfdan, charter witness 186
Halley's Comet 53, 54
Hamburg-Bremen 44, 208, 221, 228
Hampshire, England 41, 63, 64, 74, 83, 87, 95, 146, 169, 184
Harald Bluetooth, king of Denmark 43, 45, 47, 52, 271
and Christianity 44, 120, 219
civil war with Sweyn Forkbeard 48, 49

and Holy Roman Empire 189, 224
and Jomsvikings 50
role in founding of Denmark 46,
121, 192, 281
Harald Fairhair, king of Norway 16,
21
Harald Hardrada, king of Norway
117, 235, 265, 270, 271, 276
Harald II, brother of Cnut, king of
Denmark 51, 52, 100, 110, 116,
119, 121, 188, 189, 197
Harald, son of Thorkell the Tall 232
Harek of Trotta, Norwegian
landowner 231
Harold 'Harefoot' later king Harold
I of England 117, 266, 267, 268,
269, 270, 277, 279
Harold II, king of England 117, 146,
148, 173, 235, 248, 265, 274, 276,
282
Harthacnut, son of Cnut, later king of
England and Denmark 134, 170,
214, 240, 267, 268, 269, 272, 273,
274, 279
arrangement with Magnus of
Norway 161
as king of England 270, 277
birth 178
in Denmark 209, 216, 232, 255,
265, 266
Hastings, Battle of (1066) 38, 144,
146, 148, 173, 200, 242, 274, 276,
282
Hastings, England 95
heafod stoccan 71
Hearthweru 145, 146
Hedeby, Denmark 47, 120, 191, 193
Heimskringla, saga 209
Hel, Viking goddess of death 232
Heligoland 191
Helsingborg 195
Hemingr, brother of Thorkell the Tall
89, 124, 156, 171
Henry I, king of England 282
Henry II, king of England 21
Henry III, Holy Roman Emperor 260

Henry of Huntingdon, chronicler 28,
67, 69, 72, 73, 96, 157, 159, 206,
238, 239
Henry V, king of England 161
Henry VIII, king of England 66, 159
Hereford, England 126, 146, 155
Herefordshire, England 85, 171, 272
Heregeld 99, 277
Herepath 143
Heriots 169
Herleva, mother of William I of
England 255
Hertfordshire, England 95, 167
Hilton, England 212
Hitler, Adolf 11
Holcombe Regis, England 115
Holderness, England 133
Holy Apostles, Church of, Rome 224
Holy River, Battle of (1026) 217,
218, 220, 222, 223, 228
Horn of Ulf 243
Hørning, Denmark 194
Horning, England 188
Horton, England 187, 212
Hrani, Viking landholder in
Herefordshire 171, 175
Hugh the Frenchman, Count 73
Humber, River, England 41, 86, 100
Hungary 173, 276
Huntingdonshire, England 132
Huscarles 146, 170, 212
Hwiccia, England 146
Hyde Abbey, Winchester 244

Ibn Fadlãn, traveller 192
Iceland 15, 60, 61, 62, 77
Ilchester, England 95, 127
infangangenetheof 169
Ingolf Arnason, Viking 61
Ingvar, Viking landowner in Devon
212
Iona, monastery, Scotland 20
Ipswich, England 93, 152
Ireland 16, 53, 54, 55, 60, 76, 164,
239
Iron Beard, ship 59
Isle of Man 53, 54, 55, 57

Isle of Wight, England 56, 64, 83, 93, 105
Italy 38, 223, 244
Itchen, River, England 247

Jaroslav of Novgorod 236
Jarrow, monastery, England 20
Jelling 46, 120, 192
Jerusalem 59, 255, 263
John of Worcester, chronicler 85
John XIX, Pope 224, 225
John XV, Pope 55
John, abbot of Fécamp 162
Jomsvikings 50, 81, 124
Joseph of Arimathea 253
Jutes 25, 42
Jutland, Denmark 42, 45, 46, 120, 191, 193, 195

Kalv Arnesson, Norwegian opponent of Cnut 256
Kattegat 45, 193
Kennet, River, England 83
Kent, England 33, 57, 91, 93, 153, 172, 186, 267
Kenwalch's Castle, England 142, 144
Ketil the Tall, Viking 58
Keynes, Professor Simon 136
Kiev 199
King Olaf Tryggvason's Saga 58
Kingsteignton, England 64
Kingston-upon-Thames, England 31
Kipling, Rudyard, poet 80
Knútsdrapa 157
Kola, king's high reeve 64
Kormak Fleinn, Viking 22
Kristianstad, Sweden 217

Labrador 61
Lakenheath, England 262
Lambeth, England 270
Lambey, Ireland 20
Lancelot, Arthurian knight 41
Lanfranc, archbishop of Canterbury 215
L'Anse aux Meadows, Newfoundland 61

Leicester, England 102
Leicestershire, England 130
Leif Erikson, Viking 61
Leo, Bishop of Trevi 55
Leofric, earl of Mercia 172, 240, 241, 269, 273, 276, 277
Leofsige, ealdorman of Essex 64
Leofsonu, retainer of Byrhtnoth 35
Leofwine of Mercia 174, 175, 184
Libentius, archbishop of Hamburg-Bremen 228
Liber Vitae (Book of Life), Winchester 244
Limerick, Ireland 54
Limfjord, Denmark 193
Lincoln, England 102
Lincolnshire, England 132
Lindisfarne, monastery, England 14, 30, 98, 250
Lindsey, England 117
Lithsmen 170, 171
Little Bredy, England 56
Lodin, Viking 56
Lodvir the Long, Viking 58
Loire, River, France 128
Loki, Viking god 43
London, England 33, 92, 93, 94, 97, 98, 129, 137, 152, 160, 169, 172, 174, 178, 182, 195, 213, 248, 249, 280
and Æthelred II 40, 91, 130
attacked by Olaf Tryggvason and Sweyn Forkbeard 42, 103
besieged by Cnut 139, 140, 141, 149, 150, 151
description of in early 11th Century 114
Long Bredy, England 56
Long Serpent, ship 58, 59
Lord of the Rings 38
Lotharingia, Germany 247
Lothian, Scotland 239
Ludham, England 188
Lund, Skåne 194, 195
Lydford, England 166, 212
Lyfing, archbishop of Canterbury 165, 179, 181, 200, 201, 203

Macbeth (Maelbeth) 239, 240, 241
Magdeburg, archbishop of 224
Magnus 'The Good', king of Norway 161, 236, 256, 270, 271, 272, 273, 275
Magonsaete people 155, 175
Mainz, archbishop of 224
Malcolm II. King of Scotland 239, 240, 241
Malcolm III. King of Scotland 282
Maldon, Battle of 33, 34, 36, 39, 41, 42, 52, 64, 77, 94, 143, 148
Malmesbury, England 135, 146
Malory, Thomas, writer 41
Margaret, sister of Edgar the Ætheling, later saint 276, 282
Matilda, daughter of Malcolm III and St Margaret 282
Medway, River, England 56
Mercia, England 13, 40, 68, 82, 106, 108, 131, 134, 153, 155, 156, 158, 172, 174, 184, 231, 251, 273, 280
and Eadric Streona 84, 85, 101, 122, 129, 166, 168, 206, 217
relations with Wessex 26, 31
Middlesex, England 95
Miklagard; see Constantinople
Milan, archbishop of 224
Minterne, England 56
Moray, Scotland 240
Morcar, noble from the Seven Boroughs 121, 122
more danico 65, 176

Narvik, Norway 62
Neatishead, England 188
Nesjar, Battle of (1016) 166, 208
Netherlands 50
Newfoundland 15, 61
Noirmoutier, island off France 128
Norfolk, England 167, 184
Norman Conquest of England (1066) 12, 25, 38, 53, 102, 182, 184, 215
Normandy, Normans 32, 42, 55, 67, 73, 77, 99, 105, 107, 114, 171, 177, 178, 183, 254, 267
North Riding, England 133

North Sea 45, 50, 59, 124, 152, 189, 193, 197, 216
Northampton, England 94
Northamptonshire, England 184
Northman, son of Leofwine of Mercia 174, 175, 184, 206
Northumbria, England 13, 21, 85, 158, 166, 241, 273, 275
and Cnut 106, 132, 134, 249, 250, 280
and Erik of Lade 184, 206
political position in England 26, 101, 102, 133, 281
Uhtred as ealdorman of 86
Viking raids on 20, 41, 53
Norway, Norwegians 49, 53, 58, 61, 63, 75, 119, 151, 166, 188, 189, 190, 222, 229, 231, 234, 235, 239, 241, 261, 265, 270, 271, 273, 275, 276, 281, 282
and Ælfgifu and Sweyn, son of Cnut 177, 255, 256, 279
and Erik of Lade 167, 168
and Olaf Haraldsson 150, 208, 236
and Olaf Tryggvason 39, 52, 57
church in 221, 233
Cnut as ruler of 38, 225, 228, 232, 237, 260, 264, 280
geography of 16, 59, 60, 62, 220, 230
Vikings from 15, 22, 42, 71, 180
Norwich, England 77
Nôtre Dame, monastery, Francia 223
Nottingham, England 102
Novgorod, Russia 231, 236, 256

Odda, English official in time of Cnut 186
Odense, Denmark 191
Odin (Woden), Scandinavian god 16, 23, 38, 43, 154, 157, 234, 283
Offa, king of Mercia 131, 163, 191
Olaf Eriksson, king of Sweden 58
Olaf Haraldsson, later king Olaf II of Norway and Saint 229, 230, 233, 235, 237, 238, 256, 276

and battle of Holy River 218
and battle of Nesjar 166, 208
and Æthelred II, king of England 114
becomes king of Norway 150
defeated by Cnut 231, 236
Olaf Skötkonung, king of Sweden 208
Olaf Tryggvason, king of Norway 33, 39, 42, 43, 52, 53, 56, 57, 58, 59, 154, 231
Ola's Island, England 157
Old Sarum, England 127
Olga, princess of Kiev 199
Orderic Vitalis, chronicler 242
Ordgar, English official in time of Cnut 186
Ordwulf 56
Oresund 17, 190
Ork, Scandinavian landowner in Dorset 211, 212, 216, 272
Orkney 231, 232, 240, 241
Orwell, River, England 152
Osbern, chronicler 213
Osgot Clapa 172, 243, 270, 272
Osgot, charter signatory 182
Oslo Fjord, Norway 190, 232
Oslo, Norway 76
Osmaer, Saxon warrior 147, 148
Oswald, Saint 29
Oswy, son-in-law of Byrhtnoth 94
Otford, Battle of (1016) 153
Óttar the Black, Viking poet 50, 157, 237
Otto I, Holy Roman Emperor 43, 189
Oxford, England 70, 93, 103, 121, 159, 181, 183
Oxfordshire, England 68, 94, 95

Padstow, England 33
Pallig Tokeson, brother-in-law of Sweyn Forkbeard 63, 69, 70
Paris, France 14
Pavia, Italy 213
Penselwood, Battle of (1016) 141, 142, 143, 146

Peonnum, Battle of (658) 141
Peterborough, England 253
Piast dynasty 263
Pinhoe, England 64
Poland 38, 50, 51, 224, 225, 263
Poole Harbour, England 126, 128
Poppo, Christian missionary 189
Portesham England 212
Portland, England 13, 33
Portsmouth Harbour, England 123
Purbeck, Isle of, England 28

Ragnarok 20
Ramsey Abbey, England 250
Ravenna, archbishop of 224
Reading, England 83
Reykjavik, Iceland 61
Ribe, Denmark 120, 193
Richard I, duke of Normandy 55, 65
Richard II, duke of Normandy 55, 57, 105, 114, 115, 179, 216
Ringmere, Battle of (1010) 94
Ripon, England 250
Robert I, son of Richard II, duke of Normandy 179, 255
Robert the Bruce, king of Scotland 223, 239, 280
Rochester, England 56, 57
rock carvings in Scandinavia 74
Rollo, Duke of Normandy 55, 99
Roman Conquest of Britain 12, 38
Rome 134, 201, 222, 223, 224, 225, 227, 237, 239, 245, 246, 281
Roskilde Fjord, Denmark 75, 76, 192
Roskilde, Denmark 49, 75, 76, 121, 192, 193, 194, 199, 208, 219, 221, 259
Roskilde, Treaty of (1658) 17
Rouen, Normandy 55, 114, 164
Rudolf III of Burgundy 224
Russia, Rus 42, 53, 75, 198, 235
Rutland, England 68
Rwanda 73

Saami people (Laaps) 60, 196
Salisbury, England 74, 127

Sandwich, England 33, 89, 91, 92, 100, 117, 126, 227
Saxland 49
Saxo Grammaticus, Danish historian 193
Scania; see Skåne
Scarborough, England 22
Scheldt, River 128
Schleswig, Denmark/Germany 120, 225
Scotland, Scots 16, 20, 22, 45, 53, 60, 86, 175, 239, 240, 241, 260
Senlac Hill, Hastings, England 144
Sermo Lupi ad Anglos 111, 200
Seven Boroughs, England 121
Severn, River 55, 157
Shaftesbury, England 29, 64, 127, 212, 258, 259, 278
Shakespeare, William, playwright 240
Sheppey, Isle of, England 128, 141, 153
Sherborne, England 96, 112, 128, 251, 258
Sherston, Battle of (1016) 146, 147, 148, 149, 186
Shrewsbury, England 85, 130
Shropshire, England 83, 85, 155
Sicily 235
Sigeferth, noble from the Seven Boroughs 121, 122
Sigeric 'The Serious, Archbishop of Canterbury 39, 54
Sigrid the Haughty, wife of Sweyn Forkbeard 51, 58
Sigvatr, Scandinavian poet 230
Sihtric Silkbeard, Scandinavian king in Ireland 239
Siward, earl of Northumbria 240, 241, 273, 275, 276, 277
Siward, Viking landowner in Devon 212
Skagerrak 45, 193
Skåne, Denmark (later part of Sweden) 16, 104, 173, 192, 194, 205, 216, 217, 231, 280
Skraelings 61

Snorri Sturluson, saga writer 43, 49, 51, 53, 56, 59, 62, 82, 136, 175, 216, 217, 229, 230, 232, 233, 246
Somerset, England 128, 142, 148, 169, 184, 247
South Cadbury, hillfort, England 95, 127, 166
Southampton, England 33, 137, 238, 267
Southwark, England 112, 172, 214
Spain 150, 164, 190, 196
St Augustine of Hippo 213
St Augustine's Abbey, Canterbury, England 66, 246
St Bartholomew 201
St Benet Holme, England 187
St Bertin, monastery, Francia 223
St Brice's Day Massacre 69, 70, 71, 72, 73, 81, 93, 122, 124
St Ciriacus 249
St Clements Church, Roskilde, Denmark 194
St Cuthbert 249, 250
St Frideswide's Minster, Oxford, England 70, 122
St George 249
St Ibs Church, Roskilde, Denmark 194
St Mildred 246
St Omer, Francia 223
St Pauls, London, England 98, 165, 213, 214, 249, 275, 276
St Valentine 244
St Vincent 246
St Wystan 246
Staffordshire, England 130
Stamford Bridge, Battle of (1066) 117, 235, 242, 276
Stamford, England 102
Stigand, later archbishop of Canterbury 247, 248
Stiklestad, Battle of (1030) 232, 236
Stockholm, Sweden 217
Strathclyde, Britain 22, 26
Styr Ulfsson, wife of Uhtred of Bamburgh 86
Suffolk, England 68, 152, 167

Index

Suneman, Christian hermit 187

Surrey, England 95, 186

Sussex, England 56, 63, 93, 131, 169, 184, 185

Sutherland, Scotland 240

Sutton Hoo ship burial 42

Svear 195

Sverri, King of Norway (1184-1202) 154

Svold, Battle of 58, 82, 231

Sweden, Swedes 42, 43, 119, 120, 173, 176, 189, 192, 208, 222, 231, 233, 234

and Cnut 217, 218, 225, 228

characteristics of Swedes 197

geography of 16

religious beliefs in 233, 234

Vikings from 71, 76, 82

Sweyn Estrithsson, king of Denmark 45, 90, 219, 259, 263, 270, 271, 273, 275

Sweyn Forkbeard, king of Denmark 37, 43, 50, 52, 79, 85, 105, 108, 119, 122, 128, 130, 139, 150, 242, 277

and battle of Maldon 42

and Norway 62, 63, 166, 231, 271

and St Brices Day Massacre 69, 70, 72, 73

and Thorkell the Tall 81, 82, 99, 124

burial of 118, 121

civil war with Harald Bluetooth 47, 48, 49, 189

death of 109, 110, 111, 116

final invasion of England 100, 102, 103, 106, 107

raid on England (995) 54

religion of 44, 45, 120, 281

sons of 52

war with Olaf Tryggvason 57, 58, 59

Sweyn Godwinson 210, 263, 265

Sweyn, brother of Erik of Lade 62, 150, 166

Sweyn, son of Cnut 106, 177, 209, 236, 255, 256, 266, 279

Sweyn, tenant-in-chief at Ashingdon 154

swinfylking, Viking battle formation 147

Swithun, bishop of Winchester and Saint 182

Tamar, River, England 56

Tavistock, England 56, 176

Telemark, Norway 190

Tempsford, England 94

Tewkesbury, England 148, 186

Thames, River, England 56, 112, 140, 151, 154, 214, 270

Thanet, England 33, 128

Thetford, England 77, 94

Thietmar of Merseburg, chronicler 98, 119, 178, 190

Thomas Becket, Archbishop of Canterbury 33, 215

Thor the Dog, Norwegian landowner 231

Thor, Scandinavian god 16, 38, 109, 157, 234

Thorasin Praise-Tongue, Scandinavian poet 230, 237

Thored, charter witness 186

Thored, earl of Northumbria 68

Thorgils Skarthi, Viking 22

Thorkell 'The Tall', Viking leader 104, 150, 156, 168, 185, 195, 200, 208, 210, 232

and Ælfheah, archbishop of Canterbury 96, 98

and Æthelred II 103, 105, 121

and East Anglia 166, 167, 184, 206, 250

and Jomsvikings 81

at battle of Sherston 146, 147

exile from England 171, 204, 209

raids on England 89, 92

relations with Cnut 82, 117, 123, 124, 211

relations with Sweyn Forkbeard 82

Thorney Island (Westminster), England 238

Thorstein Ox-Foot, Viking 58

Thrond Squint-Eye, Viking 58
Thrum, Viking 97
Thurbrand the Hold 132, 134
Thurgils Sprakaleg, Viking 210
Tola, wife of Ork 211, 212
Tolkien, J. R. R., writer 38
Tolpuddle, England 212
Torksey, England 121
Tosti, Viking raid leader 82
Tostig, earl of Northumbria 102, 265, 276
Tovi the Proud 172, 243, 265, 270, 272
Tovi, Viking landowner in Devon 212
Trelleborg, Denmark 47, 48
Trent, River, England 100
Trondheim, Norway 62, 230, 231, 232, 233, 235
Ty, Viking god 16
Tyne, River, England 86
Tyri, sister of Sweyn Forkbeard 58

Ufegeat, son of Ælfhelm, ealdorman of Northumbria 85
Uhtred of Bamburgh, ealdorman of Northumbria 102, 116, 130, 131, 132, 241, 250
  becomes ealdorman of Northumbria 86
  killing of and subsequent blood-feud 133, 134, 168, 252
  son-in-law of Æthelred II 100, 101
Uhtred of Bebbanburgh 11
Ulf of Boresta, Viking 82
Ulf Sprakaleggson, brother-in-law of Cnut 90, 171, 209, 216, 217, 218, 223, 226
Ulf, Viking landowner in Devon 212
Ulfcetel Snilling ("The Bold") 77, 78, 94, 99, 124, 156
Unwan, archbishop of Hamburg-Bremen 197
Uppakra, Skåne 195
Uppsala, Sweden 234

Varangian Guard 198

Venerable Bede, English historian 20
Viborg, Denmark 193, 194, 216
Viken, Norway 15
Viking ships 75, 76, 77, 125
vikingar 15
Vikings language 16
Vikings motivations of 19
Vikings origin of name 15
Vikings religion of 20
Vindland 51
Vinland, North America 61
Visby, Gotland 196
Vistula, River 208
Vitae Edwardi Regis 132, 205, 210
Volga, River 76

Wagner, Richard composer 11
Walcheren, island 128
Wales 20, 53, 55, 97, 141, 260
Wallingford, England 103
Waltham, England 243
Waltheof, grandson of Ealdred 134
Wareham, England 29, 126, 127, 128, 166, 212
Warwickshire, England 129, 184
Watchet, England 33, 56
Waterford, Ireland 54
Wear, River, England 250
Wells, England 251
Wendred, Saint 156
Wends 51
wergild 164
Wessex, England 31, 82, 101, 103, 108, 131, 134, 138, 155, 184
  and Cnut 126, 128, 129, 166, 168, 169, 172, 183, 186, 251, 252, 280
  and earl Godwin 210, 211, 273
  and Edmund Ironside 141, 148, 158
  relations with Mercia 26
  royal bloodline of 23, 173, 258
  Viking raids on 13, 21, 71, 94
West Riding, England 133
Western Isles, Scotland 239
Westminster Abbey, England 248, 272
Wexford, Ireland 54

Weymouth, England mass grave near 70-72

William I, king of England 38, 109, 148, 165, 176, 248, 255, 259, 282

William II, king of England 259

William of Jumièges, chronicler 73, 177, 254, 255

William of Malmesbury, chronicler 26, 28, 82, 98, 104, 135, 137, 159, 244, 252, 277

William the Great, duke of Aquitaine 253, 261

William Wallace 239

Wilton, England 74, 127, 138, 252, 278

Wiltshire, England 74, 94, 95, 128, 142, 146, 169, 186

Wimborne, England 128, 186

Winchester, England 51, 83, 88, 103, 182, 187, 246, 248, 260, 262, 264, 267, 272
  and Cnut 182, 195, 203, 244, 245, 247, 249, 251, 259, 278
  and Edgar 23, 24
  and Emma 68, 266, 275
  and king Alfred 84

Winterbourne Abbas, England 56

Witland, Prussia 208

Woden; see Odin

Wolfred, English missionary 233

Wolin, Baltic island 50

Worcester, England 146, 170, 251

Worcestershire, England 175, 270

Wulfbald, Anglo-Saxon subject 136, 137

Wulfheah, son of Ælfhelm, ealdorman of Northumbria 85

Wulfnoth, abbot of Westminster 249

Wulfnoth, South Saxon 91, 92, 185, 268

Wulfric, benefactor of St Benet Holme 188

Wulfsige, abbot of Ramsey 156

Wulfstan, archbishop of York, homilist 80, 90, 112, 165, 220
  and Cnut 181, 201, 202
  and the *Sermo Lupi ad Anglos* 111, 200
  at Enham

York Gospels 202

York, England 109, 121, 134, 167, 197, 241, 243, 276, 282
  as a Viking city 76, 86, 102

Yorkshire, England 184

Zealand, Denmark 191, 192

About the Author

W. B. BARTLETT is a finance management consultant advising nations such as Rwanda and Fiji on behalf of the IMF and World Bank. He is the author of several medieval history books including *Agincourt: Henry V, the Man at Arms & the Archer, The Mongols, Assassins: The Story of Medieval Islam's Secret Sect, An Ungodly War: The Sack of Constantinople & the Fourth Crusade* and *The Crusades*. He lives in Bournemouth.

Also available from Amberley Publishing

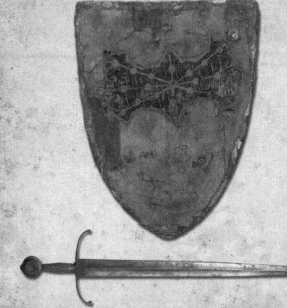

Praise for W. B. Bartlett's *Titanic*: 'The best and most level-headed telling of the whole story I have ever read' *INDEPENDENT ON SUNDAY*

AGINCOURT

HENRY V, THE MAN-AT-ARMS & THE ARCHER

W. B. BARTLETT

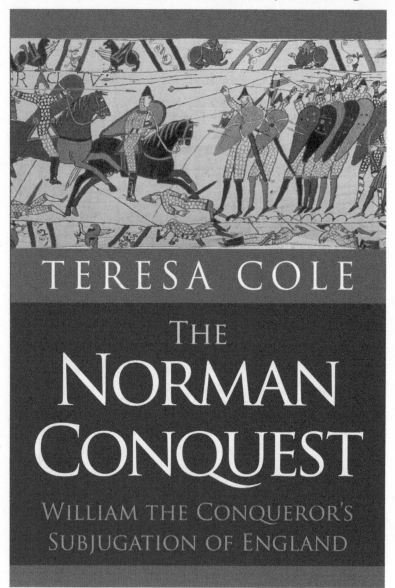

TERESA COLE

THE
NORMAN
CONQUEST

WILLIAM THE CONQUEROR'S
SUBJUGATION OF ENGLAND